PVO

Beyond the Headlines

AF584242

Peter van Onselen PhD

Published by:
Wilkinson Publishing Pty Ltd
ACN 006 042 173
PO Box 24135
Melbourne, Vic 3001
Ph: 03 9654 5446

enquiries@wilkinsonpublishing.com.au
www.wilkinsonpublishing.com.au

Copyright © 2022 Peter van Onselen

All rights reserved. No part of this publication may be reproduced, stored in a retrieval system or transmitted in any form by any means without the prior permission of the copyright owner. Enquiries should be made to the publisher.

Every effort has been made to ensure that this book is free from error or omissions. However, the Publisher, the Author, the Editor or their respective employees or agents, shall not accept responsibility for injury, loss or damage occasioned to any person acting or refraining from action as a result of material in this book whether or not such injury, loss or damage is in any way due to any negligent act or omission, breach of duty or default on the part of the Publisher, the Author, the Editor, or their respective employees or agents.

Title: PVO Beyond the Headlines

ISBN:9781922810113

eBook ISBN: 9781922810212

A catalogue record of this book is available from the National Library of Australia.

Design by Spike Creative Pty Ltd
Ph: (03) 9427 9500
spikecreative.com.au

Printed and bound in Australia by Griffin Press.

Contents

Introduction

The last two and a half years of Australian politics has been tumultuous to say the least. This collection of columns with author notes littered throughout traverses an unprecedented period in politics and public policy making.

Former Prime Minister Scott Morrison's appalling initial response to the bushfires of 2019/20. The onset of the pandemic and the shutdown of democratic institutions while executive government had its way with us. Cooperation and contestation between the Commonwealth and the states over exactly how we should manage lockdowns and the economy in a time of crisis. During this period the need for economic reforms to modernise the economy only grew, but the political willingness to stare into this need was all but non-existent. This laid bare the cracks within the government on this issue. Then we had the vaccine rollout, which failed before it succeeded, undercutting the Coalition's claims that it managed the pandemic well.

Yet Australia remained the lucky country throughout this time, doing comparatively well on the global stage on most economic and social indicators. But would that alone be enough to re-elect the Morrison government? In the end it wasn't. The polls which appeared to get it so wrong three years ago got it right this time. Voter fatigue with the Coalition government, personal dislike of the PM and all manner of unresolved policy problems came together to overwhelm a government seeking a fourth term in power under the leadership of its third prime minister.

Morrison failed to win re-election, unable to pull off another miracle comeback. Peter Dutton now leads the Liberal Party in opposition,

Anthony Albanese is our Prime Minister. Despite winning the election with a record low primary vote, and a slender majority of 77 seats in the 151 seat House of Representatives, Labor is planning for at least two terms in charge. And why not, the Opposition holds just 58 seats in the House. The Coalition in opposition is left to lick its wounds and work out what needs to change and what must stay the same for the self-described natural party of government to return to the treasury benches.

Readers of this collection of columns can work their way backwards in time through the tumult of the last two and a half years. So much has happened in terms of the daily grind of political debate, and our lives have been profoundly altered by the experiences of the pandemic and the way it shifted our thinking. But the challenges which existed before Covid struck — economically and socially — are still there, unresolved and more urgently in need of attention. Labor has always been the more progressive side of the major party divide. We will see soon enough if it is prepared to take on the social challenges the conservatives weren't interested in tackling. On this score I have high hopes, but not as high as activists who will inevitably feel let down by a Labor government that should be savvy enough not to lurch too far to the left moving away from the Morrison years. How the social media mob handles that will be interesting viewing. In the short-term picking over the carcass of the opposition will satisfy their lust.

The economic challenges, unlike social changes which I expect to see at least partially tackled, are unlikely to be properly dealt with at all. The rusty can of economic reform will most likely continue to be kicked further down the road. Australians are about to go through a post-pandemic period of economic uncertainty. Rising inflation, interest rates and debt will compound cost of living pressures on Australians. Labor wants to see wages rise to help combat that cycle, but no one wants a 1970s-style wage price spiral. What happens to house prices and rents will play a significant role in the way the major political parties square off at the next election, as will the debates over energy prices. Predicting where these debates go will be difficult.

One howler in this collection was my prediction that the teal independents were more likely to crash and burn rather than succeed. In the end the big six receiving the lion's share of attention all won, knocking off a collection of largely moderate Liberals who thought their only care was how to position themselves for promotion or factional procurement going forward. Their seats were supposed to be blue ribbon electorates providing the right of politics with ballast. Instead they have further exposed a soft underbelly within the right: its failure to satisfy women, those who want climate change activism and integrity in politics. But are such issues at the vanguard of how voters in key marginal seats feel? Post-material voting tendencies traditionally fall away when the economy moves front and centre, but in our modern world issues once considered post-material now have material consequences.

The environment and its degradation has tangible economic impacts. Women want equal pay and equal treatment in the workplace, rights which help with economic security. Integrity in politics can play an important role in cutting out pork barrelling and improving productivity, thus helping the budget bottom line.

The growth in the size of the crossbench, in the senate and the house, is a key development from the last parliament to the current one. Within that envelope of change we cannot ignore the surge in support for the Greens, taking seats from both major parties in inner city areas and growing its senate base. How the Greens flex their political muscle in this parliament will be interesting. How Labor responds when they do will be important.

Australians are clearly sick of politics as usual. Unfortunately, going hand in glove with such despair is a lack of tolerance for major reforms which don't provide instant gratification. My worry is that the path of least resistance for the political class is to therefore promise little and do even less. Avoiding the risk of being accused of breaking election pledges. If parties win elections with small targets, going on to do anything much at all could be classified as a broken promise. On the campaign trail Albanese said that he wanted to under promise and over deliver, an idiom often held up as good practice. But with where we now are in Australian politics such good intentions could land him in hot political water, accused of over-extending what mandate he has.

I believe these sorts of issues are likely to drive debates and discussions in the years ahead. This collection looks back, giving readers the opportunity to snack on debates from different moments in time during a period none of us have lived through before. It also highlights how quickly things can change, and how frustratingly similar some call outs for action not being taken by the political class can be, year in year out.

Don't dismiss Dutton's ability to rally troops

28 May 2022

There is always understandable euphoria when a change of government happens. In Labor's case, this is only the fourth time it has won its way into government from opposition since World War II. Anthony Albanese is therefore already a Labor hero.

Nevertheless, the new Prime Minister needs to be careful not to underestimate Peter Dutton, who is certain to take over as opposition leader. Scott Morrison made the mistake of underestimating Albo after Labor's 2019 devastation.

Things can change quickly in politics and the new government is in for a rough ride managing a budget burdened by a structural deficit and a global economy on the brink. If that wasn't hard enough, rising inflation and interest rates will test the patience of voters struggling with cost-of-living pressures.

Dutton and the opposition will pounce on such hardships, notwithstanding the Coalition's failure to manage the strains on the economy during its time in power.

To be sure, Dutton's job will be hard too. The internal divisions defeat brings to the fore won't be easily managed. And new governments don't tend to lose after one term. The last one-term government to be defeated was back in 1931 during the Depression, James Scullin's Labor government.

The Coalition and the Liberals have much to work out before being able to hold Labor to account convincingly. Which policy scripts do they keep and which do they throw away? How do they calibrate their parliamentary line-up better, in terms of gender for starters? Do they moderate in a bid to reclaim teal seats or do they push towards policy positions that appeal to electorates they must win off Labor in the outer suburbs?

Right now there are question marks over Dutton's suitability to lead. The defeat of Josh Frydenberg in his traditionally blue-ribbon seat of Kooyong narrowed the options. Perhaps the biggest problem for the Coalition is the lack of talent on its frontbench. Slim pickings would be an understatement.

But Dutton can't be easily dismissed. He has built a long-term political career occupying senior cabinet and parliamentary positions, and he has done so while holding what really should be a Labor seat. There is a lot of talk about Dutton's unelectability as an alternative prime minister, but most of it comes from people who wouldn't vote Liberal in a pink fit. We've seen similar references made about past leaders who have gone on to win elections.

While Dutton is the unofficial leader of the hard Right within the Liberal Party, he's more moderate on religious policy than people may realise. For some reason that hasn't crimped his appeal to right-wing Liberal constituencies.

His next step is to broaden his appeal, but he won't do that with a disingenuous shift to the left that moderates (the few left in the parliamentary party) would like to see. That would cause more problems than it solves, it pains me to admit.

The most difficult question Dutton faces is this: how does he credibly pivot without losing his base? Walking the line between the increasingly divergent "broad church" that is the Liberal Party — or that was before the teal revolt — without fracturing the Coalition with the Nationals?

Dutton should do OK managing the Coalition. As a Queenslander with the world view he has, that part of the puzzle is somewhat easy relative to other challenges.

Barnaby Joyce doesn't deserve to be removed as Nationals leader based on the junior Coalition partner's performance at the election. While Liberals lost seats to the teals and Labor, the Nationals retained all their seats. But Joyce suffers from the same perception problems Morrison did and he represents the past, not the future. His appeal in Queensland is also of downgraded importance with Dutton the Queenslander as opposition leader.

A big challenge for Dutton is finding more women to promote, including around him in key leadership roles to help with his image and policy development, to show the Coalition is serious about addressing the fact women turned off the party in droves at this election.

He can't conjure up more women in the parliamentary ranks, and the defeat of Katie Allen, Celia Hammond, Amanda Stoker and Fiona Martin won't help either. Even if he can convince good women to join the Liberals and contest key seats at the next poll, that's three years away and it won't help here and now.

There is a risk Marise Payne retires from politics. Linda Reynolds remains damaged in the eyes of the public. Senators Jane Hume and Anne Ruston are on the rise but they are in the wrong chamber to be visually front and centre. In fact all four are senators. Karen Andrews needs a key portfolio but she isn't close to Dutton. They duked it out for preselection many years ago when she first entered parliament. Sussan Ley may become Dutton's deputy as the only viable senior woman in the lower house.

One thing the lack of firepower in Liberal parliamentary ranks among the blokes does do is help reduce the chances of Dutton being immediately undermined by ambitious alternative leaders within. But never underestimate the capacity for wannabes to believe in themselves. Angus Taylor sits at the front of that queue.

While Dutton needs to approach the next election aiming to win, starting on 59 seats and needing 76 to form majority government suggests a two-term strategy is more likely. But new leadership rules that protected Bill Shorten and Albanese from internal challenges don't apply to the Liberals in opposition. Morrison established similar rules for the Liberals but only in government — another one of his self-interested moves.

Dutton's strategy will be to go after Labor in the hope of taking away its majority at the next election. Win two seats off Labor without losing any and the majority is gone. Win a half-dozen and things get interesting. Labor would have to form minority government in collaboration with remaining independents and Greens. Perhaps Dutton wins back a few teal seats along the way, pushing Coalition seats north of 65.

In the aftermath of such a crystal ball election three years from now Albanese would be damaged and Dutton would be seen to have performed well. Teals would have to declare their allegiances.

It would be a version of the 1984 election in which Andrew Peacock exceeded expectations, without someone like John Howard lurking in the wings. Unless Frydenberg fought his way back into parliament at the next election. Ponder that for a moment.

But for now, assuming Dutton takes over and the Coalition doesn't descend into a period of complete madness (of which there are no guarantees), he'll try to position himself as tough on China, tough on boats and experienced on the economy (he was assistant treasurer to Peter Costello in the final term of Howard's prime ministership). Expect debt and deficits suddenly to matter again.

Dutton's image is one-dimensional, but there is a reason his colleagues came so close to selecting him as their leader in government against Malcolm Turnbull and Morrison, and why he has defied the odds to win a marginal seat time and time again. On the hustings Dutton is far more personable than the wider public or his critics realise.

He is therefore not to be underestimated, which is not to understate the challenges he faces.

Western Australia key to Labor second term, vital target for Liberals

27 May 2022

Western Australia was both the key ingredient in Labor's federal election victory and the vital state that Liberals must now target if Peter Dutton is to turn the Coalition's fortunes around in three years' time.

The WA Premier Mark McGowan deserves the lion's share of credit for Labor picking up four seats in the west and thereby delivering Anthony Albanese majority government — which is not to diminish the new PM's role in success in the west. He recognised its importance, challenged the Morrison government's decision to initially support Clive Palmer's high court borders case, backed the WA GST changes Scott Morrison implemented and took the unprecedented step of launching Labor's election campaign in the west with three full weeks of campaigning left.

But it was Mr McGowan's popularity in WA that cemented the electoral success that followed. Winning Swan and Pearce was the low hanging electoral fruit, but Labor has talked big without success in the west before and failed on this front. This time, the low-hanging fruit was picked off, as was the tougher task of gaining further seats.

Hasluck was picked up and remarkably so was the traditionally safe Liberal seat of Tangney, which saw Scott Morrison's right-hand man, Ben Morton, lose his seat. Moore was also almost lost by the Liberals, and Canning is again now a wafer-thin marginal Liberal seat.

Winning four seats in WA alongside the absolution of the Liberal seat of Stirling (which also would have been lost had it not been) now sees Labor holding nine of the 15 WA seats on offer, the first time it has held the majority of WA seats in decades.

While state and federal politics don't always overlap, especially in the west, it turns out that Labor winning the recent state poll with around 70 per cent of the two-party vote — decimating the state Liberals in the process — absolutely counted at the federal election, as did the Labor premier having personal approval ratings in the clouds.

This is also why what happens next in the west will be so important to the coming three years. The global economy is uncertain, the relationship with China is on edge, the GST deal is due for renegotiation and Mr Dutton the Queenslander will fancy his chances of building bridges with WA voters. Queenslanders and West Aussies are kindred spirits of sorts, mining states with conservative values.

The odds are that Mr McGowan won't be as popular three years from now as he currently is. How could he be, he holds holy status in the west right now for the way he managed the pandemic. Mr Dutton will look to claw back votes in WA and rebuild the party such that the federal opposition can competitively capture at least three of the seats it just lost across the Nullarbor. If that happens, Mr Albanese will instantly lose his working majority unless he can pick up seats elsewhere around the country.

To be sure, the federal Labor caucus will have more MPs and senators to help make the case for looking after WA internally, but if that doesn't materialise in policy outcomes WA voters will surely notice, and Mr Dutton will look to exploit the consequences. Mr McGowan and Mr Albanese get on well, and Albo is no fool: he'll pander to WA if only to protect his government. But Mr McGowan equally won't be afraid to use his megaphone to call out bad decisions in Canberra if they hurt his constituents.

Make no mistake, how the west was won locked in Labor's federal success on Saturday night, and it's the key to the new government's capacity to bed that success down for a second term in three years' time.

Albo's got this — now Libs need a good think

21 May 2022

Predictions in politics are always fraught with danger. Three years ago Scott Morrison took great delight rubbing my nose in getting it wrong. But I'm happy to have another go and predict that Labor will form government after Saturday's results are tallied.

It should be able to form majority government, but at the very least looks set to govern in minority. The Coalition has had wars on too many fronts to pull off another victory coming from behind.

Teal independents are likely to win a few seats off Liberal MPs but, irrespective of whether they exceed those expectations or underwhelm, they have sapped much-needed resources from the Coalition's contest with Labor.

The aftermath will require the Liberal Party and the Coalition to have a long, hard think about who they represent and their ideological lines in the sand.

The Liberals and Nationals are holding up reasonably well in Queensland but bleeding seats in other parts of the country. You would think the government's best-case scenario would see it losing around four to six seats to Labor, not counting any losses to the teals. The worst-case scenario could go anywhere.

While there are Labor seats being targeted, and one or two may fall, for the most part Labor pick-ups are going to be a bridge too far for a prime minister on the nose — one whose own colleagues have labelled him everything from a "horrible, horrible person" to a "complete psycho", "hypocrite" and "fraud".

The personal assessments were a dagger in the heart of a leader who needed everything to go his way to orchestrate a comeback. But no one can take away his remarkable 2019 victory.

Of course my prediction that Labor wins includes the potential for a close victory to become a blowout on the night and result in a resounding win, remembering Labor never wins with majorities to match the Coalition's.

Gough Whitlam's majority was just five and Kevin Rudd won with only an eight-seat majority. For context, Tony Abbott won the 2013 election with a 15-seat majority and John Howard won in 1996 with a majority of 20.

What won't happen at this election is a Morrison comeback like in 2019. A second miracle is off the table. I make that prediction in full knowledge that it will be thrown in my face by conservative commentators and government insiders alike if I'm wrong. But I won't be. Anthony Albanese will be the next prime minister of Australia.

Which will leave the conservative side of politics to ponder: what went so wrong? A prime minister who was popular during the pandemic saw his personal numbers collapse. An opposition leader who struggled at the beginning of the campaign and was viewed as a seat warmer when he took over a shattered party after the 2019 loss will become only the fourth Labor leader to lead the party into government since World War II.

Many saw the 2019 defeat for Labor as the start of what might be a period of clean out. But after Saturday's results are tallied, that election will come to be seen as more analogous with the Liberals' 1993 defeat, which was followed by a win just three years later.

Paul Keating became too confident after his 1993 win coming from behind, just as Morrison did after the 2019 victory. Australians didn't endorse either leader with their victory; they rejected the other mob. Three years later, Howard cut a safe figure on whom voters could gamble.

Albanese has modelled his small-target strategy similarly, pushing towards the centre as Morrison thrashed around on the right.

The problems Labor will inherit are immense: a lost decade in which economic reform was put in the too-hard basket; rising debt, inflation and interest rates; the likelihood that the AAA credit rating will come under scrutiny during the coming 12 months; sagging productivity; and divisions on social issues.

It's not hard to imagine the sort of campaign Liberals will run in three years attacking Labor. It could be effective if the threadbare elements of the Coalition can hang together between now and then. Governing is going to be tough.

This outgoing Coalition government has lost so much standing from the Howard and Peter Costello years. The notion that its economic credibility is in the same ballpark as the Coalition government before it is just laughable.

It will be interesting to see if the Liberals in opposition can reclaim their reforming zeal. To do so they have to be willing to emulate the depth of thinking the wets and dries of the 1970s and '80s displayed. I question whether the personnel in parliament today have what it takes to do that on the conservative side — even more so if some of the MPs under threat from the teals are defeated.

For many of the senior Labor MPs soon to be sworn into cabinet, this is their second chance. They were seen as collectively talented 15 years ago when Labor butchered its return to government, overtaken by infighting and a cultural malaise that saw them remove prime ministers on the whim of bad polls.

If the group I'm talking about lives up to its potential it will need to match up to the first cabinet of Bob Hawke, which undertook important micro-economic reforms to set up the prosperity Australia continues to enjoy. Such are the challenges the country faces.

But that prosperity is waning after a lack of reforms in recent times. I just don't know if the incoming Labor government has what it takes to modernise our economy. After the small-target campaign it certainly doesn't have a mandate to do so, which means that if Liberals oppose reforms in a search for popularity they might dissuade Labor from doing what the country needs.

In defeat Morrison presumably will retire from politics, still in his early 50s. Malcolm Turnbull aside, Morrison will be the first former PM not to hit the road with a lifetime prime ministerial pension, which perhaps will keep him in the political game a little longer. More likely he'll do something else for a crust. I don't agree with the removal of PM pensions.

This campaign has been memorable for its vacuousness, the lack of serious policy contestation, the growth in sound bites and gotcha questions, the extent to which voters tuned out. Politics is broken and there is collective blame for that: on MPs, the media and the public. Perhaps a fresh start can help restore the civil society we need for democratic governance to thrive. We aren't the only country battling a democratic decay.

Economic reform gets filed under too hard

6 May 2022

Neither major political party has anything resembling a plan to balance the budget, much less pay down government debt. And that's before even discussing their collective unwillingness to reform the economy.

For years we had to listen to vacuous debates about the urgency of budget repair when these claims were largely a furphy; claims made by the same politicians who now preside over record-breaking debt and deficits without a hint of a blush. There is nothing wrong with debt as long as it is manageable and targeted at meaningful spending: for example, productivity-enhancing infrastructure or social goods that enrich our society.

But right now the deficit is structural. Recurrent expenditure is outstripping taxation returns. Unless this is addressed, debt will continue to grow. We are on course to have more than $1 trillion of national debt in the coming years, and neither major party is prepared to chart a course back towards a balanced budget. Debt as a percentage of gross domestic product is higher than it was when Gough Whitlam was prime minister, and his administration is still held up as economic vandals by conservatives. At least the Whitlam years produced lasting social reforms.

The Coalition has committed to a tax-to-GDP cap of 23.9 per cent, as though that is some sort of gold-star promise. Spending to GDP is currently up at 27.8 per cent. Unless these percentages are brought into line with each other we will continue to rack up government debt, just as inflation and interest rates are rising, which in time will make servicing the debt more difficult.

Were it not for the political manoeuvring both major parties are engaged in to try to win the election, some Liberals would like to slice into spending and some within Labor would like put up taxes. Or, to be less binary, both major parties would welcome the opportunity to do a little of each to help balance the books.

But that's not going to happen with an election just around the corner, and perhaps not even in its aftermath. Having played the rule-in-rule-out game all campaign, it will be hard for either major party in government to deviate from their do-nothing campaign commitments.

Fiddling with the books without acknowledging the need for significant reforms to the tax system and the federation misses the point anyway. We are overdue for a rewriting of both, overdue for a tax summit to put all ideas on the table. But I see no evidence this will happen, irrespective of which party forms government in two weeks.

Developing nations can grow their way out of debt by enlarging their economies, so debt as a percentage of GDP falls even though they continue to run budget deficits. India, for example, has done this for many years with only modest levels of economic reform. But a developed country such as Australia can't do that because we can't deliver consistently high enough economic growth figures, coming off such a high base to begin with.

There is no escaping the reality that developed countries can stay fiscally responsible only by keeping one eye on structural deficits and the other on continual economic reform. At the moment we are doing neither. Our political leaders are failing the nation they serve and not living up to the legacies of those who came before them.

The major parties claim a hung parliament risks chaos because the crossbench would hold each to ransom. For what? It is not as though either party has an economic agenda for change worth embracing, such that the crossbench would thwart it. You have to be doing something meaningful in the first place for the crossbench to play the role of villains.

What the majors really mean is a hung parliament will put on the agenda some policy requirements they don't want to discuss. In the Coalition's case, this includes an integrity commission with teeth. Perhaps budget repair also could become a negotiation point, particularly if the so-called teal independents were to control the balance of power and support Labor in government because Scott Morrison wouldn't budge on an integrity commission.

The teal independents are running in electorates with high levels of economic awareness, traditional safe Liberal seats. These independents are focused on what political scientist Ronald Inglehart termed "postmaterialism" in his 1977 book The Silent Revolution. The thesis is that when material wellbeing is satisfied, people can vote according to their postmaterial value structures — beyond hip-pocket tendencies, or any other fear threatening their security.

The wealthy electorates in which teal independents are challenging Liberal MPs are the traditional Liberal heartland where voters have become disillusioned with the lack of small-L liberalism in the modern Liberal Party. Their focus in this campaign has been on climate change, gender rights and integrity. But many traditional Liberal voters in these electorates are just as dismayed at the lack of economic-reforming mongrel within this government; it's just that such policy disagreements don't capture the attention of the media or special interests.

Perhaps teal independents could justify backing Labor in minority government if it committed to serious budget repair? Or they could force the Coalition to reclaim its one-time mantle as responsible economic managers to win their backing? I don't have high hopes of either; these independents appear focused elsewhere, just like the rest of the parliament. The search for MPs or wannabe MPs with economic-reforming convictions is a seemingly fruitless endeavour, the crossbench included.

Our leaders like to remind us that Australia is doing comparatively well economically on the international stage. Debt levels in like-for-like developed nations around the world are much higher than here. This is true, but other nations doing extremely badly managing their finances doesn't justify us doing the same.

While economists on the fringes are advocating for Modern Monetary Theory, few politicians are willing to do the same. MMT essentially argues that nations such as ours don't need to be constrained in their spending. In other words, print money and let the good times roll! No need to even issue bonds when accruing debt. Former US presidential candidate Bernie Sanders advocates this approach, if you can believe that. Think about how close he came to becoming president, and Donald Trump suddenly doesn't look so uniquely bad.

Members of the political class here, while unwilling to sign up formally to the radical theory, are borrowing from its logic as they use spending promises to chase votes, almost entirely unconstrained by the structural deficit. It remains to be seen how viable this is into the future, politically and economically, with rising inflation and interest rates.

The better manager? Pull the other one

30 April 2022

It is hard to establish on what tangible basis the Coalition can lay claim to the title of superior economic manager. While such wording implies a binary choice between the major parties, and merely requires the Coalition to best a lethargic Labor Party, I'm not even certain that's true.

Let's go through the reasons this government isn't a worthy flag-bearer for those that came before it. As I see it there are four clears reasons the Coalition should no longer be seen as economically competent: the misuse of how it allocates taxpayers' money without adequate due process; a lack of meaningful and necessary economic reforms; fiscal profligacy the likes of which we've never seen before; and counterproductive policymaking that often makes bad situations worse.

The divisions between Nationals and Liberals are crippling any Coalition claim to fiscal conservatism.

The extent of pork-barrelling on display to accommodate the regional junior Coalition partner is obscene.

Not that this government confines pork-barrelling to the regions; there also have been schemes that have targeted urban marginal seats, such as the community sports grants program and the commuter carpark scheme.

Funding allocations are no longer determined on a needs basis or via good public policy. Campaigning and political advantage trump all comers, as does back-of-the-envelope decision-making, such as the $400m Great Barrier Reef Foundation grant awarded when Malcolm Turnbull was prime minister.

The net result? Waste and misuse of taxpayers' money.

We've also seen how politicking can make it difficult to recruit quality candidates; recall Scott Morrison's parliamentary bluster that led to Christine Holgate's departure as Australia Post chief executive.

Then we have the insipid unwillingness of the conservative parties to pursue meaningful tax and industrial relations reforms. John Howard was the last Liberal prime minister to put his back into such efforts. Waterfront reforms were achieved on his watch alongside a host of other changes before the electorate decided Work Choices went too far.

Since that time there has been no ideological muscle on the right of politics when it comes to IR reforms, and opportunities to enhance productivity and international competitiveness have been lost.

We often hear lip service paid to the notion of tax reform, but in truth the Coalition doesn't have the stomach for it. The system needs a recalibration. Instead the best we get is the occasional realigning of company and income tax rates to accommodate bracket creep. It is woefully inadequate.

Perhaps the biggest furphy is the spin that only the Coalition knows how to balance the books. Given that debt has skyrocketed on this government's watch — and did so long before the pandemic made a bad situation worse — the current Coalition government is trading on the earned reputation of the previous one. Not a single minister in this government even sat around the cabinet table of Howard's administration, learning from the likes of Peter Costello and Peter Reith.

Ideology is rarely a reason for future MPs to choose a career in politics, and this is starkly so when comparing the timidity of the current crop to those who fought the internal ideological battles in the 1970s and '80s between dries and wets.

It feels like political satire listening to the current economic leaders in the Coalition spruiking their fiscal credentials at the same time they hand down a $78bn budget deficit with no plan to repair the underlying structural problems. As national debt ticks towards $1 trillion, the same names were lamenting a "debt and deficit disaster" when debt was one-third the size it is now.

Consider the 23.9 per cent tax to gross domestic product cap pledged this week. Given that spending is currently 27.8 per cent of GDP, all the government is doing is committing to long-term structural budget deficits without a plan to reduce spending in line with the tax cap simplistically promised. That's fiscally reckless. But because fear of electoral defeat is the primary concern, the Coalition hopes to cash in on voter misconceptions that it knows how to manage money, rather than cut spending in line with taxation streams so the budget can correct itself.

And remember, all of this is going on in a climate of rapid inflation and soon-to-be rising interest rates. In other words, the spendathon designed to buy votes is exacerbating the inflationary pressures that may cost people their homes when mortgage payments are affected and house prices fall.

Don't forget one of the policy announcements made early in this campaign was to ease lending restrictions for first-home buyers so they could borrow more with a smaller deposit. These new homeowners will be saddled with rising repayments.

Oh, and wages are stagnant, which means inflation pushing up the price of goods is even more debilitating for most people. The government crows that the unemployment rate is low at 4 per cent, which is a truism. And yes, it would have been nice if the Opposition Leader knew what it was on day one of the campaign. But trivial pursuit aside, you aren't counted in the unemployment data if you work as little as one hour a week, and underemployment remains a real problem.

Besides, the reason for the low unemployment rate has more to do with the temporary pauses in migration during the pandemic than any economic whiz-banger, by the government.

The simple fact is this government has refused to reform the economy meaningfully, it has spent up big and not with prudence, and it has pulled policy levers that have done more harm than good. As it begs, borrows and attempts to steal its way into a fourth term, all it really has left is a legacy from a bygone era to draw credibility and a scare campaign built on Labor's mistakes in the past. Mistakes, by the way, that are dwarfed by this government's poor decision-making.

I don't know if the other lot is up to the task of serious reform and budget repair. I suspect it isn't. The problems in politics appear generational and institutional, engulfing both sides. The system is working against its own needs to the detriment of all of us. But guess what? Labor can't be any worse than this lot. And who knows, maybe a stint on the wrong side of the treasury benches will help Liberals in name learn to become liberals by nature. Economically if not socially, given the permanent need to appease conservative tendencies in the Coalition.

Independent threat isn't all its cracked up to be

23 April 2022

There is growing speculation a hung parliament is in the offing. This inevitably brings with it claims by both major parties that they won't do deals with the crossbench, in a bid to convince voters to pick between them and not risk wasting their vote on a minor party or independent candidate. The majors also claim a hung parliament risks being unstable.

In fact there can be significant benefits to power-sharing arrangements. For a start, more stakeholders get a say on what the government might do, and generally speaking the crossbench is more interested in transparency than the government ever is.

One of the conditions Julia Gillard's government had to meet to win support from the crossbench in 2010 was to improve parliamentary processes. While the incoming Abbott government dismantled many of the changes, some stayed and the parliament is better for it.

It is in the interests of the major parties to claim a vote for an independent is a wasted one, but that's nonsense.

For a start, independents work for their local communities in a way major party MPs often do not.

Independents don't join ministerial ranks, which means they don't use their backbench role as a self-interested springboard to higher office the way major party MPs often do.

And when traditionally safe major party seats come under threat from independents, they inevitably get more electoral attention from the party fighting to save or win back the seat. That means more election pledges and more dollars going into the local area. It is a truism in Australian politics that marginal seats get the lion's share of local grants. Safe seats can be neglected by the other side because they know they can't win these seats, or they get taken for granted by the party that holds them. Independents shake up that reality.

While independents might support a government with a different partisan complexion to the one usually supported in the seat they hold, it is not as if the independent MP is unaccountable for such actions. Three years later the electorate can cast judgment on their choice.

Don't pay any attention to Scott Morrison or Anthony Albanese ruling out doing deals with the crossbench in the event of a hung parliament. The allure of power will be enticing enough for the pair of them to break that promise. But I would be surprised if anyone wanted to formalise power-sharing arrangements, as happened back in 2010. Doing so invites attacks from the opposition as it attempts to wedge its way into government three years later.

The narrative that Tony Abbott successfully prosecuted about chaos during the 2010–13 parliament was politically powerful but factually misguided. More legislation was passed during that term than in any other — not that I regard an overflow of legislation as necessarily equating to good governance. But it does dispel the myth of gridlock brought about by crossbench control.

There is a conundrum for voters in the inner-city seats where independents are seriously challenging sitting Liberal MPs. These seats include Wentworth, Mackellar, North Sydney, Goldstein and Kooyong. The last of these is occupied by Treasurer and deputy Liberal leader Josh Frydenberg.

The MPs in all these seats are what you might call moderate Liberals. Even if none has done enough to support moderate policy issues, a Liberal Party without any or all of these MPs will lurch only further to the right and therefore away from moderate policy positioning.

So what do voters do? Punish these MPs for not being vocal enough on everything from climate change action to the airing of bigoted rhetoric by the captain's pick candidate for Warringah, Katherine Deves, thereby worsening the hard-right complexion of the Liberal party room in the process? Or reward their collective timidity by re-electing them, therefore missing out on all the local advantages that an independent MP offers?

Judging by the way Morrison has chosen to campaign during the first two weeks on the hustings, it would seem that he isn't fussed about positioning the government in a way that would help save these moderate-held seats.

Rather, the Prime Minister is targeting his messages at the outer metropolitan electorates he needs to win against Labor: both seats he holds and seats he is going after, such as Macquarie, Parramatta and Greenway in Sydney's west.

Before the campaign started I predicted that few of the independents challenging moderate Liberals would win. While I still believe that to be the case, Morrison's actions aren't helping me get the prediction right.

Irrespective of how many, if any, of the non-incumbent independent candidates ultimately win, their presence is bleeding dollars and human capital from the wider Coalition campaign. These traditionally safe seats usually would be expected to raise funds to be distributed among the outer metro marginal seat campaigns, with local Liberals also expected to use Google maps to find their way to the marginals to help campaign. All of that won't happen because of the challenges afoot in these inner-city seats.

We will know the full extent of the damage done to the Coalition's chances of holding on to government only in the aftermath of the campaign. It could be a case of moderate Liberals winning their seat-by-seat battles at the expense of the wider political war with Labor. Morrison's strategy of ignoring these seats and targeting his rhetoric at the mortgage-belt electorates instead is all about avoiding that outcome.

If, however, the Coalition doesn't win enough seats to govern in its own right (but neither does Labor) Morrison will be forced to go cap in hand to the crossbenchers pleading for their support, as will Albanese. Under such circumstances you would have to think Labor is likelier to form minority government than the Coalition. But if both major parties secure the same number of seats well short of a majority, it is possible neither leader will be able to secure enough crossbench support to govern responsibly in the Westminster tradition.

If that happens Morrison could carry on until there is a vote of no confidence against him on the floor of the parliament. Were that to happen he could then call another election, hand the leadership over to someone the crossbench is willing to support, or Labor could be asked to form government with crossbench backing. By that time Albo might no longer be Labor leader.

Or this election campaign could be quickly followed by another one, without the parliament even sitting. But that could backfire on the major parties, delivering more, not fewer, crossbench MPs if voters really are sick and tired of the major parties.

It sounds messy but it's not. It's called democracy.

Property scheme is poor policy

19 April 2022

The Coalition's home loan guarantee scheme is a classic case of the superficial winning out over prudent policy development. Good politics trumping good economics.

Just watch as the individuals who have signed up to this scheme begin to suffer with rising interest rates and falling property prices.

The bottom line is that it is a market-distorting mechanism designed to win votes, nothing more. The political equivalent of a popularity contest driving policy development. With property prices on the rise nationally in recent years, the Coalition decided to guarantee home loans for new entrants into the housing market who weren't able to secure large enough deposits without government help.

In some cases, participants need only a 2 per cent deposit to buy a home under the scheme. Putting to one side the fact that the scheme logically flies in the face of the banking royal commission recommendations to lift lending standards, in the inflationary climate we're now in it is doubly bad policy.

The Coalition likes to crow about 60,000 Australians having signed up to the scheme. It hopes that number will rise with Monday's announcement that it is increasing the size of loans those buyers can access. For example, the cap in Canberra was $500,000 but it is rising to $750,000. In Sydney and major regional centres it rises from $800,000 to $900,000, taking effect on July 1 this year.

So just as economists are in universal agreement that interest rates are on the rise, the government lifts borrowing caps for people who ordinarily wouldn't be able to save sufficiently to secure the deposit the banks say they need. People for whom paying a monthly mortgage is a new thing.

It is crazy. Mortgage payments will sharply rise in the coming years, and houses are likely to lose value.

Few experts in the housing sector believe prices are going to do anything other than fall as rates rise, which courtesy of this scheme could mean we have thousands of new homeowners living with negative equity in the years ahead.

And for the rest of us not eligible for this scheme, we are on the hook for any defaults within it, because the government (that is, taxpayers) is guaranteeing the loans.

Inflation figures from overseas are deeply worrying, especially out of the US. Our own inflationary pressures are also high. Interest rates are tipped to rise four times this year alone, and keep on rising next year. Because rates have been so low for so long, such a lift in rates could see some mortgage payments lift by 50 per cent or even more. It will shock many, especially those new to paying a regular mortgage and who wouldn't ordinarily financially qualify were it not for this scheme.

Sadly, Labor has supported the scheme, which speaks to the political value of it rather than its economic worth. They don't want to be painted as the enemy of first home buyers. The superficial wins out again.

We often lament horserace journalism and a lack of policy rigour in the way elections get covered. This is a classic example of poor policy that needs to be rigorously picked apart by the media and experts alike. At every level it is wrong: it leverages new home buyers beyond their means if interest rates go up; it puts them at risk of negative equity if house prices fall; it defies the recommendations of the banking royal commission and it leaves the rest of us covering losses by those who access the scheme because of the taxpayer guarantees within it.

Major parties have no plans for updating engine of ageing tax system

15 April 2022

This really is a Seinfeld election campaign: it's about nothing, certainly when it comes to the economy. Neither major party has a plan for the future, despite the significant challenges we face.

Don't be fooled by the bluff and bluster of the opening week of the campaign.

Anthony Albanese's gaffe on the unemployment and cash rates was certainly a bad look but ultimately meaningless to the heavy lifting required to ready our economy for the future.

Equally, the Coalition might benefit from perceptions that it is the better economic manager, but after eight-and-a-half years in office it has next to nothing to show for it; no substance to support the perception voters have.

In truth, the national economy has been largely on autopilot since the heady days of the Bob Hawke-Paul Keating reforms and what John Howard and Peter Costello did to build on that legacy. The latter pair would take exception to being described as an addendum, which probably undersells their importance, but there is no denying the initial importance of the micro-economic reforms and modernisation measures instituted during the 1980s.

Through the years I have interviewed, talked privately to and studied the records of all four of these giants of modern Australian politics, and I can tell you that each in their own way has been critical of how little has happened since their day. Howard is the most polite of the four about politicians of today, but even he knows how underperforming Australia's political leadership has been for a decade and a half when it comes to managing the economy.

There are differences between the agendas of the two major parties fighting this year's election. These include substantive points of difference — on climate change, the structure of a national integrity commission, funding levels for services such as aged care and childcare — that voters can look at when determining who to support.

There are also different priorities when it comes to infrastructure plans, perhaps on border protection too.

But the heart of the economy is the tax system, and neither party has anything resembling a plan to make it fit for purpose for the coming decade. It is antiquated and overdue for an update.

2GB Radio host Luke Grant says the Labor Party have not "left themselves any room" to get things wrong as they head further into the election campaign. "A big part of this is the fact that every chance they've got, for three years they've thrown mud," he told Sky News host Rowan Dean.

Think of the Australian economy as a car and the tax system as the engine, the most important component. Both major parties are polishing the exterior, debating what colour and shape it should take, even arguing about the layout of the interior. But the engine is old, outdated and in need of a major overhaul.

At the moment there is a disproportionate reliance on income and company taxes, buttressed by a whole host of complex and inefficient taxes to go with that, spread between tiers of government. There is stamp duty, which discourages the buying and selling of property (which will matter if there is a downturn or interest rates go up); and payroll taxes, which discourage businesses from employing more staff. These won't change without federation reform, which has been taken off the table.

Income taxes dominate revenue streams for federal governments. When their budgets get out of control, bracket creep is used slowly to fix the structural deficits so politicians don't have to do anything meaningful.

Recently we have seen cuts to income taxes. But doing so without widening the reform remit has added to the structural deficit in the budget that exists well into the future. Company taxes have come down, but not enough to mirror like-for-like economies around the world. That risks offshoring, in the same way high income taxes risk a brain drain.

But you can't make such taxes more internationally competitive by cutting them without lifting taxes elsewhere, unless a government is prepared to reduce the size of government. At the moment there is a cultural shift towards citizens expecting more, not less, of government, so the days of economic liberals downsizing the role of the state no longer jells with community wants. That, at least, is my reading of the situation.

So what can governments do? There are many prudent internationally tested tax reforms that could be embarked on, but neither major party is willing even to have the debate because the sorts of reforms that should be on the table are considered taboo.

I'm talking about inheritance taxes; taxing the family home; reforming the superannuation system so the ageing population of the future pays its way rather than leaving a debt burden and recurrent expenditure problem for younger generations. Sin taxes are worth a closer look, too.

The tax burden can't result in a shift to consumers, however. Businesses have to pay their way, especially if the broadbased company tax rate is to come down. That could involve targeted industry taxes, for example: super-profits taxes or environmental penalty taxes where offshoring isn't an option. But we need a rigorous scholarly debate first so outcomes are robust and not driven only on a whim.

Unfortunately, in Australian politics, any party or politician who seeks to start a debate about any of these issues is shot down almost instantly. They wouldn't get their ideas into the internal party debate, much less be permitted to ventilate them publicly, secure something like a tax summit to do so more formally, then embark on a sales pitch to win a mandate for reform in an electorate.

Even if they did get that far they would likely lose the election in which such issues were fought because, in campaigns, fear of change trumps hope and prudent planning for the future.

So what is left? Nothing; no plan by either side to tackle the reforms previous leaders did. The current generation of politicians presumably was drawn to their vocation because of those who inspired them in the past and because of issues they fought for.

On the Labor side, I suspect too many of the current generation really were inspired only by Gough Whitlam, who despite embarking on many important social reforms after decades of conservative governance, didn't really pay much attention to economic settings.

To the extent Hawke and Keating were inspirational to current Labor politicians, it was their charisma, their capacity to win elections and dominate the floor of parliament, that shone brightly — in other words, the theatre of politics. I don't hear too many Labor politicians today lauding the economic reforming credentials of Hawke and Keating beyond using them as a punch line. If it were more than that, they would aspire to do more now because otherwise they are no credit to the past leaders they look up to.

It is no better on the conservative side. Liberals, in particular, like to hold themselves up as fiscal conservatives, the better money managers. But they do nothing to support such a claim. Economic reform, making the tax system fit for purpose and able to support what government does, is how you live up to the mantra of being a fiscal conservative. If Howard hadn't legislated the GST and reformed industrial relations, he wouldn't have been able to pay down debt and balance the budget. Both areas, instead, would have been a drag on the economy.

This Coalition government is asking for a fourth term having done next to nothing to modernise the economy since it came to office, and it certainly has no plan to change that pattern of neglect if it wins again.

Which way will the pendulum swing?

19 March 2022

The closer we get to the election the more we'll see the major party leaders focusing their attention on key marginal seats: those they hope to win off the other side and those they need to retain to form government.

Electoral politics always boils down to a simple numbers game. For the most part it will be Scott Morrison on the defensive trying to hang on to seats Labor is targeting. However, because his majority is wafer thin, for the Coalition to have any hope of holding on to government it needs to go after some marginal Labor seats.

At the top of that list is the seat of Gilmore on the south coast of NSW. Former state minister Andrew Constance is attempting to move into federal politics, despite making scathing comments about the Prime Minister's response to the bushfires two years ago.

The magic number for Labor to govern in its own right is 77 seats, assuming it wants to control the floor of parliament and select one of its own as Speaker. If it gets to 75 it also wins because it is very hard to imagine Adam Bandt or Andrew Wilkie supporting a Coalition government.

Anthony Albanese might be able to lead a minority government with even fewer seats, but that would require the support of independents occupying traditional conservative seats, which is no certainty.

Labor starts the campaign with 69 seats, assuming you give it the newly created Victorian seat of Hawke, projected to be a safe Labor win. That leaves Labor needing to net eight seats on polling day to form majority government, six to govern with the support of the Greens and Wilkie. Remember these figures.

It is important to note that if the current polling is replicated on election day a seat-by-seat analysis becomes all but meaningless.

The most recent Newspoll had the opposition ahead 55–45 per cent on the two-party vote. That would mean a move is afoot and seats not currently on Labor's radar would fall its way. It also could mean the primary votes of Liberals in safer seats fall low enough to put them at risk from independent challenges.

Late in the campaign such a blowout result would see the Opposition Leader visiting seats much further up the electoral pendulum. Morrison would stop visiting ultra-marginal seats, instead campaigning in safer electorates at risk as the Coalition attempted to save the furniture for next time.

However, if the polls tighten, as they usually (but not always) do, the pathway to victory for the opposition becomes narrower. Which is why hard heads within Labor aren't getting ahead of themselves. They know the risks a campaign presents, alongside the mother of all scare campaigns.

Working our way around the country, there are nine seats Labor regards as the lowest hanging fruit: Flynn, Brisbane and Longman in Queensland; Reid in NSW; Chisholm in Victoria; Bass in Tasmania; Boothby in South Australia; and Swan and Pearce in Western Australia.

As long as Labor holds Gilmore it can afford to fall short in one of these contests and still form majority government; for example, win just two of the three seats it's targeting in Queensland but pick up all the others around the country.

Four of the nine seats mentioned are occupied by retiring government MPs. Swan at 3.2 per cent is the most marginal WA seat and coupled with the retirement of Steve Irons looks lost for the Liberals.

Boothby and Flynn become much harder to retain because of retiring MPs. Flynn, however, is held with an 8.7 per cent margin — a large amount of electoral fat that could help save it for the government. But Labor has preselected an excellent candidate. Boothby is very marginal at 1.4 per cent, but it is a traditional Liberal seat, which means support is not as soft as it can be in swing seats. Nicolle Flint faced a vicious (and sexist) campaign last time, a major reason she isn't putting herself through another one.

Pearce at 5.2 per cent will be a tough hold for the Liberals because of the controversies surrounding outgoing member and former attorney-general Christian Porter. But his retirement probably gives the new Liberal candidate a better chance of retaining the seat for the government than if Porter had sought re-election.

The remaining two Queensland seats of Longman and Brisbane are held with margins of 3.3 per cent and 4.9 per cent respectively. Longman's margin makes it appear the more vulnerable of the two; however, its demographics suits Morrison's persona much more than Brisbane's and the floods may make holding Brisbane that much tougher for the Prime Minister.

The Tasmanian seat of Bass (0.4 per cent) and the Victorian seat of Chisholm (0.5 per cent) are the two most marginal Coalition seats anywhere in the country.

It was a miracle the Liberals held Chisholm last time; if they do so again the Coalition will secure a fourth term. It is a must win for Labor. Bass is a traditional swing seat and the closeness of the margin suggests it's a likely Liberal loss even if Morrison retains the prime ministership.

But Bridget Archer having defied the Prime Minister in support of a federal corruption watchdog and over religious discrimination laws could hang on with a strong personal following. How ironic would it be if her willingness to thumb her nose at Morrison got him re-elected?

Reid in NSW is a traditional Labor seat first won by the Liberals back in 2013 when Craig Laundy entered parliament. It was a surprise hold by Fiona Martin in 2019 when Laundy retired. Labor expects to pick it up this time and I can't find too many Liberals who are hopeful of retaining it.

Conservatives are hopeful Morrison can do what John Howard did in 1998 and win the election with less than 50 per cent of the popular vote, holding on in the seats that matter. Howard won the 1998 election with just 48.9 per cent of the two-party vote, sandbagging enough key marginal seats to retain a surprisingly healthy majority. But Morrison starts this campaign with far fewer seats than Howard going into the 1998 campaign, dramatically increasing the degree of difficulty for his re-election.

When you run through the seats it becomes easier to see why Labor is nervous it may fall short of victory if the move isn't on. That said, on any calculation it's hard to find enough seats for Morrison to again govern with a majority. For that to happen he'll need to pick Albanese apart the way Howard did Mark Latham in 2004. But Albanese is certainly no Latham.

Aged-care crisis looms as vote changer

26 February 2022

On Tuesday it will be 12 months since the Royal Commission into Aged Care Quality and Safety final report was handed down. The crisis is real, systemic and won't go away when the pandemic dissipates. The sector was in crisis long before the pandemic struck.

Problems in aged care were always going to get worse as a growing number of baby boomers entered the system. They started hitting retirement age about a decade ago, which means now they are beginning to encounter the aged-care system also.

Developed country populations are ageing as modern medicine helps us live longer. While this presents policy challenges, it's certainly better than the alternative.

The baby boomers are a generational bubble, with a spike in births in the aftermath of World War II. They have long been an important voting cohort because of their relative size compared with other generations. These twin particulars of ageing and baby boomer retirements are putting added strain on a sector already under immense pressure.

As a generation, baby boomers are less stoic than those that came before them. That isn't a criticism; it points to the fact they won't accept substandard care, nor should they. They are a modern generational cohort, burning into the socially liberal society most Western developed countries have become.

As the oldest members of the baby boom generation start to enter aged-care homes, their children are experiencing the trauma of the sector, too. Generation X therefore is starting to sit up and take notice of the problems afoot.

That's my generation, but I had an early entree into the challenges the sector faces because my mother was the matron of an aged-care facility and we lived on site. It was one of the better publicly run aged-care homes at the time, and it was 30 years ago now, but the problems we see today existed in a microcosm then.

When my mother suffered from early onset dementia and needed professional care, she was adamant she didn't want to enter a broken system. As difficult as it was, we had the means to care for her from home, but that isn't a realistic option for most people – nor should it be. We need the sector to be inviting and trusted, not seen as an option of last resort that represents abandoning loved ones.

Traditionally there has been a view that issues in aged care don't shift votes, but perhaps that is changing now that larger cohorts of new generations are coming into contact with the sector. This reality, coupled with the exposure of problems during the pandemic and the shocking findings of the royal commission, presents an opportunity and a risk for the major parties at this election.

Ignore the need for wholesale reforms at your peril, major parties; it could risk your electoral chances. Embrace the need for change (alongside a significant injection of public funding) and perhaps take political advantage of an emerging zeitgeist. Could this be the first election at which aged care takes centre stage as a vote shifter? It should.

The royal commission found that up to two-thirds of residents are malnourished or at risk of being malnourished. Page one of the interim report (titled Neglect) stated: "This cruel and harmful system must be changed... Older people deserve so much more." Forty per cent of submissions to the commission raised concerns about neglect. The commission cited "major quality and safety issues", including but not limited to "inadequate prevention and management of wounds", "poor continence management", "dreadful food, nutrition and hydration", "a high incidence of assaults by staff on residents and by residents on other residents and on staff" and "patchy and fragmented palliative care for residents who are dying".

These horror stories represent official findings about a sector most of us, like it or not, will come into contact with one day if we haven't already. In modern Australia, one of the wealthiest nations on the planet. And the worst of it? They are findings from a multi-year investigation that has only worsened in the past 12 months.

There are many things that need to change when it comes to how aged care is provided, most of which are linked to the need for wider tax reform to help fund the sector into the future. We also need to have a serious debate about the size of government, what we expect of government, and depending on the answer to these questions what role private capital should play in the provision of aged-care services, and how that should be constituted.

Governments may need to be bold, embracing policy reforms that otherwise get ruled out too quickly because they are open to negative scare campaigns come election time.

The biggest issue that needs to be addressed to start improving the sector has to be the pay of those employed in it. Aged-care work is tough and often complex. It is hard to attract quality staff and even harder to retain their services.

Many people living in aged care aren't just elderly and fragile; they also suffer from cognitive conditions including dementia. Routines matter, certainty matters. The inability to attract and retain good workers has a profound and direct impact on these patients.

Aged-care workers are among the lowest paid workers across all sectors in the economy. Attracting and retaining staff is especially problematic in the regions, yet where are the Nationals spruiking for change? Their silence is deafening.

The Committee for Economic Development of Australia has predicted that because of the expected increase in demand in the coming years a net increase of 17,000 workers in aged care is needed just to maintain current standards — standards that have been exposed as woefully inadequate.

While Greg Hunt took over aged care in conjunction with his ministerial responsibilities for health, Richard Colbeck remains the junior minister at the vanguard. How he hasn't been sacked is beyond me. But achieving change is beyond his abilities; the real problem comes further up the line because the sector needs ministerial representation at the highest levels of government. It should be a stand-alone cabinet portfolio held by a senior member of the government. Why Anthony Albanese hasn't put his aged care spokeswoman Clare O'Neil in shadow cabinet is beyond me. Labor should commit to doing so in government if it wins the election, to show how serious it is about repairing the sector.

If I am right and this important policy area is emerging as a vote changer, the opportunity is there for Labor to give voters a genuine policy alternative, avoiding accusations that it is playing to a small-target strategy. Equally, if fixing the sector became a genuine Coalition priority, it could facilitate its political salvation.

Let's hope both major parties make aged care the priority it deserves to be.

Reading the below column back knowing that Scott Morrison lost the election relatively comfortably is a reminder how cautious we all were. Having been burnt once by his capacity to come back and defy consistently bad polling in 2019 few commentators were prepared to write him off this time. In hindsight trailing 44–56 per cent in the polls three months out from the election really was a bridge too far for a PM on the nose and a government long in the tooth.

PM's down but don't count him out yet

12–13 February 2022

Don't write off Scott Morrison just yet.

Yes, the government is trailing 44 to 56 per cent on the two-party vote according to the polls and the Prime Minister's personal numbers have headed south dramatically. When a leader's net satisfaction rating plummets well below that of the opposition leader — and they are neck and neck on the better prime minister ratings — the incumbent leader is no longer a positive drag on their party's vote. That makes playing catch-up much more difficult.

Yes, Morrison's colleagues have lined up to describe him variously as a "fraud", a "liar", a "hypocrite", a "horrible, horrible person" and even a "complete psycho". And on Thursday it was revealed that Morrison was rolled in cabinet last Monday, on a political judgment call no less. The cabinet humiliation in turn was leaked to the media, a sure sign of instability at the top.

None of this bodes well for the election. Just for starters, Labor will use the colourful descriptions of Morrison in campaign advertisements and polling booth paraphernalia. The comments by former NSW premier Gladys Berejiklian labelling Morrison more interested in politics than people's lives will be especially damaging in seats affected by the Black Summer bushfires.

But writing off Morrison would be a mistake. He has come from behind to win before, and the evidence from the past tells us that when conservatives lose elections they lose them only narrowly. They are always in the fight, even when appearances suggest otherwise. With a little more than three months to go until polling day this election is still up for grabs.

Don't forget, Labor has openly won its way into government federally only three times since World War II. That is an appalling record of failure. Anthony Albanese has been on the wrong side of almost every internal Labor leadership showdown he has been involved with during his political career. As a member of the Left, failure is second nature. He jokes about it as a practical problem but a sign that unlike so many modern politicians at least he stands for something even if that stand results in defeat.

The government will launch a vicious scare campaign against the man they call Albo, a nickname he grew up with, unlike the calculated decision in recent years to manufacture ScoMo as the Prime Minister's nickname of choice. (For the record, PVO was my schoolboy nickname.)

The recently launched campaign targeting Albo attempts to lampoon him as unprepared for the rigours of being prime minister, seemingly forgetting that he has served as deputy prime minister and was a long-term leader of the house and infrastructure minister for the duration of the Rudd and Gillard years — including during the post-global financial crisis reconstruction phase. Infrastructure spending and decision-making will be a key issue as we come out of the pandemic.

But facts don't always matter in politics or political advertising, and the Coalition will likely score points with voters when it raises concerns about Albo's capacity to manage the economy. His economic degree from one of Australia's top universities will count for little. Labor has lost the economic debate ever since it walked away from the record of micro-economic achievement during the Hawke and Keating years after its heavy 1996 defeat.

The Coalition is the preferred economic managers, and the election in May is timed to follow an early budget and the post-budget sales pitch. It's likely the economy will become the central issue.

Morrison is damaged but Josh Frydenberg remains an electoral asset. He'll take the lead selling the budget to soften the government with voters before the official campaign begins. After which Morrison will move front and centre and seek to do to Albo what he did to Bill Shorten in 2019: come from behind to pull off a miracle.

To be sure, it will be harder this time, but Morrison doesn't deserve to be written off.

This election will be fascinating on so many levels. State by state differences are hard to calculate. Will border restrictions in Western Australia still exist? Either way, will voters emulate what happens at state level around the country or arbitrage by voting differently federally?

We have a state election in South Australia next month. Queensland is dominated by wall-to-wall Liberal National Party-held seats, and the old adage is that whichever party holds Queensland forms government. Once upon a time there was a view Morrison could win as many as a half-dozen seats off Labor in NSW alone, his home state. That now looks unlikely. Does that cost him re-election?

Strategists on both sides of the major party divide believe if an election were held this weekend Labor would win somewhere between 80 and 82 seats. While that would see the party form majority government, it still represents only a six-seat majority, smaller than you might have expected. Larger (just) than Gough Whitlam's 1972 win, but smaller than

Kevin Rudd's eight-seat majority. Few inside Labor believe Albo has the popularity of a Whitlam or a Rudd in their time, notwithstanding his compelling backstory. What effect does that have?

In the time until polling day, the Coalition's first task is to find a way to take away Labor's majority. Losing to a Labor minority government is better for the future than losing to a Labor majority government not beholden to the crossbench. Turning around six seats between now and polling day doesn't sound that hard. Not given the low ebb the government is at or considering the fertile ground the budget is likely to shift the focus to. It's all upside surely?

The harder equation for the Coalition is finding the remaining seats needed to claw back into contention in the virtual tallyroom. This calculation is made harder courtesy of the difficulties inner-city Liberals are facing staving off independent challenges.

Even if none of these seats is lost to independents, which looks increasingly less likely, the financial effort alone retaining them represents a resource allocation opportunity cost in key marginal contests against Labor.

There is little doubt Morrison is up against it to return to power after the May election. But he's a long way from out of the fight. The betting markets, for example, are exaggerated in the odds they're offering. We know Morrison is a good campaigner: on message and in synch with party headquarters. This will count for something if the contest becomes a seat-by-seat dogfight.

My mum ran an aged care home and never wanted to end her days in one

8 February 2022

While the Prime Minister might have only recently acknowledged a crisis in aged care, accidentally spitting the words out at a media conference the other day, it's a sector that's been on the brink for decades. With the ageing of the population the demands on aged care homes will only grow in the years to come.

The impact of Covid has led to staff shortages and higher mortality rates, to a point where yesterday Scott Morrison called the military in to help. But that is a short-term band aid fix at best. Even as we learn to live with Covid, and the pandemic becomes endemic, the aged care sector will remain in crisis. The Royal Commission highlighted just how systemic the problems are.

My mother ran a public aged care home in the 1980s, and we lived on site, allowing me as a child to see firsthand the challenges afoot. Overheard conversations about it around the dinner table. Staff shortages were utterly crippling. The salaries offered made it hard to attract and retain talented people. I recall my mother up late trying to make the rosters work, putting through desperate last-minute calls to plug staffing gaps. Relying on the goodwill of those who worked there. Trying to stretch the budget to ensure the food on offer was as palatable as possible. To build in functions and activities to enrich the lives of the residents.

The home she ran was unusual in that it was set at an amazing location which gave the residents a beautiful aesthetic. It had harbour views if you can believe that. A public nursing home to be sure. In the end all of that led to it being closed down, as the government of the day sought to sell off the land, shifting the residents to a far less ideal aged care setting. One more like all the others. Politicians doing what they do I recall her saying "this government's next policy will be to give everyone a razor blade when they turn 65", so aghast was she with the state of the sector. Hard and pointed criticism, yes, but reflective of the frustrations felt by someone at the front line trying to make the system functional.

That was more than 30 years ago, the situation has only gotten worse since then. We know that from the findings of the Royal Commission. The predictions are that the downward spiral of the aged care sector will accelerate without major reforms and huge injections of funding where it is needed most.

In a perhaps ironic twist of fate mum was diagnosed with early onset dementia herself but was adamant she didn't want to end up in an aged care facility. She was losing her faculties, but not so much as to be blinded to the grim reality of ending up in a home. My wife and I were fortunate to have the means to avoid that, living with her and arranging the necessary support structures to make doing so manageable. But it wasn't easy. Respite care was important for our own mental health.

Of course, not all facilities are awful, far from it. And ultimately dependent care can become unavoidable. It can be a lottery for people with no choice but to put loved ones into care. As a society we have a responsibility to make sure the aged care sector is a top priority, not a forgotten policy area the responsibility for which gets handed to a junior minister without adequate pull within government. That has long been the case when prime ministers hand out portfolios.

One of the challenges in aged care is the shared responsibility between state and federal governments. We know co-operation between tiers of government is strained at the best of times. These are the worst of times, in a sector hit hard by current events and adversely impacted by demographic changes which are evolving.

If there is a positive to come out of the Covid disaster in aged care, it must be the attention now focused on the sector — an opportunity to demand change. Especially right before an election.

As the population ages the odds are that most of us will end up in some form of care one day. Self-interest alone should dictate that we demand improvements.

Scott Morrison's miracle win Mark II will be harder to pull off

4 February 2022

This week hasn't gone exactly the way Scott Morrison would have wanted in the lead-up to next week's return of parliament. He'd hoped to use his National Press Club address on Tuesday as a reset, but that certainly didn't happen.

Instead the Prime Minister will go into the sitting fortnight forced to dismiss suggestions there are divisions (and rats) in his ranks, and that's before we get to all the policy challenges (and failures) he'll be held accountable for. What's happening in aged care will surely be a focal point.

The looming federal election is high stakes. Whichever major party loses will face serious soul searching, with divisions in its aftermath likely to hit fever pitch. This is common for parties in defeat, but the fallout will be greater than usual for the loser this time.

If it's Labor, not only will it guarantee the party is out of office for at least a decade this electoral cycle but it will be the second election in a row where Labor has led comfortably and consistently in the polls before going on to lose.

The Coalition is behind 44 per cent to 56 per cent according to the latest Newspoll. It would be a brave commentator to sign Morrison's political death warrant after his come-from-behind victory three years ago, but pulling off such a win a second time will be even harder.

If that happens it will mean Labor has secured a parliamentary majority in just one of the past 10 federal elections — a poor performance likely to spark a major clean-out in Canberra.

If the Coalition loses, the factional and personality divisions that are just below the surface will bubble up. Electoral success was the reason John Howard was able to maintain control over the Liberal Party and the Coalition for so long. Tony Abbott managed to contain divisions in the lead-up to 2013 on the anticipation of victory, but in doing so he only papered over problems that never really went away.

I'm talking about serious personality differences among prominent MPs, many of whom are still there. And the factional and policy divides that exist from state to state and between the Coalition parties are arguably greater than ever. Mavericks on the right and left will feel free to express themselves in opposition in a way that incumbency naturally curtails.

Morrison is only just holding together those divisions now. There are plenty of reasons his hold is weakening, among them his falling personal support in the polls. Last election the Coalition won because of Morrison. This time it will need to win despite him, unless those personal numbers turn around. Just imagine how much worse the tensions will become in defeat.

It wasn't that long ago that incumbency during the pandemic looked likely to help, not hurt, Morrison's chances. Despite missteps along the way, sitting premiers around the country secured their re-elections and most commentators assumed Morrison would too. But that's no longer a certainty.

Despite Australia avoiding the worst of the pandemic compared with death rates in other countries, the vaccine rollout was botched. While Morrison seemed to overcome those problems and sidestep a serious fallout from failures to plan for better quarantining, Australia's ultimately high vaccination rate didn't get followed up with adequate forward planning for what had to come next.

The lack of access to rapid antigen tests was a federal blunder that should have been avoided, plain and simple. It has become a distraction from the government's need to shift attention to the economy, which is its most powerful electoral weapon given we know voters trust it more than Labor to manage the economy. Josh Frydenberg must be pulling out what's left of his hair in frustration.

Problems in the aged-care sector during the pandemic are again taking centre stage. Aged Care Services Minister Richard Colbeck remains hapless and his senior minister, Greg Hunt, seems to have checked out early, having announced plans to retire at the election. Morrison has yet to tells us who may replace Hunt if the government can find a way to get re-elected.

These problems of substance for the government are challenges that sit side-by-side with obvious evidence of instability and backbiting in its ranks.

While it's inevitable speculation surrounding which senior colleague of Morrison described him as a "complete psycho" in a text exchange with former NSW premier Gladys Berejiklian, as I revealed at the National Press Club, trying to weed out who it was is an exercise in futility.

Former Prime Minister Malcolm Turnbull captured that reality perfectly, and playfully, on ABC's 7.30 program when Laura Tingle asked him: "Have you got a theory who might be the texting minister?" Turnbull responded: "Yes, I will name the culprit. It was Colonel Mustard in the library with a smartphone."

More interesting is the conjecture surrounding what might have motivated the leak. In trying to understand that I've seen questions asked about the timing of an old text exchange being leaked now. I was provided with the exchange contemporaneously during the bushfires of 2020, two years ago. But the source did not authorise me to use the text messages until more recently. They were provided to me at that time for the purpose of convincing me that there was widespread anger with how

Morrison was treating people during the fires.

As you would imagine I regularly checked in trying to convince the source to let me use the texts, given their explosiveness.

I wanted to include them in the book on Morrison that Wayne Errington and I published in March last year but wasn't given the green light. I tried again in late July last year when interviewing the Prime Minister on Network Ten's The Project. It would have been a perfect opportunity to press him, with no way out of the discussion. Berejiklian was still premier. But again the source would not release me to do so.

Late last year when it was speculated Berejiklian would contest the seat of Warringah was another perfect opportunity, but again I couldn't use the texts. The National Press Club on Tuesday was the first chance I had to ask the Prime Minister about the texts since being allowed to reveal them. Using them earlier would have breached the terms on which I was provided with the exchange, which I was never going to do.

The election is likely to be called for Saturday, May 21. It's not a lot of time for Morrison to turn around his political fortunes, but he has done it before. If history repeats, comeback Mark II will be extraordinary to watch.

SMS turns Scott Morrison's reset into painful rewind

3 February 2022

Scott Morrison's National Press Club address was supposed to be his reset moment ahead of the election.

Instead, the Prime Minister is being forced to answer questions about which current senior minister texted disparaging comments about him with Gladys Berejiklian.

The former NSW premier was a willing participant in the whinge-fest about Morrison but because the minister hasn't been named, attention has turned to who the other party in the conversation was.

While it's understandable that journalists will ask questions about it, politicians will of course line up to deny it was them, and others will demand the responsible minister out themselves; that's never going to happen.

Why? Because the minister is the source, which is also why the veracity of the text exchange isn't in question. It wasn't passed on by a third party, for example.

I'm the only other person who knows who the minister is and that's the way it will always be. Journalists protect their sources.

The PM wouldn't have appreciated learning that someone he's described as a close friend, Berejiklian, texted that he's "a horrible, horrible person".

Especially when that person is a former NSW premier he wanted to run for a federal seat at the next election. But it's a story.

When the other half of the conversation is a senior, current minister who described the PM as a "complete psycho" and "fraud", that raises the understandable concern that someone has chosen to leak something damaging about him and they are still "lurking in the ranks", as an MP described it to me.

Others will speculate about their motivation in leaking the texts. The exchange speaks for itself: during the bushfires two years ago, the minister and Berejiklian were seething about Morrison on a number of levels.

The National Press Club was the best opportunity available to put the messages to the PM and get a proper response. At a news conference, he would have dismissed that question long before it was over.

Submitting questions to his office would have resulted in all manner of backroom discussions followed by a carefully crafted response late in the day. Probably without any comment from the PM.

We wouldn't have been able to see how Morrison really felt upon hearing what was said about him. His reaction told its own story. He looked shocked, concerned, and even hurt. Who wouldn't be?

But there is only one thing the government can now do: get over it and get on with business.

A witch hunt will get them absolutely nowhere.

Agree to disagree on the road to change

28 January 2022

What are the topics we are still allowed to debate versus those that have become so taboo that differences of opinion aren't acceptable? It feels as if differences of opinion on contestable propositions aren't as tolerated as they once were — almost ironically given society is becoming increasingly diverse and open to new ideas.

It could be a case of the loudest voices are the least tolerant, meaning that the appearance of less tolerance for contrarianism in modern society is nothing more than a social media mirage, amplified and reproduced by sections of the media that don't reflect the mainstream.

If, however, we actually are becoming less open to debate, it is perhaps partly a function of increased polarisation, or absolutism in intellectual thinking.

Perhaps it is explained via lost civility, reflecting a lack of innate courtesy (a generational thing perhaps) or emblematic of understandable frustration by some with slow progress as they clamour for change.

In other words, the backlash phenomenon could be such that contrarianism has no place when it butts up against the zeitgeist.

Yet history tells us shutting down differences of opinion rarely achieves lasting outcomes. Or, put differently, ends rarely justify means. Unintended consequences also can be perverse. Who gets to decide which topics are open for debate (as well as polite disagreements of opinion) and which are not?

We have laws preventing prejudices such as racism and sexism when they do lead to discriminatory behaviours, but we can't control the minds of those who hold such abhorrent views. Former attorney-general George Brandis once indelicately made the point that people "have a right to be bigots". The hope is that in time bigoted sentiments will fade away — at first less frequent, then less obvious, eventually non-existent — partly as a consequence of discrimination legislation.

In the meantime, should we be allowed to stifle the free speech of those who hold such views?

Yes, I say, to a certain extent at least. There are "freedoms from" not just "freedoms to" as part of the social contract we all sign up to as citizens in a democracy.

People have a right not to be racially abused or sexually harassed, just as others have a right to think and (to some extent) say what they think.

But what happens if you oppose change that some see as important to continue overcoming racial and sexual prejudices, such as changing the date of Australia Day or the enacting of gender quotas?

I happen to be in favour of both of the above and will vigorously argue (and have) the case publicly for change. But if I can't change the mind of those with whom I disagree, I can politely agree to disagree. That's becoming rarer in our modern world, where issues increasingly are seen as black and white rather than having multiple shades of grey.

Agreeing to disagree has long been a hallmark of civil society, but it seems fewer ideas and topics are tolerated as contestable than was once the case.

Is it acceptable to still oppose same-sex marriage? It's the law now, having been supported overwhelming by nearly two-thirds of Australians. We were late to the party as a Western democracy, but we got there eventually. I first advocated for such change back in 2003 when doing so was significantly less popular than it is now.

But surely holding a view that opposed the legislative shift now in place is still tolerable, if only on religious grounds? Scott Morrison walked out of the chamber when the parliament voted for it.

Taboo views clearly include supporting once accepted policy scripts such as apartheid or gender exclusion from working roles. I can't believe clubs that exclude on gender are still allowed to operate that way. They certainly aren't allowed to do so on racial grounds anymore.

Extreme "isms" should be taboo, such as fascism and perhaps communism, but not conservatism or socialism for example. Nor liberalism, which can result in advocacy for civil liberties such as the right not to be vaccinated. It's not my cause du jour, but such advocacy shouldn't be taboo either.

Universities have long been bastions for debates that sometimes court controversy, but even our institutions of higher education are becoming less tolerant of contrarians. Peter Singer is one of the world's leading philosophers and has logically argued for all manner of contrarian causes. Yet even he is now lamenting the stifling of free debate on and off university campuses.

To some extent the rise of political correctness has stifled contrarianism, which is not to criticise political correctness. It has a valuable place helping overcome unreasonable conduct, especially towards minorities. It offers a positive and healthy injection of civility into debates, most of the time.

Yet, in an ironic twist, some who would consider themselves politically correct break ranks from it whenever they find themselves in opposing arguments with someone they regard as detestable.

On the positive side, if we go back far enough, contrarians were lynched, burned at the stake or put on public trial for their heretical views. That doesn't happen anymore, at least not in civilised societies. Which is just one reason civility matters.

But what happens when we get to a point at which reforms and progress appear to slow down, unacceptably so for many who want modern Australia to address problems long overdue for fixing: climate change, violence against women, lasting reconciliation with Indigenous communities? Can ends ever justify means or do we risk what we already have if we trample over civil discourse in the pursuit of change?

There are no guaranteed right answers to these important questions, and we can agree to disagree (hopefully) on our preferred pathways to achieve change. Different people with different backgrounds, ideologies and political affiliations will want to trial different options on the table. We may get it wrong before we get it right.

Because achieving change isn't easy and it usually doesn't happen quickly. And achieving lasting change that brings people along for the journey, without causing a counter-productive backlash, is even harder.

As Australian of the Year, there is no worthier winner than fighter Dylan Alcott

26 January 2022

The Australia Day Council are to be applauded for selecting Dylan Alcott as the 2022 Australian of the Year. It is hard to think of a more worthy winner. Apart from his prowess as an inclusive sporting champion, his advocacy for disability issues has already been life changing for many Australians. His contribution will now only grow even greater.

Let's throw in what a wonderful positive human being Alcott is, despite the challenges life has thrown his way. The way he carries himself will ensure he's able to use his platform this year to increase awareness about the causes that matter most to him, bringing the nation with him. Causes that deserve greater attention and action.

Make no mistake, Alcott will be loud and proud speaking out to demand better disability outcomes. He won't be afraid to hold the government to account for failures in need of fixing.

Most Australians would know Alcott for the sporting champion that he is, but he has also been a tireless worker for charity throughout what has been a glittering sporting career. He's fought hard for better disability services, improved awareness about the support Australians with a disability need, but importantly also framing his advocacy around the need for the rest of Australia to treat anyone with a disability as fierce and capable contributors. To describe him as an inspiration would be an understatement.

We know that, for example, the National Disability Insurance Scheme (as a worthy as it is) needs improvement. Who better to shine a light on exactly how that can happen and in what ways than someone like Alcott. This is a debate he's already positively contributed to over a number of years. But there is so much more to be done and he'll help achieve those improvements I have no doubt.

It is hard to believe that in more than 60 years there has never been an Australian of the Year selected who has a disability. The time it has taken to change that is a sure sign that the cause deserves greater attention. But Alcott winning this award isn't the time to reflect negatively on that oversight. The chance to improve things is now.

Despite the challenges administering the NDIS has had in recent years, since it was conceived and implemented it has helped raise the profile of what can and must be done to break down barriers. It has helped ensure more fiscal muscle is behind disability support services. Alcott has also flagged the need for greater disability representation across fields in this country, showing his awareness for the important mix of practical and symbolic achievements. It is a passion he'll no doubt focus on further this year.

And with Alcott soon to retire from tennis (hopefully with one last Australian Open under his belt, but he's achieved more than enough in his sporting career even if that doesn't happen), he'll have more time than he otherwise might to throw himself into the job of being Australian of the Year.

Few columns I have written have caused the stir the below one did. I remember how it came about. I saw on social media the way Grace Tame had responded to Scott Morrison when attending the event at The Lodge for the state-by-state Australians of the year. I didn't agree with the acclaim being sent her way for snubbing him. As the article makes clear, I just found it unnecessary and over the top. I thought hard about not writing the piece, because I really wasn't up for another round of online hate I knew it would evoke. But then I thought to myself, the day I stop expressing views I hold because I'm worried about a pile on is the day I will stop writing opinion pieces and enjoy everything else life has to offer. In sharp contrast to the social media responses and those with a platform seeking to appear virtuous, I have never had more people come up to me randomly expressing that they quietly agreed with my views. Maybe these so-called "quiet Australians" really are a thing! And I can assure you the keyboard warriors on social media would lose their collective shit if only they knew some of the high profile people who privately said they agreed with me. Politicians and journalists they would NEVER expect.

Grace Tame: If your disdain for the PM is so great, why go?

25 January 2022

The footage of Grace Tame meeting the Prime Minister at his residence in the nation's capital for a reception today was embarrassing, for her that is.

She was ungracious, rude and childish, refusing to smile for the cameras, barely acknowledging his existence when standing next to him. The footage tells the story free of overstatement.

She didn't have to play the role of court jester, or be a fake. Just be a decent human being, that's all. If that wasn't possible, why bother to attend at all? At his Canberra house no less. It isn't like the person who lives there wasn't going to be there.

If your disdain for the man is so great (understandable perhaps) that you can't even muster basic and common courtesy, then just don't go. That would be reasonable. Plenty of people would understand. It would cause a stir, but justifiably so given her criticisms of the PM. But acting like a child displaying a lack of basic manners when coming face to face with him in a meet and greet was unbecoming and unnecessary.

That's the case whether she was caught by surprise or deliberately played up to the cameras, hoping for attention such as this. To excite the mob on social media, for example. Before the dogs bark and the caravan moves on to the new Australian of the Year.

Yes the cameras were there and no doubt it suited Scott Morrison to smile for them and congratulate Ms Tame on her recent engagement. He has an election soon remember. Perhaps she was worried he'd use a smiling photo of them together on the campaign trail. I highly doubt that, but if he tried that on tweet up a storm and condemn him. That would be reasonable.

But to look as forlorn as she did in response, rudely and deliberately looking away from the photographer, was an act of juvenile dissent. The video of the exchange leaves no doubt about what happened. This isn't a case of making a mountain out of a mole hill. It was brazen and not for virtuous reasons.

If she was caught by surprise that is surprisingly naive for someone who has used her year as Australian of the Year to tactically succeed in drawing so much attention to her worthy cause.

The only caveat to my criticism of the outgoing Australians of the Year is if she was tricked into the happy snap moment. For example, if as a well-known critic of the PM she flagged before attending the event at his house that she did not want to be photographed with him, nor forced to shake his hand on arrival, but she was manoeuvred into doing so against her will. Having received an assurance she would not be put in that position.

If that is what happened, power to Grace Tame. Apologies for all the criticisms above. Her actions make sense and were appropriate. Anything short of that, however, and she has proven herself the lesser person on this occasion, which is quite a feat.

Complaining about Morrison's response to sexual abuse and sexual harassment allegations and necessary law reform is one thing. I don't disagree with much of what she's had to say. Her use of his first name when addressing him, given Morrison's tendency to use women's first names all the time, is also a good retort.

Tame's style and actions have a place in modern Australia, as polarising as they may be at times.

But if her anger on these various fronts is such that she can't even bring herself to look at the PM and shake his hand in the way people have done throughout time, at an event at his house, then avoid finding yourself in such a situation and just don't attend. Simple. That of itself sends a powerful message without being childishly rude and demeaning yourself.

But you can't do that in front of the cameras and receive mob acclaim on social media I guess.

What has this Coalition achieved to warrant re-election

21 January 2022

At the forthcoming election the Coalition is seeking a fourth term in office, just shy of nine years in power. Only three previous governments have achieved the feat, most recently John Howard's Coalition government. The question is, what has this Coalition achieved to warrant re-election? Beyond voter apathy, or fear of what the alternative Labor government might look like?

These are important questions, and they are best addressed comparatively. Howard led the conservatives into a fourth term when he won the 2004 election against then Labor leader Mark Latham. The victory guaranteed Howard would become the second-longest serving PM in Australian history.

The Coalition's 2004 win was as much a repudiation of Labor as it was an endorsement. Conservatives often draw on fear of the other. That is, presenting themselves as "safe" administrators in comparison with a risky progressive alternative.

The Latham we know today is very different to the Labor leader he presented as in 2004. Back then he was an advocate for gay rights, a protege of Gough Whitlam, and his signature policy at the election was "Medicare Gold", a plan to ensure free and accessible quality health cover for retirees.

Howard warned that Latham was inexperienced and managing the economy was beyond his competence. The fear campaign worked. Expect Scott Morrison to mount a similar campaign against Labor and Anthony Albanese this time around, but the circumstances are different, and this

Coalition government's economic track record is nothing like Howard's.

Latham also had no experience in government, whereas Albanese is a former deputy prime minister who held the infrastructure portfolio throughout the Rudd and Gillard years. The team around him is also experienced. In contrast, it is the current government that is weighed down by retirements and a lack of quality frontbench personnel left to do the heavy lifting.

Health Minister Greg Hunt is retiring, as is former attorney-general and leader of the house Christian Porter. The former finance minister and Senate leader Mathias Cormann already left half-way through the pandemic.

Who will take over as health minister? Surely in the midst of a pandemic we need to know this sooner rather than later, well ahead of the campaign.

Howard reduced government debt to zero and oversaw significant tax and industrial relations reforms. The current Coalition government has accumulated record levels of debt, shunned serious industrial relations reform and rather than improve the tax system, white papers it commissioned on tax and the federation were jettisoned before Morrison even took over as PM. There was a brief flirtation with updating the GST system (long overdue) before that too was abandoned.

Morrison didn't lead this Coalition government into power in 2013; he's only been PM since shortly before the last federal election. It was a prime ministerial team effort for the Coalition to stay in office this long: Tony Abbott won the 2013 election, Malcolm Turnbull won in 2016, and Morrison overcame expectations to defeat Bill Shorten in 2019.

Not achieving anything meaningful as a government is a collective failure. Legislating same-sex marriage certainly doesn't count — Australians did that for themselves via a plebiscite, because our elected politicians didn't have the courage to do their parliamentary duty without a prod. And two out of the three Liberal prime ministers mentioned walked out of the chamber rather than vote to endorse the plebiscite, one of whom was Morrison.

He will be the first PM since Howard to serve a full term when he contests the next election, which is a sure sign of divisions within conservative ranks over the life cycle of this government. Abbott was voted out by his electorate at the last election, and Turnbull is now one of the government's biggest critics.

Nonetheless, you'll hear a lot between now and polling day from the Coalition about "achievements" in office. It will claim credit for steering Australia through the pandemic. For the (relatively speaking) strong state of the economy compared to how other nations are coping. Coupled with these positive messages will be a warning not to shift your vote to Labor, lest all the good work gets undone. This claim will skirt over the failures associated with hotel quarantine, the early days of the vaccine rollout or being prepared to transition to the use of rapid antigen tests.

There also won't be references to the divisions which plagued national cabinet over the last two years, as we watched our political leaders squabble.

To be sure, not all of this is the fault of Morrison, but it did occur on his watch. Of course we can't be sure Labor would have done any better had it been in power. Voters could well decide that the Coalition is the lesser of evils compared with the opposition, sticking with them for another term despite shortcomings.

More meaningful perhaps is what comes next. Does the government have a vision for the future and does the opposition have the courage to present its own alternative vision? Probably not after Shorten's big target strategy failed in 2019. But a bold agenda for post-pandemic reform is what the nation needs right now, even if it doesn't know it.

Voters are understandably fatigued because of the last two years, which will inevitably make them wary of voting for a major party promising more tumult. The paradox of this reality is that it's precisely because so little meaningful has been achieved on the policy front over the last nine years that the next term must embrace serious reform — the federation, the tax system, a co-ordinated response to climate change, and a restructuring of our social security settings to ensure fiscal sustainability.

In terms of national moments, the urgent need for meaningful reform right now is arguably greater than it was in the 1980s when the Hawke government embraced micro-economic reforms that set up the prosperity we've enjoyed ever since.

Without a renewal of that purpose, Australia risks being consigned to the secondary ranks of developed nations in the coming decades — a fate that would have befallen us in the 1980s had it not been for the policy might of Hawke and Paul Keating, ably followed up by Howard in the first half of his prime ministership.

I get little sense our politicians even recognise this urgency, much less have the political courage to do something about it. On both sides of the divide. Minor parties and independents recognise some of the challenges, but not others, cherry-picking what they regard as urgent and what's not. If they control the balance of power after the next election — a genuine possibility according to the polls — they will get action on climate change, but meaningful economic reforms which are less popular but just as important will be even harder to achieve.

The below column proved to be true come election night. Confidence in Labor's majority only developed once the four seats Labor won in WA became obvious. I picked Tangney as one to watch, and it was probably the big surprise for many on the night. That's what good Labor sources can do for you.

Seats in the wild west to determine election

8–9 January 2022

Winning the west will be the key to winning this year's federal election. That is, the western suburbs of Sydney and West Australian electorates. Yes, every seat is important at elections, and it is easy to find reasons to focus attention elsewhere.

The conservatives hold the lion's share of seats in Queensland, for example. If there is a move against the government there the election will be over soon after counting begins.

Tasmania is vulnerable for the opposition according to Labor insiders, but there are very few seats south of Victoria.

Melbourne has been one of the most locked-down cities in the world, so pandemic management will be hotly debated on the campaign trail.

And if you're a Coalition strategist hoping to pick up seats to offset losses elsewhere, the NSW Hunter Region has three seats potentially on offer. Why do you think Anthony Albanese has promised high-speed rail between Newcastle and Sydney?

So yes, there are interesting contests right around the nation. But WA and western Sydney are the places to watch most closely. While there are seats the Coalition can win in the Hunter to offset losses elsewhere, that's also the case in western Sydney. Macquarie is the most marginal Labor-held seat across the country and, with the local Labor MP in Parramatta retiring, Liberals will fancy their chances there too. Equally, retaining the western Sydney seat of Lindsay will be tough for the government, especially if pandemic management woes persist. It's a bit of a bellwether electorate.

The possibility of what happens further west, across the Nullarbor in WA, could see Australians having to anxiously wait for hours until booths close and west coast counting begins.

There isn't much of a tradition of federal elections reflecting state results in WA. But these are unusual times, and the WA pandemic experience has been very different to elsewhere, especially along the east coast. Scott Morrison is sometimes sarcastically referred to as the PM for NSW, his home state. That line of attack resonates in the highly parochial west. And when you consider just how popular Premier Mark McGowan is locally - ironically he was born and raised in NSW — the adopted West Aussie's loathing of Morrison could count for something on polling day.

There were 16 seats in the west up for grabs in 2019, Liberals winning 11 of them. But in the redistribution since the last election one seat was abolished — Liberal-held Stirling. It was replaced with a notionally Labor seat in Victoria. So Liberals are defending 10 of 15 seats in WA. Yet at the state election last year they won only two of 59 seats in the Legislative Assembly. A record worst performance. In other words, plenty of West Australians who voted Liberal federally in 2019 voted for McGowan's Labor Party last year. Will they think about voting Labor again this year?

McGowan will campaign strongly for Anthony Albanese. To be sure, they aren't especially close. But as Captain James T. Kirk from Star Trek once said: "The enemy of my enemy is my friend." The origins of that phrase run deeper than Hollywood science fiction, of course. It can be traced right back to a 4th-century South Asian treatise on statecraft, which translated reads as: "My friend, the enemy of my enemy."

Premiers and prime ministers of different political complexions often get along, even benefiting from party political opponents at different tiers of government doing well. Geoff Gallop, for example, didn't mind when John Howard vanquished Mark Latham in 2004 a year out from his own re-election campaign.

But McGowan will want to see Morrison suffer at this year's election, including for his own political self-interest. If the Liberals lose federal seats off the back of having won just two lower house seats at the 2021 state election, the party will be brought to its knees. That will make McGowan's third-term re-election even more certain than it already is.

Besides, the barbs flying between the WA Premier and Prime Minister have been more hostile than usual during this pandemic. For a time there, the prospect of a federal government challenging the WA government's right to control its borders in the High Court was on the cards. There is a chance McGowan won't even let Morrison into WA to campaign, depending on what happens next during this pandemic. He didn't even bother to dial in to this week's national cabinet meeting.

When you survey the 10 seats the Liberals currently hold in the west, as many as half of them are winnable for Labor: Swan, Pearce, Hasluck, Tangney and even Canning. What makes this risk most fascinating is that WA often doesn't follow the national trend.

For example, in 1996 when Howard was winning seats around the country on the way to defeating Paul Keating's Labor government, the Coalition lost seats in WA. In 2007, when Howard was shown the door, even losing his own seat, Liberals picked up a seat in WA. It is entirely possible Morrison recovers ground between now and election day along the east coast but has to nervously wait for the WA results before knowing for certain if he's retained his majority.

The two WA seats most at risk for the Liberals are Pearce and Swan.

The former was held by former attorney-general Christian Porter, who is retiring. Ordinarily a 5.2 per cent margin would be considered relatively comfortable, but not after the controversies engulfing Porter. Steve Irons is retiring as the local MP for Swan, and it is the government's most marginal WA seat at 3.2 per cent. Hasluck is the third-most marginal government seat in the west, on 5.9 per cent. Ken Wyatt is a popular local MP but, at 69 years of age, speculation abounds that he yet might pull the pin on running. His personal following would be sizeable.

Tangney (9.5 per cent) and Canning (11.6 per cent) are notionally safe seats for the Liberals. But Labor strategists are surprisingly hopeful in Tangney, even though it is a traditional conservative seat. Their belief comes back to its boundaries overlapping with state seats now held by Labor. Canning is held by a double-digit margin, and Andrew Hastie is a potential future conservative prime ministerial candidate. But Canning has swung from one election to the next by double-digit margins before. It's a volatile seat that is safe until it's not.

Realistically, Pearce, Swan and Hasluck are the seats to watch most closely, but three WA seats on a knife edge is enough to leave east coast Australians glued to their television screens unsure which party has won until WA voters decide. And after last year's state results, it would be a brave federal Liberal MP who sits back confident on election night that their margin in 2019 will hold up in 2022.

Driven by distractions as year winds down

5–6 December 2021

A confluence of circumstances turned the penultimate parliamentary sitting week of the year into an unusual affair. Distractions, albeit some important ones, were the focus of attention. Next week is likely to be different. Scott Morrison was in isolation, bunkered down in the Lodge, with his official photographer of course, sitting out 14 days of quarantine after returning from Japan. Perhaps that situation contributed to the Prime Minister's decision to up the ante the way he did when it came to China. A Chinese foreign ministry official known for incendiary rhetoric posted an offensive fake image on Twitter of an Australian soldier slitting the throat of an Afghan child. Rather than leave it for one of his ministers to express disgust, Morrison took up the challenge, calling a media conference from iso and demanding everything from an apology to the tweet being taken down. Morrison's political impotence in the face of a rising China was laid bare. Of course, if Morrison had said nothing his critics would have attacked him for being weak. Because the Prime Minister wasn't in the parliamentary chamber for most of the sitting week, Labor made the tactical decision to ignore him, directing questions at his ministers instead. This let Morrison off the hook for the robodebt debacle. On Wednesday the official third quarter gross domestic product numbers were released, showing a 3.3 per cent bounce back in the economy. Good news, albeit off a very low base. Australia has recovered nearly half of the economic growth lost during the six-month recession, but the economy is still 3.8 per cent smaller than it was during the corresponding period last year. While Josh Frydenberg tried to paint the numbers as good news, the simple fact is the economy is hanging by a thread. A deficit of more than $200bn, debt ballooning past $1 trillion and a decade of more deficits to come is hardly good news. Throw in the trade war with China and a million Australians out of work, with millions more employed with the assistance of the JobKeeper spendathon, which runs out in March, and fragile is the best word to describe the situation. Morrison ambled out of quarantine on Thursday, with his suit pants on this time, only to discover that China had censored his WeChat post aimed at addressing Chinese Australians directly. Not that anyone should be surprised; China is an authoritarian dictatorship with only limited respect for free speech, a free press, international law or the rule of law domestically. It murders its own citizens, it locks up journalists who don't toe the Communist Party line and it has imprisoned hundreds of thousands of Uighurs in concentration camps. It's a far cry from the "historic" move towards democracy Tony Abbott hailed when President Xi Jinping visited Australia in 2014. Next week parliament sits for the last time this year; it returns in the first week of February. Labor should go after Morrison on robodebt, given the death and despair the scheme caused, as highlighted in the class action statement of claim. The Coalition set up a royal commission into the failures of Labor's home insulation scheme during the global financial crisis, a process that cleared the government of responsibility for the handful of deaths. The deaths and devastation caused by Morrison's decision to enact robodebt are on a scale well beyond anything that happened during the rollout of the so-called pink batts scheme. Morrison will stonewall any demands of accountability for the failures of robodebt because he was the scheme's architect, having conceived it as social services minister, used it as treasurer to spruik a looming surplus, and as Prime Minister fought against claims it was illegal. It was only when the government had no moves left to make that it parted with $1.2bn of taxpayer money to try to make the scandal go away. While most Australians have been unlucky during the pandemic, Morrison has benefited from it as it took attention from his failures during the bushfires and acts as a shield from responsibility for robodebt. As Newspoll again highlighted this week, Morrison is popular and the government is ascendant: a sure thing to win the next election. It is Labor and Anthony Albanese under pressure as the year comes to an end. Which brings us back to next week's final parliamentary sitting. Morrison will reshuffle his frontbench once the week is over and the Opposition Leader will have to respond with his own reshuffle. Albanese may come under some pressure, with growing speculation within the opposition that were it not for Labor's leadership rules protecting the incumbent, a move against the leader might be in the offing. That could happen anyway, but it is unlikely next week. One senior member of Labor's frontbench — without an axe to grind or interest in the leadership for themselves — told me Albanese can't afford to make a misstep across the summer. Doing so could become a trigger for change, the same way Kim Beazley referring to Rove McManus as Karl Rove was used as an excuse to move against him back in 2006. For Morrison's part, his reshuffle is a further chance to put his stamp on the government he inherited from Malcolm Turnbull. Mathias Cormann's departure allows for a limited reshuffle, unless Morrison wants to really shake things up, which he could do by demoting duds such as Richard Colbeck, for example. The Prime Minister could promote the likes of Nicolle Flint or Sarah Henderson if he wants to beef-up the number of women on the frontbench. Backbenchers such as Dave Sharma and Tim Wilson are deserving of frontbench promotion, but Morrison may not value that both think for themselves and aren't afraid to express opinions. Perhaps the trickiest decision the Prime Minister has to make is whether to promote Ben Morton further up the ministerial ranks. Morton, a Morrison mini-me, is assistant minister to the Prime Minister. It is a role that allows Morton to work closely with Morrison, which the latter values very highly. But Morton is ambitious and unlikely to take kindly to being overlooked. John Howard alway s used to say reshuffles are one of the most delicate political calculations a leader has to make.

The below column was without double my pre-election howler. In fairness I wrote subsequent pieces recanting my certainty that the teals would crash and burn, but I left this one in the collection and those out simply because this was my (albeit incorrect) judgement before a conga line of opinion polls proved I was off the mark, after which I hastily tried to rewrite history with extra musings. While wrong on most counts, I was at least right when it came to the candidacy of Jo Dyer in Boothby. She polled in single digits, no surprises there. Pretty much everything else, however, was me missing the early signs of revolt in traditionally safe Liberal seats. So sit back, and enjoy the kiss of death at his best...

Mavericks are likely to crash and burn

18–19 November 2021

The gaggle of "independent" candidates contesting inner-city Liberal seats at next year's election is receiving no small amount of media attention. But how realistic are their chances of success? Not very, is the answer. In the recent past, when such seats have been picked up by independents unique circumstances have precipitated the change.

The three one-time Liberal strongholds currently held by the crossbench are Indi, Mayo and Warringah, respectively by Helen Haines, Rebekha Sharkie and Zali Steggall. All were lost in extraordinary circumstances unlikely to be mirrored in 2022.

Indi was lost by Sophie Mirabella, a polarising conservative MP out of step with the values of the electorate she represented. It is also a rural seat. Tony Abbott's defeat at the hands of Steggall was similarly unique: a former PM seen to have overstayed his parliamentary welcome who was too conservative for many of his electors. Jamie Briggs lost Mayo having been under a cloud and dumped from the ministry. A former staffer won the seat as an —independent.

Put another way, in each of these instances the Liberals lost traditionally safe seats to independents because of perceived failures attached to the serving Liberal MPs. At next year's election, the pitch to dump Liberal MPs and shift support to independents is less enticing.

The seats being targeted include Wentworth, North Sydney and Mackellar in NSW. In Victoria, the independent collective is aiming to pick up Goldstein and the Treasurer's seat of Kooyong. All are held by moderate-leaning Liberals, which diminishes the reason for throwing them out on the grounds they are out of touch with their inner-city electors.

This week, an advocate for Christian Porter's accuser, Jo Dyer, announced she would be running for the seat of Boothby in South Australia. Liberal MP Nicolle Flint is retiring. A seat with a retiring MP is always more vulnerable, but Dyer is an activist who doesn't exactly fit the moderate small 'l' liberal other women contesting seats as part of the independent alliance do. It's hard to see her polling ahead of Labor in Boothby, much less the Liberals.

Other than Dyer, Liberal attacks against independent candidates running in these seats are neither fair and accurate. Federal Liberal Party director Andrew Hirst has sought to paint all of them as left-wing stooges masquerading as moderate. Dyer aside, that's a false narrative. It is true, however, that the Liberal Party has drifted to the right. It is also true that moderates aren't as effective within the Liberal party room as they should or could be on issues such as climate change.

But unless circumstances uniquely conspire against Liberal MPs, defeating them on home soil in safe seats is a tall order. None of the MPs under attack is what you might call odious.

To be sure, if Scott Morrison loses the election with voter support ebbing away even further than it already has between now and polling day, a number of these so-called independents (centrally funded, a point for another column) should fancy their chances.

A big shift in voter sentiment would cause electoral carnage all over the seat-by-seat map. But under such preconditions Morrison is a loser anyway, and Labor wouldn't need to work with the crossbench, or at least not new crossbenchers when the likes of Andrew Wilkie and Adam Bandt are guaranteed to support a Labor government.

One of the myths in Australian electoral studies is that when government's lose they lose big. That is only true of Labor governments. Conservative governments, on the three occasions they have lost power since World War II, have done so with perhaps surprisingly narrow margins. Certainly on two occasions. That's in contrast to the way Labor governments lose, with thumping defeats at the ballot box. Perhaps the progressive side of politics falls harder when it fails.

Labor defeats in 2013, 1996 and 1975 all saw huge swings against the government with large majorities for the incoming Coalition governments.

In 1972, when Gough Whitlam won the "It's time" election, there was much fanfare with the end of 23 years of continuous Coalition rule. However, the majority secured was just five seats strong, and that was after campaigning against perhaps the worst PM in Australian history, William McMahon. Granted, the two-party vote was strong for Labor, but prising individual seats off the Coalition proved to be more difficult than the headline numbers suggested.

It was the same in 2007, despite the theatre of the Kevin 07 push and the long-in-the-tooth leadership of John Howard. While Howard lost his own seat on the way to defeat, Rudd's majority was just eight in a parliament significantly enlarged from 1972.

Again, the two-party vote for Labor was strong, but the Coalition managed to sandbag enough seats to contain the swing against it.

Bob Hawke's majority of 13 in 1983 was more in keeping with the way the Coalition wins its way into office, but it was still smaller than all four Coalition wins since the war. Tony Abbott won in 2013 with a majority of 15, Howard's 1996 majority was 20, and Malcolm Fraser won in 1975 with a 17-seat majority. Robert Menzies even secured a 14-seat majority in the smaller parliament of 1949.

Today's House of Representatives has an additional 30 seats.

The point is that the conservative side of politics is good at sandbagging seats, helped along by no small amount or pork barrelling. That's a major incumbency advantage that helps a government retain key marginal seats.

Independents can and do win seats of major parties, but circumstances have to conspire against the major party under siege.

While theoretically an independent needs only 25 per cent of the primary vote and they can make up the other 25 per cent with preferences from Labor and the Greens, doing so isn't easy in seats considered blue-ribbon Liberal seats. Many independent candidates struggle even to get their primary vote above that of Labor such that preference flows can work in their favour.

While the independent collective targeting safe Liberal seats will be a distraction for Morrison, and it will force the party to devote money and manpower to retaining seats it otherwise would have taken for grants, we're unlikely to see many (if any) of them fall.

Scare tactics that go bump on election night

11–12 November 2021

Scare campaigns are always a feature of election countdowns, and more often than not they are bogus. But they can work. In 2016, Bill Shorten disingenuously argued that a re-elected Coalition would abolish Medicare. No such thing has happened, nor was it ever going to.

The success of Labor's scare campaign reduced the size of Malcolm Turnbull's majority, leaving the accurate impression that ousting Tony Abbott as PM led to a disastrous election outcome. Victorious, yes, but pyrrhic all the same. A majority of just one sparked endless speculation about Turnbull's leadership, culminating in his removal.

Shorten was never going to win the 2016 election, but his scare campaign worked.

John Howard was the master of scare campaigns, using them effectively for a decade to retain power. Claims of Labor economic mismanagement was his pathway to victory in 1996, despite the Labor government he ousted legislating the most profound and important macro-economic reforms in the nation's history.

In 2001, national security and Labor's supposed lack of ticker on such matters was held up as a reason not to change the government. In 2004, concerns over Mark Latham's inexperience was the foundation of his undoing. This is probably the right time to note than scare campaigns aren't always based on a false premise. Vanquishing Latham as a prime ministerial candidate may well be the greatest service Howard did for this country.

In 2007, Kevin Rudd knocked off Howard with the mother of all scare campaigns: hammering WorkChoices into submission before dismantling it once elected. Last year's election saw a return to the false premise used for scare campaigns when Scott Morrison claimed if Labor was elected it would introduce an inheritance tax. That rubbish made Shorten's Mediscare campaign appear a comparative truism it was so egregiously false. But Morrison backed that fallacy with a truth voters ultimately baulked at: if you vote for Labor, you'll get Bill Shorten as prime minister. It was enough to re-elect a dysfunctional Coalition for a third term.

Fast forward to today and the Morrison scare campaign shaping up as a central component of his re-election strategy in 2022 is to tether Labor to the Greens in a bid to dislodge swinging voters from the Labor camp in key outer metro marginal seats. Greens leader Adam Bandt fuels Morrison's strategy when he tweets and talks about the power the Greens would have in an alliance with Labor in government.

Such rhetoric serves the Greens well, but it is the last thing Anthony Albanese wants dominating attention. It also happens to be deeply untrue. Whatever Albo's faults as a politician, he's been fighting Greens for years in his own electoral backyard of inner-city Sydney. While a creature of the Labor Left, and therefore more sympathetic to Green issues than most within Labor, Albo knows full well that Labor cannot give the Greens an inch. He has already dismissed even the prospect of negotiating with the Greens on emissions policy. He won't negotiate with them to form minority government, nor on anything else for that matter.

Albo knows that playing footsies with the Greens opens Labor to a scare campaign that will erode its vote in the centre. It is a lesson he's learnt over a lifetime of staving off Green threats in his electorate. He was a vocal critic of Julia Gillard's decision to publicly spruik her alliance with the Greens after the 2010 election as she sought to build momentum towards forming minority government. He knew where it would lead: right into Tony Abbott's scare campaign at the following election. Abbott duly used the deals done to hammer Labor at the 2013 election, which saw the Coalition returned with a sizeable majority.

While any scare campaign linking Labor and the Greens ahead of next year's federal election will be a false one, that doesn't mean it will fail to resonate. A false premise is not necessarily an inhibitor to success. Which is why Albo needs to strike hard at the false premise and not give an inch when doing so.

One of the reasons scare campaigns often succeed is because they go unanswered for too long, only responded to long after they have become a political problem for the party under attack. Turnbull initially chose to ignore the Mediscare campaign because he found it so preposterous. By the time the Coalition took it on the sentiments underpinning it were well established in voters' minds.

The problem for Albo is that mainstream concerns Labor is in bed with the Greens are somewhat entrenched. Morrison doesn't need to build the false narrative to cement it. It already exists as a real historical narrative. It just so happens that Albo is a very different Labor leader who despises the Greens and what they have done to erode the left flank of his beloved Labor Party. His task is to find a way to penetrate that fact into the subconscious of the mainstream without appearing like some sort of political figure disinterested in the goals of the environment and social justice. Not an easy task, even for someone who has forged a political career promoting exactly those values.

While Albo has his problems countering a scare campaign about the Greens, Morrison and the Liberals need to worry about the plethora of independents challenging moderates in inner city seats, particularly in Sydney and Melbourne. The loose alliance of female independents spruiking their environmental and transparency credentials is a distraction Morrison doesn't need. It will require fundraising in seats the Liberals can usually take for granted, and it will see MPs under threat in those seats use their voices to disrupt Morrison's louder message designed to attract votes in less progressive marginal seats.

But aside from a distraction (even one capable of costing the Coalition the election) it is hard to see any (or many) of these so-called independents winning their way into parliament. If they do, it will be because the Coalition is on the way out anyway. In other words, there is a national move already happening costing Morrison in the seats that matter.

If the election is close, these independents will most likely strike granite as they attempt to dig deeper into traditional Liberal support in these blue ribbon seats. They will reduce margins, perhaps even coming close to winning. But when they strike granite with a few percentage points to go to claim the 50 per cent plus one required for victory, things get tough. It happens, but not often. Most headlines about a conga line of well-funded independents will end up as clippings in the bottom drawers of those who ran and failed.

That said, for the most part I wish them well, because the Liberal Party is nothing like the party Menzies founded. And moderates in its ranks are by and large weak and voiceless. The irony is they will become even weaker and more silent if the independents' collective succeeds, because every Liberal MP being targeted is a moderate rather than a conservative.

Coalition's pathway to re-election narrows

6–7 November 2021

Will the economy be front and centre during next year's federal election campaign? That is the only question that matters. If not, Scott Morrison doesn't have a pathway to victory, given how small his parliamentary majority is and how strongly broader issues are running against him.

There's no "electoral fat" to absorb a hit, as they say.

However, if the campaign does focus on the economy — jobs, wages, growth, house prices, interest rates, inflation — then the Coalition is certainly still in with a shot, even if the pathway to re-election remains narrower than Coalition hardheads might like.

Which is why you will see a rapid attempt by the government to shift the debate back onto the economy now that the PM is back from overseas. On his first day back, the Treasurer called a media conference to talk about tax cuts.

To be sure, the summer will be politically sleepy, but that could work to Morrison's advantage as he attempts to block out broader failings. It is what happens on the other side of Australia Day, when both major parties move onto a campaign footing, that really matters. Will voters sharpen their focus such that Labor's current lead in the polls (54 per cent to 46 per cent) narrows? Will failures early on in the vaccine rollout become irrelevant, courtesy of the new reality of borders opening up and life returning to normal? And if these changes do happen, does the economy come sharply back into focus?

Politically, it may not even matter what the academic answers are to questions about which side of politics has the better policies and ideas to address economic challenges. It is about which leader can sell their messages, inject fear into voters' minds about their opponents, and whether or not historic voter bias — when it comes to judging the economic management of the two major parties — repeats.

The Coalition are perceived to be the better economic managers; politically, it's that simple. Labor's track record of major economic reforms during the Hawke and Keating era doesn't penetrate the subconscious of mainstream voters. Many probably aren't even aware of them. Nor does the fact that Rudd's administration avoided recession during the global economic crisis, saving heaven knows how many jobs by doing so.

A calculated appraisal of the economic policies Bill Shorten and Chris Bowen took to the 2019 election wasn't relevant to mainstream voters, when Morrison talked up the risks such settings posed to people's economic wellbeing. The banked credibility the Coalition enjoys as the better economic managers decided who won, with a healthy amount of misrepresentation thrown in for good measure. Remember Morrison's references to Labor's death taxes policy? No such policy even existed.

This time around, Labor has advantages when it comes to repelling the entrenched economic advantages the Coalition enjoys. For example, armed with the knowledge of the damage done to Team Shorten for its big-target strategy, Anthony Albanese looks set to adopt a small-target strategy, hoping to minimise the damage the Coalition can inflict. Misrepresentation by a PM with a trust deficit should be harder to make stick.

There are also known unknowns going into next year's campaign. While we know the historical advantage the Coalition has on economic management, we do not know if that has been dented by its (mis) handling of the Covid crisis. And, indeed, by its more than eight years in office. Debt has risen, wages growth has stalled. JobKeeper saved jobs and businesses, certainly, but there have been rorts along the way.

What will mainstream voters chose to focus on? These are the unknowns.

We also can't be sure if distractions from the economic debate will continue to dog the government, and the PM in particular. Question marks over trust, for example. John Howard faced similar challenges ahead of the 2004 election, having lost trust over the war in Iraq and the children overboard scandal. But he cleverly turned the trust debate around into one of who do voters trust to manage the economy. They unequivocally chose him over Labor and Mark Latham.

Morrison has a relatively large amount of baggage for a one-term PM. Scandals in Parliament House, frictions within the Coalition, tainted ministers and backbenchers, an unhealthy number of retirements, a "women's problem", failure to set up a federal watchdog, and now a disastrous trip to Rome and Glasgow overshadowed by a war of words with the French President and questionable climate-change credentials.

Morrison needs these problems to fade into the background and be overtaken by a focus on the economy, even if Labor thinks this Coalition government's track record managing the economy hasn't been a good one.

Political scientists have long known that post-materialist voting tendencies usually come a distant second to the selfish voter gene. For issues such as the environment or ethics in politics to trump the economy, they need to either directly impinge on the economy, or the economy needs to be stable enough such that other issues can come to the fore.

While climate change, for example, is certainly an economic as well as environmental challenge, I'm not convinced mainstream voters see it that way. Especially not in the seats that usually decide elections. Voters living in these electorates are more likely to shift their support away from the coalition for other reasons — such as state-by-state factors related to the federation.

There is little doubt that economic challenges in 2022 and beyond should be front and centre, irrespective of whether you think the Coalition or Labor are better placed to handle them.

The housing bubble will burst sooner rather than later. Inflation and a change of approach by the Reserve Bank will almost certainly cause interest rates to head north, with all the attendant consequences. Trade wars will continue to impact the Australia economy, and the build-up of national debt (public and private) will again become an issue.

How the post-pandemic recovery plays out will profoundly impact on people's daily lives, their job security and their prosperity. Whatever way you slice and dice it, the economy should be the focus at the next election. But we know from experience what should happen doesn't necessarily happen. Also, the Coalition is seeking a fourth term in office. It is always possible that as the election gets closer, the "it's time" factor grows stronger.

If that happens, nothing will save the Morrison government.

Our political class lacks depth and conviction

30–31 October 2021

There was never really a golden age for Australian politicians, however much we tend to look back at different eras with rose-coloured glasses. The political class has always been trusted about as much as used car salesmen. The proceeds of mining booms have been squandered many times before. They've certainly always broken promises, and they have long been hypocritical. But the situation does appear to be getting worse.

The decline of the political class is accelerating, which in turn is diminishing institutions and processes, as well as killing off the moments in history when leaders can leave their mark by standing up for what they believe in.

In the past, political leaders could rely on a robust public culture based on political parties with deep roots in the labour movement, the business community, and the professions. The era of the mass political party is behind us now. Gone are the days of major parties with hundreds of thousands of members who reflect the views and values of millions of their countrymen and women. At first, this shift was held up by political scientists as a consequence of the professionalisation of politicking and perhaps not a bad thing. Rather than relying on mass party memberships to spread the word and campaign, major parties crafted themselves around professionals: pollsters, party officials and a growing cohort of staffers. Such professionalism was seen as a good thing, but it soon had perverse implications, such as the -politicisation of the public service.

The consequences of the shift has largely been negative. The Labor and Liberal parties are now shadows of their former selves, dedicated to advancing the interests of career politicians instead of bringing leaders and policies from the whole of society into the highest reaches of public power. Professionalisation became an agent for disconnecting those who represent us from the mainstream. It has therefore added to societal divisions, rather than addressed them meaningfully.

Widespread loyalty to parties once gave political leaders a head start in their efforts to win majority support for any given policy. The nation was made and remade a number of times throughout the 20th century. But voter dealignment now sees a larger voting centre willing to pivot between parties. To be sure, some of these swinging voters think for themselves, rather than blindly follow, but it is the less virtuous reaction from the politicians that is decaying the system. In chasing these voters, political leaders all too regularly abandon what few convictions they still have. Following is easier than leading.

Today, governments start with a smaller base of support and must compete with a cacophony of media-savvy interest groups, think tanks and corporate PR for public attention. Money talks, cancel culture often wins out, the noisy few misrepresent themselves as the mainstream worth listening to.

More importantly, the combination of compulsory voting and new media often puts elections in the hands of voters either disenchanted or simply uninterested in political debate. Not that the disenfranchising of so many in non-compulsory voting systems is necessarily a better way to go.

Australia is increasingly divided between a handful of politics tragics who have any number of ways to satisfy their thirst for political news, and a growing group of voters who can shut news about politics out of their lives altogether. Trying to understand and reach these voters through focus groups and spin is simply no substitute for a political party with deep connections to civil society. That is how communities really get heard in a liberal democracy, not just via the ballot box once every three years as an elected dictatorship. This lost connection between politicians and those they are supposed to serve is at the heart of the demise of the political class, not just here in Australia but to greater and lesser extents right around the democratic world.

More than a decade's worth of leadership instability might be a sign of things to come in the way that our political culture will have to evolve in order to build majority support in an ever more complex and diverse society. Not that there appears to be a brighter side when leadership stability returns. Scott Morrison is the first Prime Minister since John Howard to enjoy certainty in the job during his time in office. But he is a long way from matching the convictions of Howard. Even modern leaders, safe from the knives of colleagues, may no longer be prepared to present as conviction politicians.

There is little sign that the present generation of political leaders is up to the task before them. The public relations machinery that governments now rely on have left political leaders unable to make an argument in defence of good but unpopular policy. Populism is now the defining trait of political leadership.

The Rudd government, which began with lofty promises of "evidence-based policy", launched the nation's biggest infrastructure project on the strength of back-of-the-envelope arithmetic. The Gillard government was more productive despite the hung parliament, yet received no popular credit for its achievements.

Meanwhile, the Coalition parties exemplify the lack of depth in Australia's political talent on an almost daily basis.

Recently, the importing of American cultural politics has added a toxic flavour to Australian political debate, which few Liberals have the guts to challenge. The party's know-nothing approach to science would have appalled Robert Menzies, whose government oversaw a tenfold increase in funding for the CSIRO. The Coalition is left with Howard's wedge tactics but none of his policy substance. Morrison is now shamelessly overseas spruiking an embarrassingly unfit-for-purpose emissions policy.

How will our timid, populist political leaders deal with the numerous challenges facing Australia? Not well, most likely. It is now a vicious cycle. Careerists who lack convictions choose politics as a vocation. It is no longer a calling. Their backgrounds are limited. Hollowed-out political parties turn pre-selections into insider affairs, ensuring the narrowness of the gene pool in parliament. The media is fixated on the horse race of politics, yet convinces itself of its virtuousness by targeting contradictions and broken promises. That focus only elevates voter cynicism, reducing trust, as well as discouraging politicians from following the advice of John Maynard Keynes and changing their minds when the facts change. Risk aversion dictates the day, killing off bold or innovative policy.

In short, we've become hostage to managerial leadership by political leaders with no pre-parliamentary career track record of good management to speak of. Uninspiring and selfish, but it's not all their fault. The media and the public must share the blame. The decline of the political class is a collective failure.

Our political record on climate is appalling

16–17 October 2021

As the Nationals consider whether or not to support a net-zero emissions target for 2050, ahead of Scott Morrison's inevitable departure for Glasgow later this month, it's worth reflecting on just how comprehensively Australia has butchered its response to climate change action up until now. And not just recently.

To be sure, we can blame conservatives for the failures, including media commentators whose stock and trade is stoking divisions. But the left and the centre are also at fault, and not only because of failures to win arguments. The perfect has been the enemy of the good too many times when it comes to designing emission-reduction policies. Let's not forget that — as worthy as the debate over what emissions targets should now look like is — the most important debate is how we achieve those targets once they are agreed upon.

Without carbon pricing in some form, if we do get emissions down it will only be because of the actions of state governments, private citizens and the private sector. Or because of reduced activity courtesy of Covid. For the most part, the commonwealth has been utterly useless.

At the 2007, election both John Howard and Kevin Rudd campaigned on a commitment to introduce an emissions trading scheme. Yes that's right, 14 years ago there was bipartisan support for the sort of market mechanism all sides in a liberal democracy should be able to support. While Howard's model was contingent on global action, both major parties (including the Nationals as part of the then government) wanted emissions trading as the best way to cut emissions. When Rudd won, as expected he immediately ratified the Kyoto agreement (largely symbolic) and began work on what an ETS in practice might look like (far more complicated and important).

Keep in mind that all of this came after the publication of the Stern Review, a 700-page report released a year earlier by conservative economist Nicolas Stern, commissioned by the British government. It reviewed the profound economic challenges of climate change and the need for environmental taxes to address these challenges. Its chief recommendation was early decisive action, because acting late would be both environmentally and economically devastating.

Is it any wonder younger generations are aghast with where we are now at? Feeling let down by anyone with a modicum of political power over the past decade and a half. Including conservatives, when one of their own (albeit overseas) was the author of something so important.

The ETS Rudd took to the parliament to be endorsed and legislated was a reasonable enough first step towards pricing carbon. While Brendan Nelson as Liberal leader started to grumble about what was on offer, he was soon replaced by Malcolm Turnbull who was certainly on board with Rudd's ETS, albeit proposing subtle amendments to improve the scheme.

But guess what? Not only was Turnbull outflanked on his right by conservatives, including the now secretary-general of the OECD Mathias Cormann, a sudden fan of the need for action, but business and mining interests were also lined up against Rudd's ETS — which is easy to forget given how supportive they all are now when it comes to emissions targets. Even the Greens wouldn't support Rudd's ETS, because they didn't think it went far enough, holding out for something that would move more quickly to reduce emissions. If they hadn't let the perfect be the enemy of the good, Australia would have introduced an ETS at a time when it was non-controversial to do so, helping to restructure our broken taxation system and embedding a mechanism which could be dialled up or down to help reduce emissions as necessary — indeed, as targets were set and reset.

Knowing that they could kill two birds with one stone, conservatives baulked and dumped Turnbull in favour of Tony Abbott, who infamously thought climate change was "absolute crap", killing off a bipartisan ETS in the process. The policy still could have been legislated if Bob Brown's Greens weren't so puritanical, but alas they were. And it still could have been legislated if Rudd had an ounce of political courage and called a double dissolution election on the issue, but he didn't. In the end Rudd was more concerned about political survival than "the greatest moral challenge of our time", as he put it.

Speaking of courage, if Labor had an ounce of it they would never have dumped Rudd when he fell behind Abbott and the Coalition in a solitary Newspoll in 2010, replacing him with Julia Gillard. And if Gillard had an ounce of political nous she wouldn't have ruled out a carbon tax during the ensuing election campaign, only to backflip and seek to introduce a fixed carbon price (otherwise known as a carbon tax) before transitioning to an ETS once re-elected.

After that, pricing carbon became synonymous with a broken election pledge. The damage was done. Abbott — arguably the best opposition leader in Australian history if the yardstick is tearing down your opponents — showed no mercy when criticising the Labor government, and its internal leadership divisions overshadowed any policy achievements, including finally legislating carbon pricing years after Stern literally wrote the book on why it was so important to do so in a timely manner.

Abbott won a landslide election in 2013 promising to repeal the carbon tax, and even though he was quickly on the nose allowing Team Turnbull to find the numbers to remove him less than two years after becoming PM. The deal to garner those numbers required Turnbull to temper his climate change ambitions. In other words, naked political ambition became more important. Australia thus found itself governed by one of the first federal MPs to seriously press for a market mechanism to address climate change, but he never seriously did so. A little like if Gough Whitlam had become PM in 1972 but decided not to pursue social reforms, lest doing so was politically risky.

In the years that followed, the mainstream switched off to the importance of climate change action, and the conservatives were happy to play the (politically successful) role of villains, warning about the costs of action rather than the costs (and opportunity costs) of inaction.

Which brings us to where we are now. Glasgow is important, yes, but only because it represents a first step towards emission-reduction targets scientists tell us are so necessary to stave off the worst effects of climate change. Only then will the heavy lifting begin trying to actually achieve the targets. Doing so will most likely require a return to the debilitating debate over pricing carbon.

Let's hope the sequel is better than the original.

Squabbling states still run their own race

2–3 October 2021

Divided we stand, but for how much longer?

Premiers have all the power at present when it comes to when or even if they open up their states, domestically and internationally. They also have all the power with respect to when or if lockdowns are put in place or lifted.

There is no quick end in sight to this power imbalance between the states and the federal government. The constitutionally enshrined rights of states to shut their borders on health grounds certainly doesn't look as if they'll be challenged any time soon.

Electorally you can see why there are differing opinions around the country, depending on the extent of COVID-19 in each community.

NSW and Victorian residents increasingly are tired of being locked out of other states. Understandably, they point to the fact they hold passports as Australians, not based on their state residency. They ask why restrictions can't be eased, at least for the vaccinated.

But it is also easy to understand why Australians living in Western Australia, South Australia, Tasmania and Queensland feel differently. Queensland especially is getting a taste of how it feels to lose freedoms when COVID-19 comes knocking.

Why would anyone in those states who is not affected by the tyranny of distance that border shutdowns create want to rush their way out of such restrictions and invite Covid into their communities sooner, alongside the attendant loss of freedoms that may follow?

Even if such states theoretically embrace the need to open up when vaccinations reach a certain level, I can understand why they want to keep raising that bar, ignoring advice coming from the federal government and knowing that Covid running through the community will result in hospitalisations, serious illness and death, including among the vaccinated.

So when will all that change? Because it has to eventually. If not when 80 per cent of over-16s are vaccinated, when? At 90 per cent? When 80 per cent of over-12s are vaccinated, or does it need to be 90 per cent of over-12s?

And what happens if vaccination rates stall below these markers? They may well in outlier states unaffected by COVID-19. The rush to vaccinate we are seeing in places riddled with the virus is more of a stroll in other states. Complacency reigns almost as an implied means to continue with border restrictions, trading travel for local freedoms.

So far during this pandemic the federal government has carried the can financially for the policy decision-making of the states, but seemingly not for much longer.

This week Josh Frydenberg announced the timeline to end Covid support for states and territories enduring lockdown based on their vaccination rates. The federal Treasurer sent a very clear message that the federal government expected lockdowns to become largely a thing of the past once Australia hit its 80 per cent vaccination target for over-16s.

Of course that may need to change, as we've seen happen around the rest of the world. Scott Morrison made a point of referencing lockdowns in nations with higher vaccination rates than ours to repel Labor accusations that his slow vaccination rollout was to blame for lockdowns.

But unless hospitalisations in a post-vaccinated Australia put undue pressure on state health systems, the federal government is sending the message that we can't live in lockdown, not when we know the damaging impact it has on people's mental health, children's education and socialisation skills, and the national economy.

But the capacity of the federal government to put pressure on states not to lock down when vaccination rates are higher is a red herring. The real divide in this country is driven by state border closures, and there is little the federal government can do to change that short of winning a High Court action to interpret the Constitution differently.

Is the Morrison government game for such a move? I doubt it, knowing how parochial some states are. Which brings us to the politics of border closures.

It is undoubtedly popular for WA Premier Mark McGowan to keep his state's border closed for the foreseeable future, which poses a problem for the Prime Minister. Morrison must retain seats in the west to retain government and he has to go to an election before June next year.

But putting politics to one side for a moment, a day of reckoning for states locking Covid out will have to come eventually. They can't just shut themselves off from the outside world forever, and even if they can there are no guarantees doing so will continue to be successful. A breach is inevitable.

If there is one thing the Delta variant has taught us it is that there is no certainty that quick lockdowns will stop Covid spreading into the community. Just ask Victorian Premier Daniel Andrews.

Andrews, like most other premiers, took aim at the soon to depart Gladys Berejiklian's decision not to lock down Sydney early as the cause for the virus spreading in NSW. Yet he locked down Victorians swiftly and more aggressively than NSW has ever done and the virus still spread, to the point that the number of Victorian cases has surpassed the number in NSW.

Will that be the experience of Queensland sooner or later? Its politicians have intimated it will, warning their citizens to expect as much, and there are risks afoot already. It's a nervous wait in the Sunshine State right now.

Federation reform was put on the table by Tony Abbott after winning government in 2013, only for Malcolm Turnbull to junk the white paper process when he took over in 2015. It has never been more necessary as we emerge from the haze of Covid after almost two years, yet achieving anything resembling consensus between the states, much less with the federal government, seems harder than at any time since I have researched and written about federal-state relations.

Parochialism is on the rise, including in NSW, which traditionally hasn't suffered the insularity shared by the smaller states.

Good luck convincing NSW to continue to carry the can the way it often does for the smaller states when most have refused to do their fair share for returning Australians or have grumbled about rushing more vaccine doses to Sydney when they were needed there. And good luck convincing other states they should accommodate NSW when it's riddled with Covid and they are not, much less when they do eventually let Covid in and blame Sydney for it.

In the coming months and years what divides Australians, not what unites us, is likely to define our relationship with each another. We're all in this together? You have got to be joking.

Don't hold your breath waiting for tax reform

25–26 September 2021

Not fit for purpose: it may not be the most encouraging way to describe Australia's taxation system but it's certainly the most accurate.

Former Treasury secretary Ken Henry has belled the cat when it comes to the deficiencies of the taxation system, doing so at an event at the Australian National University.

The after-effects of the pandemic have heightened the need to recalibrate how Australia taxes. We have vastly more debt, greater expectations on government and dwindling sources of taxation revenue beyond relying on productivity-sapping bracket creep. Even then, legislated staged income tax cuts will erode that windfall.

Neither major party is prepared to embrace GST reform; it was thrown in the too-hard basket long ago. Rent taxes, which Henry advocated in his tax review for the Rudd government more than a decade ago, aren't palatable either.

And with national cabinet revealing deep divisions between the federal government and the states, don't expect federation reform — which would include realigning taxation arrangements between tiers of government — anytime soon.

We'll continue to hear protests from political leaders that they are serious about reform, highlighting everything from tax transfer adjustments to new business concessions and auditing provisions. So what? These are minuscule adjustments that low-level bureaucrats recommend in internal papers that politicians seize on to show they are doing something, or reforms that special interests spruik for marginal benefits.

The whole system needs a revamp; a system no longer fit for purpose requires profound changes, not tinkering. As debt continues to balloon, the structure of our system does not allow us to tax high enough to cover what government must spend.

As Henry put it, our tax system is "not capable of raising sufficient revenue to fund the activities of government".

Perhaps we first need a philosophical debate: what is the purpose of government, and are community expectations realistic? Do we need to restructure the tax system in line with higher expectations, which means higher taxes, or are expectations too high, thereby requiring re-education about what the role of government in a liberal democracy should be?

Either way, change must soon follow, otherwise our system will splutter along, making the eventual need for reform that much harder when it finally happens.

Imagine how much more difficult the micro-economic reforms the Hawke government initiated would have been had they not happened for another decade. Australia truly could have become the banana republic Paul Keating warned us about, incapable of rising to the middle-power status and prosperity we now enjoy.

This moment is similarly crucial, yet the capacity for our politicians to think outside the square when it comes to reform is limited. The media is shallower than it once was, more reactionary in how it reports the mere prospect of change, in turn exacerbating the timidity of the political class. And voters are fatigued, partly because of Covid. We've also seen major reforms scuttled because they weren't legislated as part of wholesale tax reform.

A carbon tax repealed. Henry's mining tax suggested, butchered by the politicians before being legislated, only to be repealed, too. Howard-era workplace reforms could have improved business competitiveness but were junked because the scare campaign was too much for voters weary after a decade of Coalition government. Even the GST ultimately legislated is a compromise version of what was taken to the 1998 election, and it's certainly inferior to the model for which John Hewson failed to win voter support in 1993.

So here we are in the back half of 2021 with a tax system incapable of doing what it must to collect sufficient revenue for government to do its job — unfit for purpose. We won't even consider rearranging taxation structures, such that the tax-free status of the family home gets looked at, death duties (like those in place all over the world) get put on the table or a new form of carbon pricing as we push for a zero-emissions target enters the political lexicon.

Why? Because as Donald Horne once lamented, we are a lucky country run by second-rate politicians. Horne was concerned our run of good luck might come to an end. Well, guess what — that time is upon us unless the political class steps up and does what it must, leading from the front. Don't hold your breath.

Finally, on another matter, it appears the Christian Porter saga will continue to be in focus when parliament returns next month, with Labor and the crossbench calling for him to resign from parliament altogether if he won't reveal who donated to a blind trust to pay his legal bills when suing the ABC for defamation. As mentioned in this column last week, it was untenable for Porter to remain a minister with unknown donors contributing unknown sums of money to his legal action. He now has resigned from cabinet.

However, in my view that's also the case for any backbencher, which means yes, he should be forced out of parliament if he won't provide details about who the donors are. But it appears the rules do not explicitly require Porter to make such a disclosure, which is extraordinary. Those rules must be changed for the long term. This episode has again highlighted the need for reform on political donations. Unfortunately away from the partisan advantage one side of politics can see when the other side is under pressure, there is little support for such reform within major parties.

But the other revelation this week courtesy of the ongoing Porter saga came in the form of news.com.au political editor Samantha Maiden publishing details from a longer document prepared by Porter's late accuser that has never seen the light of day. It included that the alleged victim believed she suffered from stigmata.

She burned the only contemporaneous diaries that existed from the time she claims to have been sexually assaulted. The diaries relied on, which were written years later, didn't even name Porter as the alleged rapist and they were heavily doctored and amended. The 88-page document that has remained hidden is also the only document Porter's accuser ever signed. Yet for some reason, despite being in possession of it, the ABC chose not to publish any of what Maiden now has. I wonder why. Perhaps because such details cast doubt on something spun to be beyond doubt.

Which is why the settlement Porter reached with the ABC to put a note under the article acknowledging what has been alleged can't be proven to a criminal or civil proof is so important. Maiden is to be applauded for highlighting what she has, when anyone who has the temerity to buck the trend of simply assuming guilt by accusation is painted as some sort of "rape apologist".

World events may decide the next election

18–19 September 2021

The Coalition is gearing up for an election campaign spruiking one simple message: don't trust Labor. Not on the economy, not on national security.

Negative campaigning is standard practice in most democracies and you can bet Labor will adopt the same approach. The opposition's focus will be on the slow vaccine rollout and problems with hotel quarantine, alongside bemoaning big companies that exploited JobKeeper.

The Coalition's strategy involves no small measure of chutzpah. For example, its economic track record is nothing like what it promised it would be when first elected in 2013. Ending the "debt and deficit disaster" has been replaced by record debt and deficits, with a recession thrown in. But do voters blame the government for events largely out of its control?

Labor is working hard to blame the Morrison government for the current lockdowns, claiming if vaccines had been rolled out more quickly lockdowns wouldn't be necessary. The overseas experience doesn't back up that claim, but will voters care? The Coalition is banking on anger dissipating before an election early next year.

On the national security front, Scott Morrison plans to use fear of China to lock voters in behind him, arguing that Labor is weak on national security. Incumbents usually do well at khaki elections, especially conservative governments. But is the threat of a new cold war akin to a khaki election?

A new submarines deal with the US was announced this week that Morrison hopes to exploit politically. But it's a deal born out of necessity and off the back of procurement failures after the Coalition comprehensively butchered its submarine contract with the French. But will such nuance be lost of voters? I suspect it will.

The third leg in the Morrison re-election strategy will be to demonise Anthony Albanese. There are superficial question marks over whether Albanese is a viable alternative prime minister, but there shouldn't be. His experience is apposite for the position.

Elected in 1996 when John Howard became prime minister, Albanese spent nearly 12 years learning the parliamentary ropes from opposition. He then spent the better part of six years as leader of the House of Representatives and a member of the leadership group in the Rudd and Gillard governments, briefly becoming Kevin Rudd's deputy prime minister when Rudd returned to the top job ahead of the 2013 election defeat.

It is an old-fashioned resume for an opposition leader, more in the mould of a Howard than a Morrison or Malcolm Turnbull, who served shorter parliamentary apprenticeships before becoming leaders. As infrastructure minister Albanese held a portfolio that put him in the thick of key economic decision-making in the wake of the global financial crisis, a time not that dissimilar to now.

However, I suspect none of these machinations is likely to decide the next election. More likely both leaders will be beholden to events largely out of their control. How does the world respond to COVID-19 in coming months? Does a new strain emerge in the northern hemisphere as it enters winter? Do vaccination rates peter out too early to open up the economy? What about the differences between the states, and the increasingly hostile relationship between some Labor premiers and the federal government?

To be sure, most of these challenges are downside risks for Morrison, not Albanese. But oppositions win elections only when there is an "it's time" factor among voters. Can Morrison avoid that sentiment even though he's leading a government seeking a fourth term in power?

While Morrison remains the favourite to win, winning a fourth consecutive term in office is never easy. Robert Menzies did it, but the Labor Party of the 1950s and '60s was hopelessly divided, with the DLP split making winning government that much more difficult for Labor. Malcolm Fraser failed in his attempt to win a fourth term in 1983. Bob Hawke won one for Labor in 1990, but only just. Andrew Peacock's opposition won more than 50 per cent of the two-party vote, just not in the seats that mattered. Howard won a fourth term against Mark Latham in 2004, but Latham imploded in a way few major party leaders do. He really was a one-off.

You can bet Morrison would relish replicating Howard's achievement by winning a fourth term for the Coalition. He'd chalk it up as a marketing coup.

Albanese's biggest problem is that incumbents tend to succeed in times of upheaval, and the pandemic is certainly such a time. And as much as it is true that winning fourth terms is hard for governments, of the post-war governments three secured a fourth term and three failed to do so. It is evenly split, and the fact there have been only seven governments during the past 70 years or so is telling in and of itself.

Finally, I wanted to say something about Christian Porter and his need to step down from the ministry for a lack of disclosure over exactly how he funded his legal bills suing the ABC for defamation.

There is no question it is intolerable for Porter to hide those donors and remain a minister. As much as you can understand why people willing to fund his campaign might not want to be known publicly — the lynch mob that has lost sight of the importance of due process is a modern reality, unfortunately, and it would come for each of them one by one — no minister can accept funding from unknown sources.

As an academic and journalist, I have called for transparency in this space for many years. The Porter saga now also raises genuine concerns about crowd-funding. Such donations are usually smaller than what we assume Porter's individual donations might have been, but they are often also anonymous, and numerous micro-donations very easily could compromise MPs who are on the receiving end of such support.

While it is unsustainable for Porter to remain a minister when receiving hidden donations, his likely downfall for having done so doesn't change one simple reality: under our legal system he is an innocent man who hasn't been accused of a crime. His settlement with the ABC made the point that its reporting did not in any way prove his guilt or even cast any doubt on his innocence. A modern-day mob, led by individuals who don't respect the rule of law despite a number of them studying it, will succeed in forcing him out of higher office. That is nothing to celebrate.

Perhaps in the fullness of time further disclosures will shed light on just how nefarious the campaign to get Porter really was.

Albanese gets short end of stick from Bill

28–29 August 2021

This week, despite all the failures with the COVID-19 vaccine rollout and associated pandemic blunders, the opposition managed to make a meal of its own political and public policy strategy when attacking the Morrison government. Anthony Albanese was forced into a back-down. His attempt to divide and conquer was re-routed by a ghost of Labor leaders past.

The Opposition Leader had hoped to side with breakaway premiers by throwing mud at the Doherty Institute's targets for lifting restrictions. He'd been working up to such a stance for weeks.

The intent wasn't to undermine the reputation of the institute. Throwing doubt on the modelling — indeed, claiming that the advice from the institute was changing, with material implications for how and when we open up — was all about making political life that little bit harder for Scott Morrison, feeding into the problems the Prime Minister has had controlling the agenda recently.

Then former Labor leader Bill Shorten entered the fray, siding with Morrison and the plan originally agreed to at national cabinet. The news landed with a thud on Wednesday, with those close to Albanese privately accusing Shorten of deliberately playing the role of wrecker. Shorten supporters weren't going to let that criticism go unanswered, reminding anyone who would listen that Albanese wasn't exactly Shorten's most loyal lieutenant during the six years the latter led the party.

With some of the premiers having attempted to crab-walk away from national cabinet's staged targets for opening back up — yes, Mark McGowan, we are looking at you — Albanese hoped to be the beneficiary of such parochialism by egging on the contrarianism. But once Shorten belled the cat, doing so would have divided the federal opposition more than it would the relationship between Morrison and the premiers.

Albanese was forced to retreat, all the while claiming he wasn't retreating. Of course the federal opposition supports the reopening plan agreed to at national cabinet.

Albanese had hoped to be able to continue to box Morrison into a corner on what happens next in dealing with Covid, but instead he was outflanked. Yes by Morrison (armed with focus group research on community attitudes showing a shift is under way), but also by Shorten (who still has a leadership baton in his backpack, as Kevin Rudd used to say).

Make no mistake, Shorten is coming for Albanese. He may not be able to seize the leadership this side of the next election or after. But he is happy to use his authority as a former leader to stir trouble when he believes he'll be on the right side of history eventually. This was one of those moments.

Either way, Shorten forced Albanese explicitly to back the national plan, and thus back the Prime Minister. Maybe we really are all in this together.

Shorten did so despite Albanese starting the parliamentary week casting doubt on the modelling and the consequences of opening up later this year.

A week is a long time in politics after all. Of course, there is a long way to go until election day, the timing of which is at the Prime Minister's discretion. By the time election day does roll around, any Australian who wants to be vaccinated will be. Those who aren't won't be able to blame the government. There will have been ample vaccinations available for long enough, such that few can reasonably complain that opening the economy up isn't fair.

That will be the climate in which the next election campaign will be fought. Because of the furore inside Labor this week, including the back-down by Albanese, Morrison will point out Albanese wanted to keep fully vaccinated Australians wrapped in cotton wool, long after the botched vaccination rollout had been fixed.

But that is a lesser of evils for Albanese compared with sticking to his guns arguing against opening things up, only to be left stranded when community sentiment shifts. Assuming that does happen — as both Morrison and Shorten are convinced it will — Albanese really should thank Shorten for the valuable service he performed this week. Messy, yes. Awkward, no doubt. Humiliating, maybe. But necessary to save Albanese from himself? Absolutely.

Most Australians do not live on taxpayer-funded salaries, guaranteed whether we are in lockdown or not, with a generous super scheme they know will get them by no matter what. They are nervous about their economic future, the mental health of their children; indeed, their own mental health. The health risks remain real but, once they are vaccinated, people aim to be hopeful. Hence Australians are rapidly shifting their thinking, wanting restrictions lifted so they can get on with their lives in a world of Covid.

Albanese has cleverly avoided Sydney since parliament rose for the winter recess, allowing him to campaign around much of the country. He therefore hasn't experienced the Sydney lockdown. It has left a blind spot.

While people are angry and frustrated with the failures of a slow lockdown in Sydney and a botched vaccine rollout nationally, the only thing that would make these failures even worse would be if once fully vaccinated we still weren't let out of our cages. That was Albanese's emerging position before Shorten intervened.

On another topic, the debacle that has been our withdrawal from Afghanistan continues to worsen. We now know many of the locals who helped us while Australian troops were deployed will not secure asylum on our shores. Some will eke out an existence under Taliban rule, others will be killed.

Morrison likes to erode the uniqueness of the welcome to country for Indigenous Australians by including a thanks to those who have served in our armed forces. I could tolerate the departure from custom if such platitudes were supported by something substantial.

For a long time our military personnel had been warning the government it needed to act with haste to secure safe passage for Afghans who supported us. They were ignored. As Morrison has said, we knew that once US troops left, the Afghan army would capitulate to the Taliban soon enough. Why then were we too late? There are no excuses.

Whatever your view on the war in Afghanistan, the manner in which we have left has been handled badly.

Assault on expertise killing civil debate

14–15 August 2021

Whatever happened to civil debate? Whether it's shock jocks' bleating commentary, chock-full of opinions on topics they know very little about, or the mob on social media dishing out anonymous vigilante justice, our modern discourse is a mess. It comes when we need more substance, not less, from politicians, commentators and the public.

While the disdain that exists between sections of the reactionary media and the virtue-signalling mob online is palpable, in many respects they are as bad as one another; two sides of the same coin. Both are happy to let ends justify means when it suits them. Both dismiss expert analysis when it contradicts their stance. Both thumb their noses at due process if it gets in the way of what they personally consider just outcomes.

And hypocrisy abounds.

Take critics of the vaccine rollout, for example. Some of the same voices condemning the Morrison government for not acquiring enough of the Pfizer vaccine have played a lead role in causing vaccine hesitancy when it comes to AstraZeneca, a vaccine we can produce here and of which we have an ample supply.

This week's Newspoll highlighted that Labor and Greens voters dominated those polled who say they want to get vaccinated but will be waiting for Pfizer. Go figure.

On the other side of the spectrum we see conservative commentators who talk tough on terrorism but won't condemn the rise of right-wing extremism.

ASIO tells us right-wing extremism now accounts for about 50 per cent of its counter-terrorism focus, up from just 15 per cent a few years ago. Yet shock jocks quick to weigh in on Islamic extremism seem to have lost their collective voices.

It is the same when it comes to how to combat climate change. We see free marketeers at the vanguard criticising market solutions such as carbon trading.

No wonder most voters are turning away from political engagement. Rational discussions aren't possible on the most important topics we face: climate change, post-pandemic reform, how to address gender failures.

Weigh in with nuance and the absolutists howl you down.

I saw this firsthand when weighing in on the historical rape allegations made against former attorney-general Christian Porter. While I declared having a friendship with him that predated his entry into politics, many of his toughest critics never saw fit to disclose their own associations with interested parties, even rejecting the need to do so when they subsequently were exposed.

The online mob turned fiction into fact. Although I declared that Porter should stand aside pending an independent inquiry, and expressed a view that he couldn't survive the allegations politically, the mob ignored my commentary. Instead I was described as a "rape apologist" because I defended the rule of law and the presumption of innocence, and journalistic ethics requiring serious allegations be put to those being reported on. All the while the mob was egged on by sections of the commentariat who frankly should know better.

When a plethora of media organisations selectively published the diary of Porter's accuser from his childhood, Kate, that was fine apparently. When this masthead did so, it was a violation of her privacy. Never mind that those parts published were the same parts her friends had already submitted as evidence for an independent inquiry (the one I supported, remember).

As if to highlight the double standards within the criticism, the Federal Court ultimately published the entirety of the diary Kate's friends submitted after she died. Did the court therefore violate her privacy?

But the double standards and hypocrisy doesn't stop there. The redacted pages filed as part of the ABC's defamation defence, 27 of them all up, were kept from public view as part of the agreed settlement between Porter and those he was suing. All parties had to agree to such terms.

This masthead, among others, sought access to what was in those sealed documents, but access was ultimately denied by the courts. Yet parties to the proceedings who specifically agreed to the redaction to achieve settlement of the case went online to bemoan the court's decision.

What utter hypocrisy. If they felt so strongly, they never should have agreed to keep the pages secret as part of the settlement in the first place.

The whole online world of fast-paced thought bubbles piling up one after the other on social media platforms goes against the cultural norms we are taught from a young age. Think before you speak; sleep on it before making a decision; don't rush to judgment and thereby rush to failure.

Platforms such as Twitter allowing anonymous comment flies in the face of the basic cultural principle of accountability for what you say.

Often it is the same people who lament the lack of public policy regard for "freedoms from" that go hand in glove with "freedoms to" in a democracy who forget themselves when posting online.

All of the above is happening in conjunction with the ongoing erosion of respect for expertise. This is in no small part the fault of the Coalition in government for constantly attacking academics as some sort of collective out to destroy one side of the ideological divide. What utter nonsense.

Major parties such as the Liberal Party would be better off reminding themselves what ideological convictions they even ascribe to these days, rather than seeing demons everywhere out to get them.

And what about the conservative commentators dismissing the seriousness of COVID-19 as they hide away in their rural retreats, surfacing only once vaccinated? They listen to experts for their own protection but spruik dangerous denialism.

There was a brief respite for subject matter experts when governments sought to hide behind official health advice to avoid accountability for political decision-making during the pandemic. But that misunderstood the nature of what is involved in listening to experts. Rarely is professional advice definitive. Rather, it's the job of policymakers to listen to experts who are prepared to challenge one another, making informed judgments thereafter.

This is how public policymaking processes should work.

The assault on expertise comes from all sides. Politicians want to use experts to paper over their own weak decision-making. Commentators latch on to only those experts whose views advance their own polemic. And, egged on by ignorant shock jocks who regard themselves as experts on everything, the public joins in when experts challenge what they would rather hear.

Covid shows how political class is failing us

7–8 August 2021

The next election is likely to highlight just how bereft of ideas both our major parties really are. Timid, unwilling or unable to set Australia up for a prosperous post-pandemic future. Both Labor and the Coalition lack the lateral thinking and political courage to ascribe the policy settings we need to lock in the stability future generations deserve in the wake of this pandemic.

We are a lucky country. Our resources and geographical positioning give us untold comparative advantages over other nations — as long as our geographic isolation from other Western democracies doesn't become a security threat that overwhelms us.

We've seen the value of our global positioning as a trading nation, and recently in the context of avoiding the worst of the coronavirus. And because we are already a developed nation, our technology, health and educational settings are such that we will continue to sit at the top of the global tree for some time to come.

But maintaining that dominance, and indeed improving on it, requires the political class to step up. To take advantage of the post-pandemic new world order and the ways in which society needs to adapt to a global construct likely to be weighed down by the ongoing impact of COVID-19, including how it will force change.

We are living through a pandemic and will be for some time to come. Make no mistake, history has taught us that pandemics don't come and go quickly.

In a sense, the pandemic of 1918–20 — as severe and deadly as it was — taught us the wrong lessons as we entered this one. It was the exception that proved the rule. It left us thinking that the worst-case scenario was significant deaths and serious illnesses over just a few years rather than a decade or more.

Because World War I preceded that early 20th century pandemic — and it was soon followed by the Great Depression and World War II — the Spanish Flu wasn't the defining moment in history it could have been. Therefore, it didn't require policymakers to step up in its aftermath the way they need to now. The focus was elsewhere.

However, when we look further back at pandemics of the past, they have lasted longer and been defining moments, impacting societies in far greater ways. This is what policymakers need to be ready for in the coming years.

A hundred years from now, when historians look back on COVID-19, they won't see it as "the 2020 pandemic". We know that even now, as the after-effects have already overtaken 2021. The COVID-19 pandemic will likely be seen as the pandemic of the 2020s. Think about that and then turn your attention to the political class charged with successfully seeing us through it.

How much faith do you have in its ability to make good decisions? To make tough decisions for the betterment of society, even if there are political consequences? And what about the media and the commentariat. Do you think they are up to the task of sifting through what's important and what's not? Evaluating serious policies and decision-making in more than a glib way? Do they have the attention span to do so, the necessary skills sets? What about voters?

Equally, is our adversarial system of government properly equipped to handle all of the above? What about the federation? Can you seriously see state and federal co-operation overcoming political differences and narrow parochialism to set us up for a more stable future?

There should be little doubt that the pillars of stability that once ensured Western democracies like ours could withstand shocks are crumbling. What's left is a decaying epicentre of a system that both underestimates the longer-term seriousness of this pandemic and couldn't adequately plan for it even if a greater consciousness did exist.

Meanwhile, the public seems unaware of how long the after-effects of this pandemic might last, if not the pandemic itself. Mutations in the virus, new strains, will pose challenges to new and innovative vaccines. The underdeveloped world's inability to adequately gain access to vaccines will fracture whole regions. Even successfully combating coronavirus risks lengthening the time it takes to defeat it: reducing the health consequences for many of us but elongating the time it takes to fade away. This is where modern society helps us survive a pandemic but doesn't necessarily reduce the length of time we have to live through it.

The Black Death plague in the mid-14th century wiped out one-third of the global population, and that was at a time when the interconnectedness of the world was nothing like it is today. It also lasted a decade, with after-effects that profoundly reshaped governance.

Back in Roman times the Antonine plague of 165AD — believed to be smallpox — lasted a full 15 years, after returning soldiers brought the disease home from afar. It killed more than five million and acted as the precursor to the fall of Rome. One hundred years later, another plague (the Cyprian plague) also hit a debilitated Roman empire, lasting two decades.

More recently, when the new world of the Americas was discovered by Europeans, plagues ripped through the Indigenous populations during much of the 16th century, killing around 90 per cent of the population.

In raw numbers these historical plagues didn't kill as many people as the Spanish Flu. But they lasted longer, affected a larger cohort of the impacted populations and profoundly reshaped the communities touched by them.

The COVID-19 pandemic won't kill anywhere near as many people as Spanish Flu either, but it has already killed millions, and millions more will die from new variants, and certainly in the underdeveloped world.

Yet this isn't the lens through which to assess the impact of COVID-19. What it does to our way of life, the world order of powerful nations, how cultures from one country to the next interact with each other, and the way of thinking younger people growing up impacted by COVID-19 subsequently approach the rest of their lives.

What restrictions from government we tolerate, how innovative policymakers become in addressing the demands citizens have of government, how the human race chooses to prioritise rights verses responsibilities, and what reach of government into our daily lives we come to accept. These social consequences are the real impact of COVID-19.

The political class now and into the future will be charged with managing all of the above. How confident are we that it is up to the challenge?

Where's the line between rights and wrongs?

31 July 2021

In the long term, one of the defining features of this pandemic, especially in Australia, will be compliance; that is, the willingness of citizens to have their rights curtailed in the name of the public good.

That may seem like a trivial change to flag as so important. Overseas, deaths and serious hospitalisations have been defining features of the pandemic. Although deaths have been nowhere near the rates experienced during the Spanish influenza pandemic from 1918–1920, millions have died from COVID-19, and millions more will die in underdeveloped countries.

New variants also are a medium to long-term risk for all nations, even for the vaccinated.

However, in Australia the number of deaths has been among the lowest anywhere. Notwithstanding the slowness of the vaccine rollout and the heightened risks attached to that, they are unlikely to accelerate to a point that elevates their significance when assessing the long-term impacts of Covid.

The policy levers used by governments, state and federal, to combat Covid have revealed a willingness by democratic populations to give up rights in sometimes unexpected ways. We have also seen how wide the range of powers available to governments is under the Constitution and via recent legislation. The Biosecurity Act, for example, gives government extraordinary powers.

Of course, erosions of civil liberties aren't a new phenomenon. In the name of fighting terrorism we've seen an uptick in rights-stifling national security laws for years. Technological advancements and the rise of social media this century have shown people are more willing to part indiscriminately with their personal information. Indeed the cultural wont to protest or strike isn't what it was decades ago, as new laws curtail doing either.

Long gone are the days of civil disobedience Peter Singer wrote about in the Oxford University thesis that became his first book. But the erosion of freedoms during the pandemic, and the ease with which people have accepted it, has been surprising.

An ability for premiers to ignore the federal government and lock down borders. Stay-at-home orders during lockdowns that have included evening curfews and limits on freedom of movement. Refusals by the federal government to grant entry to Australia for citizens abroad because of arrival limits. Forced quarantine for those who can successfully return home. Whole sections of the business community shut down because the services they provide are deemed "non-essential". With the media classified as an essential services (the fourth estate and all of that), too many of us with a microphone and a pay cheque have undercooked the significance of this last point to people's livelihoods.

Before China used lockdowns in Wuhan, democratic policymakers didn't consider such a course of action feasible. It wasn't part of their forward planning for a pandemic. Even then they wondered if populations used to having rights would refuse to comply with such measures after they watched it succeed in Wuhan. Yet here we are, 18 months later, using them as a first response to news that Covid cases have infiltrated the community, with only pockets of noncompliance.

My point isn't that it has been wrong for populations in democracies such as ours to come together for the greater good — it's a form of utilitarianism, to be sure, accepting the loss of rights and freedoms to bring the virus under control for everyone's benefit. I'm not part of the protest movement or fringe commentariat, fighting the longer-than-usual arm of the law during Covid. You can highlight these developments as a profound cultural shift with potential consequences, where ease of compliance with government rules could lead to shifts for the betterment of society but almost certainly won't, and what that says about our governmental structures.

Where is the line when it comes to giving up freedoms? How far is too far? Unfortunately there aren't enough serious scholars in this space willing to sully themselves in public debate, presumably because what's left of public debate is often found wanting. This is its own issue, but it becomes an accelerating part of the problem when it reduces qualified voices prepared to challenge continued erosions of rights.

Interestingly, just as the government embarks on expanding restrictions on our freedoms in the name of protecting us, it won't protect us in non-pandemic areas where saving citizens from themselves could be a public good.

These could include curtailing gambling, especially online; or properly monitoring underage access to pornography online, if not banning online pornography altogether; or doing more to legislate sin taxes beyond smoking, where such measures have led to a clear decline in smoking rates — evidence that logically should lead to an expansion of sin taxes, providing a chance to cut productivity-sapping taxes elsewhere.

We regularly are told such measures wouldn't work, however. Prohibition is bad, consumer freedoms are good. Regressive taxes may worsen social cohesion and exacerbate inequality. The rejections are often glib.

Civil libertarians wouldn't want an expansion of the so-called nanny state, but why won't the political class embrace it in the wake of the pandemic? The answer is simple: it is beholden to special interests in the sectors that would lose out to such reforms. Politicians will only act courageously with a pandemic to justify radical policy responses.

Perhaps, conscious of the dangers of rights continually being curtailed, we should be grateful for that. Plenty of philosophers want rights protected. Or maybe it should concern us, knowing our leaders will quickly erode freedoms and rights when a sudden crisis justifies it but not when we boil slowly over time, such as when there is a lack of consensus on climate change action.

What about young men accessing pornography — surely a contributing factor to sexual violence among youth? Pervasive access to online gambling can't be a good thing when the cost of living is going up and inequality is on the rise. As our nation continues to become more obese, putting more pressure on the public health system, why won't politicians consider a sin tax on sugary goods?

In the aftermath of this pandemic, when we get the chance to pause for thought and evaluate what our society looks like, it will be interesting to judge the limits of what has changed, and the boundaries that have been pushed further out.

The below column received plenty of criticisms from those who couldn't see how we might learn to live with Covid. But fast forward to today and sure enough, its message is right. Lockdowns and the like needed to become a thing of the past once vaccination rates rose.

Are we ready to make the hard decisions?

17–18 July 2021

At some point soon the Australian population is going to have to come to terms with the realities of the new Covid world; that is, in the context of full availability of vaccinations.

Of course we aren't there yet and likely won't be until the end of this year or early next. But it won't be long before a reality check is needed among the wider population and politicians.

Our two largest cities are in lockdown. In the case of Sydney, it may be a relatively long one. Melburnians have been through this before, too many times, and will be hoping theirs is short. Either way, we are fast approaching the time when lockdowns must become a thing of the past.

A fully vaccinated Australia will need to say no to lockdowns and state border closures, and it also will need to start to open up to the outside world. That means a near free flow of international movement. The notion of long periods of quarantine also will need to be looked at. They are stifling and ultimately pointless if the country is going to try to live with the virus once vaccinated. They must become the exception, not the norm.

To be sure, becoming fully vaccinated really means the unequivocal opportunity to be vaccinated, when we all can no longer complain about a lack of supply or time to get the two doses into our arms. Because we know, like it or not, many won't consent to Covid vaccine jabs. It will be a sizeable cohort and they vote, but we can't let their fears ruin life for the rest of us.

But the biggest thing citizens and politicians need to accept once we hit this point is the sickness and death associated with COVID-19. It won't be on the scale we saw overseas last year when Covid ripped through unvaccinated communities in places such as the US, Italy and Britain. But it still will come as a major shock to a country that largely has avoided the worst of this virus.

If we apply to Australia what is happening abroad in countries with near adequate vaccination rates and adjust the numbers to our population size, thousands of people will be infected with Covid every week — which could then lead to dozens of deaths.

The difference vaccines make is they dramatically reduce the death rate to what has long been considered an acceptable level during flu seasons, or at least in bad flu seasons, albeit with much higher infection rates.

Are we ready for that? Are our political leaders willing to explain the necessity of tolerating such an outcome? What about the media; will it avoid sensationalising higher death rates and much higher infection rates? It is hard to see the bandwagon bleating of social media tolerating such an outcome without simplistically using it to ascribe political blame on partisan adversaries.

Let's hope as a country we are mature enough to overcome such nay-saying because, if not, we soon will lag behind the rest of the world economically, which will cause all manner of other negative effects on a society.

Lockdowns and border closures eventually will lead to us falling behind other wealthy nations in a post-vaccine world. It never ceases to amaze me how many people can't see past their own noses sometimes.

It can be only because they haven't read enough history. If we allow ourselves to make bad decisions too many times and for too long, our wealth and status as a nation can drop dramatically. We can become a less prosperous society, as happened in Argentina, once the sixth wealthiest country.

Because other parts of the world were so badly ravaged by COVID-19 last year, their gratefulness for fewer deaths and fewer serious illnesses among those who catch the virus today means their tolerance level for such outcomes is higher than ours may be.

This is why we won't see any of what I mention as a necessary evil until after the next federal election. Scott Morrison knows that politically it is going to take time for Australians to adjust to the realities of living with COVID-19. His government will want a full term in office to manage an election out of the other side of that — assuming he can overcome current criticisms to win re-election in the first place.

Besides, as Prime Minister, Morrison has only a limited say in what a post-vaccinated Australia looks like. The federal government needs state governments to accept the reality spelled out above. Even if Morrison accepts it, will the likes of West Australian Premier Mark McGowan? Or will McGowan keep West Australians locked off from the rest of the country, and the world, long after other states reopen?

The difficulty is that if not all leaders realise what has to come next, there will be a political contest. Deaths and sickness will be used as a political weapon to claim some leaders are mismanaging the situation. It will be an unbecoming spectacle. Unless, perhaps, there is such a sizeable community backlash against closed borders.

While it is easy to see communities that have had to lock down repeatedly wanting that to end once a vaccine is widely available, states that barely have been touched by lockdowns may not be so unwilling to embrace the risks of Covid running through their communities, at least not initially. Especially knowing that variants of the virus can find their way around the protections vaccines offer. Risk-aversion in these states may win out against the need to return to normal.

This far into the pandemic — it has been more than 18 months — it is easy to forget that lockdowns were never seriously considered an option by democratic countries until they saw them used effectively in China. The assumption was that citizens with rights wouldn't be compliant enough for them to work, much less tolerated.

Then we have the often-forgotten reality that the federal government's health advice never recommended state border closures. Rather, state health officials, in conjunction with their politicians, made such calls — dividing the nation in a way we haven't seen since federation.

Many Australians now would see themselves as citizens of their state first and foremost, their country second, and that is no exaggeration. Why not, when you are denied the chance to travel freely in your own country as a citizen and are unable even to get to major family events or tragically are denied entry to states where loved ones are suffering and dying? That can have an impact on one's psyche.

Our subservience to the state has been a feature of this pandemic, perhaps the chief feature of it. In time the legacy of such subservience could become the next chapter in human history.

Politics of Palaszczuk just reckless needling

3–4 July 2021

Queensland Premier Annastacia Palaszczuk and chief health officer Jeanette Young (who the Premier recently appointed Queensland's next governor) used a media conference on Wednesday to deliver a reckless and self-serving message.

They verballed the Prime Minister and downright misled the public. Their actions undermined confidence in vaccinations, leading anti-vaxxers to jump with joy.

I rarely defend Scott Morrison, and I certainly don't defend the errors the federal government has made rolling out vaccinations. But Palaszczuk and Young appeared to try and take advantage of those failures, using them to distract from their own problems: an unvaccinated 19-year-old worker spreading Covid in Queensland and forcing the state into lockdown.

That was a state government failure, so the Premier used a "look over there" strategy to deflect criticism. It was brazen but worse still, its consequences were alarmist in a way that will damage public confidence in vaccines.

Palaszczuk claimed Morrison wants to set up commonwealth mass vaccination hubs for AstraZeneca. That is absolute rubbish. He has not sought to do that privately, nor has he made one public utterance to that effect.

The Premier also refuted alleged claims by the PM that national cabinet made a decision to roll AstraZeneca out for people under 40. The problem with her rebuttal? He did no such thing.

Queensland's Health Minister claims a shortage of Pfizer vaccines is behind the PM's amplification of AstraZeneca as an alternative: "Maybe this is why the PM has come out and suggested that under-40s get AZ." That statement is probably right; Australia does have a surplus of AstraZeneca and a shortage of Pfizer. Whether through bad luck or bad management (I lean towards the latter), that is where we find ourselves.

All Morrison did was remind people AstraZeneca has been approved by the TGA and could therefore be available for those under 60. He said people should consult with their GP. "If they wish to go and speak to their doctor and have access to the AstraZeneca vaccine, they can do so." The commonwealth is moving to indemnify nervous doctors who might otherwise recommend AstraZeneca for their patients. Granted, there needs to be more meat on the bones of this decision.

However, the reaction to the PM's entirely reasonable statement has been to claim he's going against the health advice, which is utter rubbish.

Last week at Wimbledon the developer of the AstraZeneca vaccine, Dame Sarah Gilbert, was given a standing ovation when introduced to the crowd. A grateful nation expressing its thanks. If she came to Australia she might get pelted with tomatoes, such is the unnecessary hysteria surrounding AstraZeneca.

And it's a hysteria Queensland's CHO added to when she said "No, I don't want under-40s to get AstraZeneca… I don't want an 18-year-old in Queensland dying from a clotting illness who if they got Covid probably wouldn't die."

It is hard to know where to start with such black-and-white rhetoric by someone so senior who should know better. But let's begin with the risk profile she's talking about.

Around one in three younger people in every 100,000 who take AstraZeneca get blood clotting. Only 3 per cent of clotting cases result in death, according to professor of public health Julie Leask. That's 3 per cent of three out of every 100,000 cases, which works out to be around one in a million.

A one-in-a-million risk Queensland's Deputy Premier described as "very risky". Ponder that fearmongering.

As far as medical risk profiles go, one in a million is extremely low, which is why the TGA approved AstraZeneca in the first place. But governments have been very cautious nonetheless. For context, in Britain, AstraZeneca is available to people under 40 but recommended for the over-40s. In France, it is fully available, as it is in many other nations. Australia is shipping it all over the Pacific, for all age groups, to help our neighbours.

As health expert Professor Nathan Grills points out, the risk of taking aspirin is "two hundred times more dangerous than AstraZeneca". Which is why the absolutist rhetoric of Young, in my opinion, is so reckless. It took just minutes after she made her statements for former deputy chief medical officer at the federal level, Nick Coatsworth, to challenge what she said, tweeting "well, I guess that puts me at odds with the QLD CHO".

And he's far from alone. Since Young's comments, a conga line of specialists has been critical of the message the CHO sent with her comments. As the vice-president of the AMA, Dr Chris Moy, told ABC radio on Thursday: "I was quite concerned, I actually thought that was inappropriate."

It is worth noting that the 58-year-old CHO herself waited for the Pfizer vaccine, even though AstraZeneca was recommended for her age group at the time.

And the Queensland Premier also got a Pfizer shot when AstraZeneca was recommended. The reason? She had to get a flu shot, her dog bit her, she might go to the Tokyo Olympics, so she needed the faster turnaround time for the second jab. These were all excuses she used.

Not to be flippant about it but there's probably a greater chance Queensland's next governor hurts herself when cutting a ribbon at an opening than there is of an 18-year-old dying from AstraZeneca. Which is not to say that it can't happen, like anything in life there are risks. In this case, a one-in-a-million risk. Public health advice includes subjective judgments, which is why it always irks me when politicians hide behind "health advice" in absolutist terms, suggesting their decisions are beyond reproach. That is not how public policy generally works, nor is not how health policy specifically works.

The reasons behind not actively discouraging young people to get AstraZeneca jabs are multifaceted. It undermines confidence; it ignores the benefits of more vaccinated Australians being less likely to transmit Covid to more at-risk communities. Young's comparison of an 18-year-old's risk of dying from Covid versus AstraZeneca ignores the risks of Covid during an outbreak, if ICU wards are at or near capacity, indeed the risks of 18-year-olds carrying Covid while unvaccinated and passing it on.

As the AMA has pointed out, even one shot of the AstraZeneca vaccine reduces the transmission rate of the virus by 50 per cent.

There are layers of nuance and responsibility attached to how health officials should conduct themselves in public, and we saw little of that at Wednesday's media conference.

Frankly, I don't know why I'm surprised. This is the same Premier and CHO who repeatedly rejected requests for a son to see his dying father, even though he was fully vaccinated, had tested negative three times, was prepared to wear a hazmat suit and fly in and out on a private jet. Despite NSW and federal health officials giving the mercy dash the green light.

Eventually, the Queensland Premier gave in, and he was able to see his dad. But only after media and public pressure was acutely applied. In other words, once a compassionate decision became a political problem in need of fixing.

That tells you everything you need to know.

Cabinet acts globally and ignores the locals

19–20 June 2021

There has been a lot of backslapping among politicians about how well national cabinet has worked since it replaced the regular COAG meetings. Scott Morrison has led the self-praise.

Of course we know that the rise and rise of national cabinet was in the context of the pandemic. Leaders at state and territory levels wanted to be able to talk directly with one another, uninhibited by the banality of bureaucratic processes. Many politicians aren't as details oriented as they could or should be. Too many party fundraisers and not enough time reflecting.

Because COAG included the bureaucrats, sometimes political leaders felt the process took precedence over the need to achieve outcomes. Forgetting that ends rarely justify means. A sweep of history confirms that reality.

There are always unintended consequences in changes to long-term processes. Even if short-term praise meets the new idea. One of the downsides to the removal of regular COAG meetings is the way in which local government has been left out in the cold. Missing out on a seat at the table.

When national cabinet was conceived the attention on who missed out was focused on the federal opposition. But it was never part of the COAG predecessor anyway.

A perhaps little-known reality of COAG was that local government had a seat at the decision-making table. It wasn't just chief ministers of the territories infiltrating the space of state and national leaders (the more high-profile representatives).

But territory heads have been retained in the national cabinet process, local government representation has not. If the saying "all politics is local", coined by former speaker of the US House of Representatives Tip O'Neill, really is true, there hasn't been much attention paid locally in this country since the start of the pandemic.

That, simply put, must change. Either a seat at the table must be found for local government, or the national cabinet should be replaced by the processes of COAG. A return to the past, as it were.

Our leaders need to understand that Australia has three tiers of government — national, state and local. Just because constitutionally local government can be overridden by state legislatures doesn't change the fact that it has important work to do. Until it's abolished it must be heard.

In fact it is local government that often (and usually) has closer contact with the daily lives of constituents than state or national MPs. Which is why it really was barking mad to exclude local government from national cabinet during the pandemic — a time when people needed their local communities more than ever.

Think for a moment about how much better informed those national cabinet debates would have been if those who represent smaller local communities were included during discussions on how border towns might be impacted by state lockdowns or border closures. The need for understanding when it comes to medical treatments between council areas locked down. How hoarding could have been better combated region by region, town by town. And what about the way city-based outbreaks often resulted in harsh shutdowns in regional centres untouched by the pandemic? A seat at the table for local government — which includes local councils in regional Australia — would have been a voice of reason against that outcome.

While it might be easy to simply say that local government is the responsibility of state governments, so the premiers can represent them at national cabinet, that misses the point. State leaders are at the table to represent their entire states, not to put various hats on and off as discussions ebb and flow. Local communities nationwide would benefit from a power structure which gives them a seat at national cabinet, not shared with other constituencies.

Besides, because vertical fiscal imbalance means the commonwealth raises most of the revenue but the states do most of the spending, local government needs direct access to the Prime Minister via national cabinet. The feds fund close to 10 per cent of local government spending.

Plus, the pandemic taught us that politicians in charge of service delivery have power scholars underestimated before the pandemic, even if they don't control the purse strings. That's the case for local governments almost as much as is the case for states. Everything from garbage collection to planning provisions to the maintenance of local roads and parks falls under their purview. It doesn't matter that state governments can legislate over the top of these councils. When states change planning laws at the macro level they often neglect the micro needs of councils.

I'm well aware local government is often forgotten. Even mocked. So when the PM sat down and came up with the idea of national cabinet on the back of a napkin one day, I'm not surprised he left this important tier of government to wither on the vine.

But the time has come to fix that mistake. And it isn't even a backflip which would see the government lose political skin. It's not, for example, as politically challenging as the decision-making around the Biloela family. Or whether or not to embrace a 2050 net zero emissions target now that a senior Nationals cabinet minister (Keith Pitt) has declared that he doesn't think his party would agree to such a policy shift.

Letting local government back in the room where the decisions are made (yes I've seen the musical Hamilton) is all upside — unless the Liberal Party has forgotten its federalist roots and is only interested in centralising power and disempowering representatives on the margins. If that's the case someone needs to alert the Nationals. As the junior Coalition partners they need to be more aware of who they are politically in bed with, given that the Deputy PM and Nationals leader is also shut out of national cabinet.

There is a strong argument that while politicians prefer the simplicity of national cabinet over the policy and bureaucratic complexity of COAG, the latter often guarantees better policy outcomes. While that might be debatable, what is not is the need to get the local government pollies back at the decision-making table. So that local communities are better represented and get heard by those in power

Outbreak we need is some government action

29–30 May 2021

"Coulda", "shoulda", "woulda" — that's the story of Australia's plunge back into lockdowns as we brace for potential future COVID-19 outbreaks.

Outbreaks that are happening because hotel quarantining is flawed, especially when it comes to protecting ourselves from virulent new strains.

Outbreaks that are made more dangerous because not enough Australians have been vaccinated — a failure of the slow rollout, exacerbated by vaccine hesitancy.

We coulda built quarantine facilities capable of containing the virus long before now, and we shoulda. We woulda accelerated the vaccine rollout and dovetailed doing so with a better public awareness campaign if we knew this is where we might end up.

But we didn't and, stuck where we now are, there isn't much we can do about it. Sure, it's never too late to get going and construct purpose-built quarantine facilities around the country. In the current budget climate it's not as though fiscal conservatism is an ideological impediment to the cost. But by the time they would be built it will be too late to avoid further hotel quarantine failures anyway.

We face many months of such failures even if the construction of purpose-built facilities started first thing Monday morning — which of course it will not.

It's hard to escape the feeling that stubbornness on Scott Morrison's part is a factor in the refusal to capitulate on these facilities.

The same coulda, shoulda, woulda lament goes for the vaccine rollout. It is accelerating. Each week beats the previous one for the number of

Australians who are being vaccinated.

But the simple fact is that one jab is only partially effective. You need two to really feel relaxed and comfortable that you won't die or get seriously ill if you catch Covid, as well as to minimise your chances of catching the virus and passing it on in the first place.

There is a 12-week wait between AstraZeneca jabs, which are freely available in great enough numbers to vaccinate everyone. But they are not recommended for those of us under 50, courtesy of rare blood clotting. Equally, courtesy of rare blood clotting, there are not enough people over 50 getting their AstraZeneca jabs.

It's an understandable emotional fear, even if the maths and the health advice tell a different story. Again, the government probably should have handled differently how that information has been distributed — coulda, shoulda, woulda.

The Pfizer jab requires only a three-week wait between needles, but it isn't freely available in the way AstraZeneca is. In short, we don't have enough of it to go around yet, so the government necessarily has to limit who is eligible and drip-feed it out.

In hindsight we needed better deals across mRNA vaccines, but on that score we were unlucky and backed the wrong horse.

This week in question time the Prime Minister admonished Labor for not embracing bipartisanship when it came to the pandemic. We are all in this together, remember?

Morrison was critical of Anthony Albanese questioning the slow vaccine rollout and the failure to construct purpose-built quarantine facilities. But it was a weak response to the Opposition Leader's valid questions.

There is no rule that bipartisanship must prevail. In fact it shouldn't. I always found such demand callow during the height of the pandemic domestically.

The whole point of our Westminster system is that we have an opposition to hold the government of the day to account, to challenge its policy decision-making. That's why parliament being shut down the way it was last year was so outrageous.

Partisanship for its own sake rightly gets called out. But Labor has legitimate gripes when it comes to failures that are exposing Australians to greater risk when Covid enters the community. None of which should detract from the fact Australia is still where you want to be. We have managed the pandemic well — and as well, if not better, than anywhere else in the world.

Labor hopes to replace that proven success with emerging failures as the narrative. It will be a fascinating political contest to watch. A government seeking re-election post pandemic claiming credit for successes early on that built the foundations for the jobs and economic recovery it now wants to focus on.

Sure, the Coalition has thrown fiscal discipline completely out the window. Hypocrisy aside, it hopes not to be penalised for that, and it likely won't be. But it will be penalised if we see rolling outbreaks and lockdowns in the months counting down to election day, especially if they hamper economic recovery and cost jobs.

In addition to its macro arguments for re-election, the Coalition is zeroing in on what are micro weaknesses for Labor. Opposing the gas-fired power plant in NSW's Hunter Valley was right on policy grounds but wrong on the politics. I realise good policy theoretically is supposed to equate with good politics, but that's not always true.

By opposing the $600 million spend in the Hunter, Labor has exposed itself in three seats in and around that region. It also gives the government ammunition to attack Labor in the twin resource states of Western Australia and Queensland. Joel Fitzgibbon knows this, which is why he has been so outspoken.

While most of his colleagues do not agree with his decision to cause havoc by going public, many privately agree with his sentiments — more than Labor's leadership team seem to realise.

They appear to be focused on picking away at problems in Parliament House. Yes, there is an abundance of issues with the toxic culture that has been exposed, but the wider public is infinitely more concerned with issues that affect their daily lives. Some within Labor haven't come to grips with this post-budget reality, hoping instead to spark further problems for Morrison on the gender front.

If Team Morrison is going to be brought down it won't be courtesy of what goes on inside the beltway. It will be because quarantine and vaccine failures that affect ordinary Australians shift votes accordingly.

The sooner those with decision-making authority in the opposition realise this is the only game in town, the better the chances they can politically exploit the situation to electoral advantage.

If that doesn't happen, Morrison will win a fourth term, and push himself into the upper echelons of Liberal prime ministers, and Labor will be left to look back thinking about what it coulda, shoulda and woulda done differently if it had its time again.

Just the shot in the arm to keep us safe and sound

22–23 May 2021

Every effort needs to be made to ensure herd immunity from the vaccine rollout is achieved as quickly as possible.

In fact the aim needs to be to get beyond herd immunity, encouraging every Australian to get the jab. The best medical advice tells us that once enough of the population are vaccinated the chances of people getting seriously ill or dying from COVID-19 are low. Lower, perhaps, than is the case with the flu.

Doctors are reluctant to make the flu comparison because of misinformation campaigns during the height of the pandemic last year, before vaccines were available. Denialism about the severity of COVID-19 led to inaccurate claims that it was little different to the flu.

However, once people are vaccinated similarities do exist, comparisons can be made. That was the point Virgin chief executive Jayne Hrdlicka sought to make, albeit clumsily, early in the week.

If Australians are vaccinated in enough numbers we can open our international borders and risk coronavirus ripping through the community. Scary, yes. Counterintuitive, you bet.

But as long as we maintain hygiene practices and use contact tracing techniques learnt during the crisis, few if any Australians should die from the virus. Managing the health impacts becomes the focus, rather than seeking to eradicate the virus as an isolated nation. But only if the country is as near to fully vaccinated as possible. Because those not vaccinated are at as much risk from COVID-19 as at any time during the pandemic — perhaps more so now courtesy of new strains popping up around the globe.

We have seen data out of countries such as Britain, torn apart by coronavirus, showing few if any deaths now that most of the population have been vaccinated. That's despite continuing high numbers of infections.

In fact, by last month the daily numbers started to reflect more deaths from flu than from COVID-19.

Australia is in the fortunate position of having managed the pandemic better than most. Our isolation and ability to shut ourselves off from the rest of the world have kept infections and death rates low. That has allowed us to take our time with the vaccine rollout, waiting to see the side effects of the various vaccines on the market and to tailor our rollout to put safety first.

But now it's time to ensure Australians realise how important vaccines are to what comes next. We need a powerful public awareness campaign to promote vaccinations. Breaking through the 30 per cent plus hesitancy in the community to get vaccinated is essential. Clotting problems with the AstraZeneca vaccine certainly haven't helped.

Yes, we must appeal to people's collective consciences, but Australians also need to understand that at the individual level they are safer once vaccinated. The chances of complications from vaccines are small compared with the risks of COVID-19 if not vaccinated. Once people understand that they can't be safe from COVID-19 forever courtesy of a Fortress Australia mentality that comparison should cut through. This is where a well-tailored public awareness campaign can help.

The Fortress Australia notion may be popular, playing into a long-time cultural appeal in this country for isolation from the rest of the world. Don't forget, as much as Australia has modernised in recent decades, we are still a country with a long anti-immigration history. The global cut-off can't and should not last forever. It harms business and, by extension, slows growth and reduces prosperity.

Public policy think tank the McKell Institute has estimated that our isolation from the rest of the world is costing the Australian economy more than $200m a day. These are the economic realities. It isn't just airlines and the tourism sector that suffer from border closures. We are seeing the effects on universities, with international student numbers drying up, and wider trade and commerce also suffers.

Which is to say nothing of the regressive mindset caused by shutting ourselves off from the global community indefinitely. Our politicians know it is popular, but they must refrain from tapping into it. We have seen premiers exploit the concept of "the other" between Australian citizens by overcooking state border shutdowns. There were some health benefits in doing so early on, but the political games behind such decision-making also were an undeniable factor.

Federal political leaders need to avoid doing the same when it comes to other nations in what might be an election year.

The government has received its fair share of criticism for the slowness of the vaccine rollout. Fair enough. But the latest figures reveal the daily jab numbers hitting 100,000, with 3.5 million Australians vaccinated.

To be sure, there is as long way to go. But it is community hesitancy with getting vaccinated that is the bigger threat to herd immunity, rather than a lack of availability of vac-cines.

I have been surprised by how limited information campaigns have been, given that governments of all stripes are usually so quick to roll out unnecessarily politicised ad campaigns when it suits them to do so.

This is one of the few times when a mass campaign has real value.

Finally, on another issue, let me debunk the myth that the amount of debt building up is OK. The absurd unwillingness of the government to get its fiscal house in order isn't merely hypocritical after the way the Coalition treated Labor in the wake of the global financial crisis — it's lazy.

Red is the new black as the budget reveals sky-high spending with no effort to get the books in order across the forward estimates. The claim is that we have been ravaged by the pandemic.

But here are the numbers in the government's own budget (Budget Paper No 1, page 359): next financial year (which starts halfway through this calendar year) tax revenue is expected to be higher than it was in the last full financial year before the pandemic (2018–19). That is, $479bn next financial year compared with $477bn in 2018–19. Yet back then payments (essentially spending) were just $478bn whereas next financial year it is anticipated to be a whopping $589bn.

That is after JobSeeker and JobKeeper and with no more crippling lockdowns. The understandable record spending during the height of the pandemic when such factors were in play was $661bn for the 2020–21 financial year. Why is it OK for spending to be so high after all of that? But it doesn't stop there. In each of the financial years that follow, spending rises year on year — to $593bn in 2022–23, $612bn in 2023–24 and hitting $629bn in 2024–25. Worst of all, the increases largely aren't productive spending. Rather, they worsen the structural deficit with debt-funded recurrent expenditure increases. It is woeful fiscal management according to the yardstick fiscal conservatives like to set. By a Coalition government no less.

Josh kicks the reform can down the road

15–16 May 2021

People underestimate the importance of Josh Frydenberg's first budget in helping the Coalition at the 2019 election, when Scott Morrison came from behind to win. The budget was brought forward to April to accommodate a May 18 election. The Treasurer put his stamp on that budget, spruiking the "back in black" mantra and fashioning the books, such that the Coalition could sell itself to the public as the side of politics that repaired the finances. It was a powerful sell.

Facts don't always see eye-to-eye with political spin. In government the Coalition at that time already had doubled the debt it inherited from Labor in 2013 and "back in black" would turn out to be a mirage. But there is no denying the role Frydenberg played in that election win, even if the Prime Minister rightly gets the lion's share of the credit. The hit job on Bill Shorten's economic credibility to lead the country was effective politicking.

Fast forward to now and a similar outcome might be in the offing after Tuesday night's budget, even if the complexion of the comparison is very different. Frydenberg is seeking to paint the Coalition as prepared to junk ideological zeal for the practicalities of addressing voter needs. But he also has framed the budget as important to support economic growth to fight rising debt.

Then there is the goal of full employment, with which even Labor concurs. But Tuesday night certainly wasn't all good news. Wall-to-wall deficits across the forward estimates. Record debt in the current financial year, forecast to come in at a tick under $161bn. National debt surging past $1.2 trillion. These numbers will be a burden for future generations, certainly if interest rates move north as they inevitably must one day.

While the Coalition has clearly overcome its fears about a "debt and deficit disaster" (Joe Hockey's words before the 2013 election), the debt-funded spending is repairing long-neglected policy areas such as aged care, childcare and the National Disability Insurance Scheme. And even though I was surprised more money wasn't spent on initiatives for women, there is cash going into programs to address domestic violence and workplace harassment too, just not enough.

Usually a conservative government finds itself playing the role of the bad guy when it comes to hand outs, crimping spending with the aim of getting the structural deficit under control. Not anymore. Frydenberg has jettisoned that mantra unapologetically and has replaced it with largesse. His critics want to focus on the backflip and hypocrisy, which is an issue.

But it isn't the issue for voters, who simply want to be looked after by their government. Too often political insiders focus on the manoeuvring rather than the outcome of said manoeuvring. Labor is left to criticise the spending priorities from the sidelines while lamenting waste along the way.

Or it can pivot right and cast itself as the safer economic managers by embracing fiscal conservatism. Anthony Albanese's budget reply speech suggests he'll try to do all of that, which risks casting the Opposition Leader as all things to all people.

We will see. It isn't an easy position for Labor to be in. But the most important outcome of the latest release of finance numbers alongside the political responses is that the reform can continues to be kicked down the road. Australians need to have a conversation about what we expect of governments.

Do we see the role of government as more interventionist in our lives than has been the case in the past? Is the safety net that modern governments have a duty to provide not cast wide enough? This is where the conversation needs to go.

I suspect most voters do want more from government, which explains why the money flowing to a greater extent than it has in the past is tolerable. But if such a brand of social liberalism is the ethos we want, everyone has to get realistic about what it takes to provide that.

Debt is funding recurrent expenditure, putting the budget in structural deficit. With more expected of government alongside challenges such as ageing and reduced migration post-pandemic, our politicians need to debate what has to change to accommodate community expectations.

Right now extra needs are being funded by extra debt. And with limited buyers of Australian government bonds on the international market the Reserve Bank is snaffling them up, which essentially means it's just printing money. Eventually this will have to put upward pressure on inflation and interest rates, which in turn makes paying debt interest more expensive.

And, by the way, the AAA credit rating — while confirmed — has been put on a watch list. If we lose it, that also sends interest rates north. If we want more from government, we need government to embrace ways of funding those additional things. That means higher taxes, but it's never that simple.

Putting taxes up can stifle economic growth. Enter tax reform. We need higher taxes to fund higher recurrent spending, but new taxes need to be designed so they don't become counterproductive and halt the expansion of the economic pie. You get that outcome only with sweeping tax reform, but there's no appetite for that, certainly not on the eve of an election at which a long-term government is seeking a fourth term.

And it won't be encouraged by an opposition burnt at the previous election that went big with reform ideas and lost. To be fair to Frydenberg there is a lot more in the details of the budget than gets widely reported when it comes to rejigging taxes to complement economic growth.

But that's still not the equivalent of major reform. I am starting to think that Frydenberg has more in common with John Howard than Morrison ever has. Morrison is perhaps more comparable to Malcolm Fraser, even if their compassionate policy scripts are polar opposites. Fraser won elections and was a hero for doing so, but ultimately led a government that plunged the country into recession and accrued debt.

Howard was Fraser's treasurer, so he shares that legacy. However, once unshackled from the Fraser years, Howard was able to spruik micro-economic reforms that should have happened under Fraser but didn't. The only problem was that Howard had to wait 13 long years to get back into government to start his prime ministership. That seems unlikely to happen again in the fast-paced environment of modern politics, even for Frydenberg, who is already approaching age 50.

Budget repair on hold with an election to win

1–2 May 2021

You have to wonder how the so-called fiscal conservatives within the Coalition's ranks feel about the Treasurer's latest pronouncement: no return to austerity until the unemployment rate has a four in front of it.

In other words, short of achieving full employment we won't see this conservative government even get started on budget repair, instead resting on its laurels that it handed down a smaller-than-usual deficit before the pandemic struck. Mission complete.

Put to one side the record deficits, debt, low wages growth and inadequate productivity growth all around us. Why? Because there is an election to win. And Australia is doing better on the economic front than most like-for-like nations. Cuts to the budget are never popular, so don't expect a populist PM to sign off on budget austerity after the last few months Scott Morrison has endured as he begins campaigning for his re-election. Especially when, in fairness, economists near-universally agree that now isn't the time to dry up government spending and move taxes higher.

Which means debt will continue to grow, as does the role of government. We will have to have the conversation eventually about what the public wants from its government. A more interventionist government asked to do more needs the revenue streams to fulfil such obligations. That means higher taxes, or at least tax reform to make how we tax more efficient.

It is a philosophical debate largely beyond the political class, certainly beyond much of the commentariat, and disconnected to the daily struggle mainstream Australians go through simply to live their lives.

Josh Frydenberg is relaxed about ballooning debt because interest rates are so low. That's not unreasonable in the here and now. But what happens when that changes? Debt repayments skyrocket. But that won't be this government's problem because the debt being purchased to fund profligate spending won't mature for decades, as articulated in Frydenberg's pre-budget speech on Thursday.

Such long-term settings kick the fiscal can far enough down the road that future generations can worry about the consequences, not us. Or at least, not us right now. And besides, the Reserve Bank is printing money, and buying much of the debt with it, so the facade of fiscal responsibility can be maintained in the face of record blowouts.

It is true that growing your way out of debt is a meaningful (and real) pathway to future prosperity. That means considering debt as a percentage of GDP rather than on the gross or net raw numbers. Developing countries the world over have long reduced debt as a percentage of GDP, all the while watching the raw figures grow. Paul Keating must have been right: growing the pie works. Now let's hear a Liberal Treasurer admit that.

To be sure, Morrison has never really been a fiscal conservative. Nor is Frydenberg, in the sense that he's a pragmatist who wants to be PM one day. He's in the same difficult position as Keating: likely to be on the wrong side of the political cycle when it's his time.

Which is why Keating struck when he did, after Bob Hawke dishonoured their Kirribilli handover pact, ousting Hawke in a partyroom coup, going on to win an unexpected additional term at the 1993 election.

Frydenberg won't be striking at Morrison anytime soon (or later, most likely). And winning the next election is going to be hard enough with Morrison still in charge. That leaves the Treasurer destined to take over a long-term government and needing to perform his own miracles to win re-election in 2025. Or he'll become a first-term opposition leader after Morrison is defeated next year.

And we know how likely it is that first-term opposition leaders become prime minister. Not very.

We might be counting down to next month's budget, but the real number-crunching going on within the Coalition right now is at an electoral level. Polling day is probably a year away, and the numbers aren't good for the Coalition.

Even if it remains deserved favourite, remembering it is already on the brink of losing its majority.

Take a look around the country. A lost seat in WA courtesy of a redistribution coupled with difficult holds in seats like Swan and Hasluck are a reality. Throw in Christian Porter's newly marginal seat as another tough hold. WA has long been at a high watermark for the Liberals federally, yet at state level the party now only holds two lower house seats.

Labor must like its chances of winning back one or both of Bass and Braddon in Tasmania. It has long targeted Boothby in South Australia and can now do so against a candidate rather than a sitting MP, following Nicolle Flint's announced retirement.

Team Shorten failed to pick up Victorian seats it hoped to in 2019, the likes of which will again be on Labor's radar. I'm talking about seats like La Trobe and Chisholm. And redistribution there hands an extra seat to the opposition.

The conservatives hold the lion's share of seats in Queensland. Retaining so many seats when shooting for a fourth term won't be easy. If Queensland falls it could deliver Labor enough extra seats to form government. But that is a big if. Federal Labor has long struggled in the Sunshine State, other than when Queensland's own Kevin Rudd vanquished John Howard in 2007.

NSW is the one saving grace for our Pentecostal PM. Team Morrison hopes to not only hold the line in his home state, but prise seats like Macquarie, Parramatta and perhaps Greenway off Labor. And return Craig Kelly's seat of Hughes to the Liberal fold, perhaps Warringah too. That's a big ask, however. Were it to happen, Morrison would almost certainly win the election. If it doesn't, the difficulties around the rest of the country are likely to either flip the result or cause a hung parliament. We would then have to turn our attention to who the remaining crossbench supports.

All of which is why this year's budget, while it might not be the last one before an election, is designed with re-election in mind. Hence no austerity, more debt and winners from pillar to post when it comes to funding initiatives. With even the mere prospect of austerity ruled out until we hit full employment.

Gone are the days of fiscal conservatives ruling the roost in the Coalition, replaced by profligate politicians on all sides. How good is Australia?

We'll all be rooned by culture of criticism

24–25 April 2021

Watching the collective hysteria because of delays in the national vaccine rollout reminds me that Australia really is the lucky country. So lucky, we will find anything to complain about. Which is not to undersell the problems attached to the rollout or the mistakes ministers have made over-promising and underdelivering.

Donald Horne asserted in his 1964 book The Lucky Country that "Australia is a lucky country, run mainly by second-rate people who share its luck". But let's get some perspective.

While Australian politicians seek to find better ways to deliver the vaccines in coming months, using better co-operation between the commonwealth and the states, other nations the world over are battling second, third and fourth waves of the virus.

These are nations that really are led by second-rate politicians, if judged against the job they have done managing COVID-19. While Australia opens a travel bubble with New Zealand — mutually enjoying our largely COVID-free lifestyles — countries such as India daily battle new cases in the hundreds of thousands and surging ever higher. More than three million people across the world have died from the virus and many more will die before it's brought under control.

You get a distorted view of things sitting here comfortably in Australia, especially when unable to travel and see firsthand how bad things are overseas.

Yes, the vaccine rollout has been hampered by problems with the AstraZeneca brand, weighed down by concerns about blood-clotting.

Better to find that out now after a limited rollout, mind you, rather than after many millions of citizens in the higher-risk category have been injected with a problematic new medicine dispatched under emergency conditions. That was the experience of Britain and many other countries. And don't forget the clotting problems are infinitesimally rare. The caution shown is a luxury of our COVID-free circumstances.

Reporting on so-called catastrophic failures with the vaccine rollout butted heads this week with the rather different opinion of US National Institute of Allergy and Infectious Diseases director Anthony Fauci. Readers will remember Fauci's regular and sober media appearances alongside Donald Trump in which he was prepared to contradict the rantings of his political master.

Fauci isn't afraid to call a spade a shovel. He did it again this week when asked about the criticisms the Australian government is facing. He told his audience that voters shouldn't be too harsh, noting how well Australia had done combating the virus (certainly compared with the US, for example, but also compared with almost everywhere else).

Fauci also pointed out how common it was at the early stage of rollouts to experience teething problems — with COVID vaccines and historically when rolling out mass vaccinations.

An acceleration in rollouts as they ramp up is common practice. On Thursday after national cabinet, armed with charts to prove his point, Scott Morrison explained how the vaccine rollout was accelerating. That is likely what we'll continue to see in the weeks and months ahead, especially now that the states are more involved. This is notwithstanding international supply issues — which most nations are facing — and despite the federal government initially breaking a cardinal rule of politics: don't over-promise and underdeliver. Had the government not made that mistake, the harshness of the criticisms being levelled at it might be mitigated.

Australian politics is dominated by a "glass half empty" commentariat hellbent on finding fault and refusing to concede good outcomes. This is one outcome of the shift in modern journalism from widespread reporting to widespread commentary.

Australian bush poet John O'Brien (his pen name) originated the phrase "we'll all be rooned" in his 1919 poem "Said Hanrahan". He was talking about the harshness of the Australian climate and its impact on farming, though the popular takeout has been usage of "we'll all be rooned" as a way to dismiss negative attacks that ruin awaits us all.

The lucky country has more to be proud of during the past year and a half than we should lament, but you wouldn't know it if you confined your reading and viewing habits to certain media outlets and social media. A culture of grievance is taking over, which has the distorting effect of diminishing legitimate and unequivocal complaints.

Failures to address gender issues is a legitimate concern, for example, even if raising problems is more common than suggesting solutions. Another legitimate grievance: the way the government approached the robodebt debacle; indeed, the way it refused to correct its mistakes soon enough.

Yet these sorts of issues get swept up in wider white noise, meaning that all mainstream voters begin to hear is criticism for criticism's sake, which many understandably decide is over the top. John Howard as prime minister faced similar overblown commentary, but that was before it became as widespread as it is now.

The reaction to inevitable problems with the vaccine rollout is playing into a mainstream voter rebellion. It helps to explain why the Prime Minister, even though he has lost support in the polls, is far from terminal. More than half the population are satisfied with his performance — hard to believe in the context of hyper-criticisms.

The culture of criticism also is feeding the anti-vaxxer campaign, which could have long-term detrimental consequences for the opening up of international borders and economic interaction. This itself is a risk for the government, which will be judged on economic performance during the coming 12 months.

Don't get me wrong; Morrison and his inner sanctum aren't free of criticism. Far from it. His line this week that he won't let inner-city types who frequent wine bars decide climate policy is the definition of divisiveness, designed to turn citizens against one another based on geography. Simply put, it's unhelpful.

I'm not interested in a blame game of "who started it", like we see in playgrounds when teachers catch children fighting during recess. The point is, whether we are talking about commentators who simply air grievances and see fault in anything and everything the political class does, or politicians who use populism as a political weapon, something needs to change — and sooner rather than later, I'd suggest. Otherwise we all really will be rooned.

The botched rollout could spell doom for PM

10–11 April 2021

The vaccine rollout is a test of competency for the federal government. With an election just over the horizon it's not a test it wants to fail. The degree of difficulty for the Coalition winning a fourth term in office is real, made more difficult by the fact it doesn't have a majority to play with. Numbers in the House of Representatives are on a knife edge.

Competent management — or at least the perception of it — is likely to be a key factor at the next election. The Coalition will look to scare voters away from Labor, blitzing the airwaves with negative attack ads. There is nothing new in such a strategy, both sides of politics do it. Labor undoubtedly will look to tap into anger at the government's (mis) handling of gender issues, for example.

But the government's attack ads will focus on the risks Labor poses as economic managers. They will target perceived incompetency from the last time Labor was in office and remind voters about policy scripts the Bill Shorten-led opposition offered up at the 2019 election.

Such negative campaign techniques are harder to sustain when the government itself is seen as lacking competence, which brings us back to the importance of improving the rollout of the vaccine. Failure on that front could spell political doom for Scott Morrison.

As with its early response to the pandemic, the federal government is being forced to loop the states in to ensure the vaccine delivery isn't botched. It was always going to be thus. Federal governments aren't experienced at service delivery. Doing so is largely the preserve of the states and for the most part they do it well.

It is an example of the 10,000-hour rule Malcolm Gladwell explores in his book Outliers: the more experience you gain, the better you get at doing something.

Since the beginning of the federation, state governments have been responsible for service delivery in varying forms. More than 100 years of such experience has honed their skills to deliver healthcare, education, transport and utilities management with world-class precision. While the public service isn't always as efficient as it could or should be, on the world stage Australian states do comparatively well.

In contrast, the federal government rarely turns its hand to service delivery and, when it does, it often botches the job. Think of the home insulation scheme or robodebt services, for example. Failures have been bipartisan.

Which raises the question: what was the Morrison government thinking when it decided to take charge and own the vaccine rollout all by itself? Team Morrison's grasp on its own limitations seemingly was lost behind a desire to win political points. Political glory was the goal, but that aim is being replaced fast by failure. The states coming to the rescue could be Morrison's salvation.

It is easy to forget that a similar process played out at the beginning of the pandemic. States dragged a reluctant commonwealth kicking and screaming towards lockdowns. Remember our Prime Minister was off to the footy and his chief medical officer was traversing the country shaking hands. It was the premiers who called for more responsible actions. They saved Australia from replicating the devastation seen in other countries that didn't react quickly enough to the virus.

Had responsibility for borders and lockdowns and restrictions of liberties been left entirely to the federal government it is likely the virus would have got out of control initially and Victoria's second wave wouldn't have been contained to just the one state. Federalism did its job last year and Team Morrison will be hoping it does its job this year, saving the vaccine rollout as the states come to the fore.

But there are still plenty of hurdles that need to be overcome.

The vaccine rollout began poorly, behind schedule and haphazardly. Despite self-confident prognosticating by the Health Minister and Prime Minister that their targets for vaccinations would be met, failure replaced misguided confidence.

I well remember interviewing Greg Hunt as he dismissed questions casting doubt on the bullish estimates the government was relying on for the speed of the rollout. While problems with vaccine deliveries from abroad played its part in slowing the rollout, it doesn't explain away everything.

Simply put, the federal government over-promised and underdelivered, thereby breaking a golden rule in politics. Estimates this week put Australia's rollout in 90th place on the global stage, wedged between those powerhouses of competent management, Albania and Bolivia.

And now we have to face up to the reality that the AstraZeneca vaccine — on which Australia is over-reliant — is being dogged by concerns about blood clotting. It is the only vaccine Australia has the technology to produce locally, even though with forward planning we had ample time to develop the capacity to produce alternative vaccines.

The government's next challenge is ensuring everyone over 50 gets their second dose of AstraZeneca on time. A little discussed potential pitfall associated with the vaccine rollout is the fact if people don't get their booster second shot on time, exactly 12 weeks after their first shot, the process needs to start all over again. That is the medical advice. The research shows that without a timely second dose, certainly within a week either side of the 12-week timeframe, the value of the first shot is lost and hence the protections the vaccine offers go down.

When you consider how behind schedule the rollout of the first dose has been, how confident are we that the federal government will get the timing right on second doses? We are told clinics are saving second doses to avoid this potential failure. Let's hope so. Perhaps we are also more confident now that the states are beginning to intervene in the process, too, but the risks haven't gone away.

Even just at the individual level this is an issue. We all miss appointments as our lives get busy. The second vaccine shot isn't something that can be delayed. The greater good relies on individuals doing the right thing.

We also need to consider the vulnerable in the vaccine rollout. The more than 100,000 Australians who are homeless, for example, need to be looked after. Ensuring they get vaccinated is challenging enough, much less guaranteeing they get their second shots. People weighed down by social and financial challenges are also vulnerable. These societal factors present risks to patients getting their second doses in a timely manner.

Let's hope the government has contingency plans in place to overcome such barriers. Doing so is an important test of its competency and social conscience.

Legal reform on table in sex assault debate

3–4 April 2021

The national conversation in recent weeks has centred on the need to address sexual assaults in this country. It is long overdue. Understandably, the focus so far has been on outrages rather than solutions. For the groundswell to lead to tangible outcomes, that's going to have to change. The national conversation will need to become a high-level debate about what can be done to address past failures.

What those failings exactly are is clear enough: low numbers of women coming forward when sexually assaulted; low numbers of cases of alleged sexual assault resulting in police action and judicial follow-through; and even when these hurdles are overcome, sexual assault convictions are rare, certainly when compared with other crimes.

The important thing about the movement for justice, as it has become known, is that the issue has finally gone mainstream. But to result in improved outcomes, new steps must be taken: the task of fixing what has long been broken must be taken up by experts, those with experience and know-how in public policymaking and law reform. And the politicians need to listen.

Surprisingly few ideas for change have been articulated this past month. It is important when it comes to debating ideas that we are prepared to think outside the box. That means moving past an environment where contrarianism gets shot down.

Activists need to give thoughtful debate a chance, just as legal purists need to overcome their conservatism towards doing things differently.

Good ideas rarely emerge without bad ones having been debated and discounted first. Without a free and open debate about possible reforms, we risk putting our heads in the sand and thus missing the opportunity to make change, or kneejerk policy reforms get enacted with unintended consequences.

There are important questions anyone wanting to improve sexual assault outcomes needs to ask themselves. In the name of catching more perpetrators, are we prepared to see more innocent people go to jail? Or get caught up in a legal process that damages their livelihoods and reputations?

I suspect the answer to that is largely yes right now, courtesy of the dial having been drawn too far in the other direction for far too long now.

Which brings us to ideas for reform. Please don't shoot the messenger, whether you think some of these are off the mark, go too far or don't go far enough.

Perhaps it is time for our justice system to move away from its adversarial origins when it comes to sexual assault cases and towards a more inquisitorial approach as we see in countries such as France. That would involve a judge presiding over sexual assault cases doing all the questioning of witnesses and directing the use of evidence to be assessed. It would take some of the hostility victims currently face via cross-examination out of the equation.

Rules of evidence could change for sexual assault cases. For example, the past conduct of alleged perpetrators could become admissible in specific cases where such patterns of behaviour are currently inadmissable. But this change would need a counterbalance. For example, under an inquisitorial system a judge could determine that the evidence just isn't there for a conviction on a single matter, but when that evidence is assessed in the context of a pattern of behaviour, a guilty verdict could be delivered. Shifting a case to allow otherwise inadmissable evidence into the frame couldn't happen in jury trials, where those sitting in judgment lack legal expertise. And perhaps for such evidence to be included, the potential sentence after a guilty verdict might need to be lowered too to reflect the reduced burden of proof when incarcerating a person.

If a judge still doesn't believe a conviction can be recorded with a burden of proof beyond reasonable doubt, are we prepared to consider adjusting the law further to allow sexual assault convictions on the balance of probabilities? That is, to a civil standard. For many this will be a bridge too far, a radical solution that causes other problems. But is the community prepared to consider such a shift in the context of the times we are in and the woeful track -record of sexual assault convictions? Maybe.

If a judge reduces the burden of proof to the balance of probabilities, rather than leaving it at beyond reasonable doubt, perhaps taking incarceration off the table can allow the change. A conviction recorded would mean future offending receives harsher penalties. While a suspended sentence, community service or a hefty fine may seem woefully inadequate for a sexual assault, for victims it beats an outcome of nothing at all. It gives them some form of justice, closure even. And it just might encourage more victims to come forward.

This informally happens already in the legal system when plea bargains are struck and the prosecution and defence present a unified recommendation to the judge.

These ideas are but a snapshot of the sorts of debates we need to have. It isn't enough for activists to simply dish out vigilante justice as a substitute for real reforms. That worsens our society and our structures. The rule of law matters, but it has to be flexible enough to suit our changing community.

There are, of course, other reforms away from the trial process itself that must go hand in glove with some of what has already been discussed. Consent laws could be changed to universally require positive consent. The Tasmanian model is worthy of close examination. Workplace reporting of sexual assaults should be mandatory.

And in the wake of revelations of alleged sexual assaults among school-aged girls, there is a strong argument for lowering the age at which students are taught about consent in schools. It has come down in recent years, but could and probably should be further reduced.

Let's also not forget boys and men need to be at the vanguard of taking more responsibility for their own actions, as do parents to educate their children. It is incumbent on parents to keep up with the times.

Finally, perhaps it is time to look at the graphic, sometimes violent, and freely available nature of pornography in this country. It might be age limited in theory but it's freely accessible in practice. Is it time to use technology to stifle access to such materials, which are surely contributing to the problems now being discussed? Is it worth giving up some liberties to achieve that goal? Many would say absolutely.

It's time to have these debates to find solutions to the problems now being widely articulated.

Re-reading the below column in the wake of the Coalition's defeat at the hands of female voters, including the devastation wrought by the teal candidates, it is hard not to say "I told you so". Yet there are still very few signs Liberals will ever get serious about gender quotas.

Quota for Coalition women well overdue

27–28 March 2021

Quotas. It is a six-letter world Liberals have near universally rejected as a solution to their "women's problem" for as long as I can remember.

Then suddenly on Tuesday everything changed, or at least I hope it did. A Prime Minister under siege remembered that he'd ruminated about quotas as an out-of-the-box solution to the low numbers of women in parliament for the conservatives before the 2019 election.

However, at the time, Scott Morrison had no authority to impose such a "radical" shift on the Liberal Party, even if it was more than a thought bubble. He was the fill-in Prime Minister, remember? Not expected to win the election.

But then he did. Victory saw the issue of quotas pushed right down his priority list, if it was ever really on it, as so often happens to issues affecting women, even though they represent more than half the population. On Tuesday Morrison was on the back foot, needing to brandish something, anything, that showed he cared about what women wanted. Quotas suddenly was pushed right up the agenda. He supports them and claims he has for a long time now.

At the 2019 election, even without quotas, Morrison backed more women into winnable seats than any recent Liberal prime minister. Of the 16 new members of the Coalition — the class of 2019 — exactly half are women. The overall numbers within the parliamentary Coalition are still below 30 per cent, compared with Labor's 50-50 fairness.

I have written about the need to impose quotas within the Liberal Party for years now. Every time I do it gets met with criticism among conservatives. Let's see if the Prime Minister has the stomach for the fight internally.

More women within the Liberal Party are now coming out in support of the shift. Cabinet minister Karen Andrews joined that list this week.

It's a nice contrast to Linda Reynolds who, when Morrison promoted her into cabinet in 2018, used her first media conference to exclaim proudly that her elevation was a clear sign women could make it in the party without quotas. It's easy to say that quotas aren't a good solution. That's just rhetoric. It's much harder to come up with alternative solutions that work to fix the gender imbalance.

The Liberal Party's Senate ticket, which is more centrally controlled, has seen a greater number of women brought into the fold in recent years than has happened in the House of Representatives. A sign perhaps that party powerbrokers recognise how serious the issue is as an electoral impediment.

Liberals now have fewer female MPs than they did in 1996 when John Howard was elected prime minister. Reflect on that. A quarter of a century later they have gone backwards, despite the uptick at the last election.

The most vacuous argument against quotas is the notion that you support a quota to improve female representation or you support merit-based selections. What utter rubbish. Quotas ensure merit wins out, unless you honestly think women are inferior to men and are therefore worthy only of lower representation. It's an illogical argument, yet the anti-quota brigade uses it time and time again.

Who seriously thinks the factional system or stacked pre-selections deliver merit anyway? Even if the argument is that not enough women are active in Liberal Party politics — hence a quota gives the few women who are an unfair advantage — then quotas should be seen through the prism of encouraging more women to engage and seek parliamentary office. It also should be viewed as a way of encouraging powerbrokers and factional leaders to seek talented women for representative roles in the first place.

That is what happened in Labor.

The other tired argument used to dismiss quotas is that they go against Liberal Party philosophy. As though many Liberals understand or have ever read political philosophy. Besides, the party's coalition agreement with the Nationals includes a quota for the number of Nationals in cabinet. Fancy that.

We also have a constitutional quota for the number of senators hailing from each state within our institutional framework. And there are informal quotas for leaders when they select their ministerial line-ups, as they look to reflect state and factional affiliations. There is even an informal quota these days to boost the number of women Liberals put on the frontbench. So why not a quota to boost parliamentary numbers?

The barriers within the conservative side of politics to adopting quotas cut across age groupings. Older generations are naturally more conservative and hence more resistant. Young Liberal men, despite having more progressive tendencies than older party members, have ambition to become MPs. Introducing quotas would reduce their chances of relying on the patriarchal system to get them there, meaning they are resistant to change too.

Which is why Morrison's intervention this week might be significant. That is, if he's prepared to put his back into forcing real change.

Once upon a time women disproportionately used to vote Liberal over

Labor. The male environment of the union movement was a turn-off for many women. But today the turn-off has flipped. The Liberal Party culture is now unfriendly to women, clearly, and Labor has a quota, which has bolstered not only female parliamentary representation but also the number of women who join the Labor Party in the first place.

And the women at the apex of the Labor Party are strong and central to party tactics, policy development and strategy. Where are the likes of Penny Wong, Kristina Keneally and Tanya Plibersek on the Coalition side?

Rattle off the names of senior women in the Liberal Party and it becomes clear there aren't any. Julie Bishop was a lone wolf and she's gone. Peta Credlin had power and authority but was cut down and never entered parliament anyway. Andrews is certainly formidable but on the outer. Look at Morrison's inner circle and there isn't a woman in sight. No wonder he misjudged the mood of women around the country in recent weeks.

Decades ago, when Labor introduced quotas, it was attacked without mercy by a Liberal Party that commanded the female vote. As that has steadily slipped away it has become obvious quotas have done their job for Labor. Yet the Coalition hasn't even taken the first step to enforce change.

It's time. Actually, it's not time, it's long overdue.

McGowan consigns WA Libs to oblivion

15 March 2021

Not since Julius Caesar uttered those immortal words "I came; I saw; I conquered" has a victory been so unequivocal. Mark McGowan's WA Labor government was always going to win Saturday's state election, but the size of the victory will reverberate for some time to come.

The Liberals look to have won only two seats in the 59-member Legislative Assembly, creating a coin toss for their next leader. The 34-year-old Zak Kirkup, picked just months ago to lead the party into the election, lost his seat and announced he's retiring from politics after his one term in parliament. There goes the future.

The Nationals now have twice as many MPs as the Liberals and aren't inclined to form a coalition. Unlike around the rest of the country, the Liberals and Nationals rarely do in WA.

Either way, Nationals leader Mia Davies will be the official Opposition Leader charged with trying to hold the re-elected McGowan government to account, leaving the two Liberals to play paper, rock, scissors in deciding who gets to be in charge of their duumvirate. Good governance requires good opposition to hold governments to account. McGowan will need to be careful not to fall victim to hubris because he won't face much parliamentary opposition for the next four years. Labor is also on track to secure a majority in the state's upper house, guaranteeing its ability to pass legislation. How on earth did it come to this? And what, if any, are the federal implications from Saturday's historic results?

Liberal powerbrokers tapped former state leader Liza Harvey on the shoulder to stand aside in November. As a deputy premier in Colin

Barnett's government she was no lightweight. Neither was the leader she replaced halfway through 2019, Mike Nahan. He was Barnett's treasurer for three years. So-called powerbrokers also partook in shoulder tapping on that occasion.

McGowan's approval ratings since the beginning of the pandemic have hovered around the high 80s and low 90s — higher than all other premiers. His parochial WA border policies have been popular. He was never going to lose this election, which is why Kirkup conceded two weeks ago.

Where was the conservative strategy for saving the electoral furniture? More Liberal voters supported the Labor Party at this election than ever before in WA. Doing so was made infinitely easier by the decision to match a boy against a man. A political lightweight against a Premier oozing experience.

The only hope the Liberals had on Saturday of saving supposedly safe seats was with someone blue-blooded voters could consider a seasoned alternative. Like a Nahan or a Harvey. Instead, the geniuses at Liberal HQ handed the leadership to a novice in his first term whose only pre-parliamentary experience was political staffing.

Losing seats such as South Perth, Nedlands and Churchlands to Labor isn't something I ever thought I would see.

By all accounts Kirkup had a lot to contribute over what should have been a 20-year career in parliament. Instead, he was elevated beyond his station too soon and has been chewed up and spat out by the Liberal Party.

McGowan might only be 53, but he's been in state politics since 1996, gaining ministerial experience in the governments of Geoff Gallop and Alan Carpenter. Yet he's always avoided factional Labor politicking, a contributing factor behind his soaring popularity. Don't forget the cabal of Labor powerbrokers who tried to blast McGowan out of opposition leadership on the eve of the 2017 election, claiming he was "unelectable". He went on to comprehensively beat Barnett before reducing the conservative side of politics to a rump on Saturday. How embarrassed they must be.

The results at state level contrast sharply with the federal sphere. The Liberals hold 11 of the 16 seats in WA, with Labor having failed to do any better than that in two decades. Scott Morrison will be rightly worried that the size of the state defeat might hamper the party's organisational capacities in the west, putting seats such as Swan, Stirling and Hasluck at risk.

The Australian Electoral Commission releases its draft redistribution for WA this Friday, and we know one seat is to be abolished because of WA's relative decline in population. The expectation is Christian Porter's seat of Pearce might be the one to get the chop.

While state campaigns are usually fought on state issues with little correlation to events in Canberra, it is hard to escape the thought that the Morrison government's woes of late made it harder for WA Liberals to engineer any sort of late campaign tightening in the polls.

Equally, there has been a confluence of state and federal political issues since the pandemic. WA voters like McGowan's tough stance on borders, whereas the federal Liberals have been critical of his positioning on that. The Coalition government was planning to support Clive Palmer's High Court challenge to border restrictions before the PM smelt the breeze and backed away.

With the Coalition holding on to the barest of majorities federally, and Labor's McGowan re-elected in emphatic fashion, Anthony Albanese will be looking west for inspiration on how to overcome conservatives on their own turf. Because with the possible exception of Queensland, WA is the most conservative state in the commonwealth, and it just delivered the state conservatives a humiliating defeat.

Few modern day pile-ons have been more unedifying to me than the one Christian Porter faced. Including by some who really should know better when it comes to basic principles of due process in law and democracy. None of us can know what really happened, and we almost certainly never will. But I do know this: some of the information that has surfaced since the allegations against Porter were made public highlights that he was subjected to what can only be described as vigilante journalism in the pursuit of vigilante justice. What concerned me most was that it could quite literally happen to anyone, irrespective of guilt or innocence. Yet so many still can't see the problems in what transpired.

Chilling and disgraceful denial of basic rights

6–7 March 2021

The way the allegations against Attorney-General Christian Porter crescendoed this week was utterly extraordinary. The denial of natural justice; the trial by media; the lost presumption of innocence; the mob mentality of convicting someone whom police didn't even charge with a crime — I have never seen anything like it in Australian politics.

It is vital when seeking to overthrow tyranny that those who start with good intentions don't themselves resort to tyranny or be used by those without good intentions in the first place. That may sound melodramatic, but in the case of Porter we have borne witness to something that hurts our institutions, our democracy, our standards of journalism and even perhaps the cause of better justice for sexual assault victims.

Ends do not justify means.

I don't know any more than anyone else whether what was alleged to have happened back in 1988, when a 16-year-old girl and a 17-year-old boy attended a debating tournament, occurred.

But I do know that whether Porter is guilty or innocent, the way it played out publicly could happen to anyone and that should concern everyone. The trite bullshit that an innocent person has nothing to fear is rubbish. Read nearly any history book to understand why.

Porter has never been contacted by police. He hasn't seen the so-called dossier prepared anonymously by the alleged victim's friends. Neither have most of us. Selected materials from the accuser have been selectively leaked to selected personnel. Then when the time came for one journalist to publish the accusations, they were never put to the person they were being levelled against, according to Porter, which to my knowledge has not been contradicted.

That is extraordinary.

That the initial publishing of the allegations was anonymous doesn't make this failure any better. It precipitated a pile-on and a witch-hunt. It put the entire Morrison cabinet under a cloud. In short, it released the hounds.

We have heard from a random collection of the alleged victim's friends, most of whom lost contact with her for most if not all of the past 30 years. We have not heard from her parents, who according to their daughter's own writings and recordings — none of which were contemporaneous to the alleged crime, by the way — questioned her claims and didn't want the issue to go public.

I can only imagine their trauma at losing a child before also having to endure this. She, according to what has been released, had deep psychological issues. But we don't know, of course, whether they were caused by a traumatic event or her reported bipolar disorder, of which delusions are a possible symptom.

Yet friends who knew her as a 16-year-old, but not for the following 30 years, are sure. So the parents who weren't so sure, and presumably have lived through their daughter's difficult life, are ignored, as are their wishes for privacy. I find that extraordinary.

One fact that isn't in dispute but does seem to get breezed over lightly is that the alleged victim withdrew her complaint. She did so one day before taking her own life. People will make their own assessments about what may have motivated her to do so, but the bottom line is that none of us will ever know. She withdrew the complaint.

Scott Morrison has said that there won't be an independent inquiry into what happened. I disagree with this. We should get line of sight on these anonymous friends and their exchanges with journalists, seeking to bring this issue into full view.

An inquiry with all the powers to compel witnesses and access electronic communications should happen in this matter. A chance to interview the alleged victim's psychiatrists to paint an accurate picture of her mental health. The fact the family released a statement on Thursday indicating they would welcome an inquiry only adds to the value of having one.

The irony is not lost on me that Porter is part of a government that denies refugee rights, used robodebt to take away the presumption of innocence for welfare recipients and fell in line behind a Prime Minister who used the floor of parliament to summarily stand down Australia Post chief executive Christine Holgate on spurious grounds. I have railed against the Coalition on each one of these fronts. But its failures to observe proper processes are no excuse for others to do the same, and in a most extreme and egregious way.

As Porter said at his media conference on Wednesday: no one is beyond an allegation. That is why allegations that were never put to him before being published, that didn't lead to charges or even a police interview for him, allegations the accuser ultimately withdrew, weren't sufficient for him to get sacked. Were that to happen then anyone could weaponise allegations to remove any politician, or indeed anyone else, with any degree of legitimacy.

Yes, I have known Porter for more than 20 years. Unlike many others reporting on this sad saga with close links and friendships with the alleged victim, I have been open about that. However, what I think about Porter's guilt or innocence on this matter became of no consequence once it played out the way it did when the allegations became public.

Which is why this is a matter for all of us. Self-interest should kick in because any one of us would want procedural fairness, which has been absolutely denied to Porter with the public tarring and feathering he has endured.

I know some of the people who have targeted him: ideological opponents who have disliked him since the moment they met him; people for whom ends justify means. No doubt Porter made it easier for them to dislike him with some of his antics.

Evidence could emerge tomorrow locking in Porter's guilt for the alleged crime all those years ago and it wouldn't change the fact that what has transpired in terms of denials of basic rights under our democratic and legal systems has been chilling and utterly disgraceful.

Opportunity knocks — open the door, PM

19 February 2021

The pandemic and the impact it has had on the budget present the Coalition government with a unique opportunity: the chance to do something. I don't mean simply preside in office, tinkering at the margins of policy or holding media conferences claiming to have achieved meaningful reform.

I'm talking about actual substantial change. Let's face it, as much as politicians like to strut around the corridors of power in Parliament House and ride in the white car with the flag on the bonnet, all the while imagining they are on the set of The West Wing, most don't leave much of a mark. The same goes for ministers, who tend to become captured quickly by their departments, no matter how many ideas they floated early in their political careers.

Even the few who rise to become prime minister don't really achieve a lot. If you think about the game-changing achievements of modern prime ministers, at best they can point to a handful of meaningful reforms they have championed.

Bob Hawke oversaw important micro-economic reforms and the Accord with the unions. Paul Keating was responsible for the introduction of superannuation. John Howard broadened the tax base with the GST and reformed gun laws. Kevin Rudd said sorry to Indigenous Australians.

Julia Gillard introduced a price on carbon, only for Tony Abbott to repeal it. Malcolm Turnbull oversaw the introduction of same-sex marriage, although by the time he did so Australia was already a global laggard and it really was the people's achievement anyway via a popular plebiscite.

Other than presiding over the pandemic, albeit successfully, so far Scott Morrison has yet to achieve anything meaningful, something he may want to discuss with Jenny this weekend. We have to go a little further back when surveying prime ministers to zero in on some of the most meaningful reform that has shaped Australia today, certainly in terms of social policy.

In the 1970s Gough Whitlam introduced universal healthcare and free university education. The former continues today, the latter has been replaced by the HECS system, but the purpose of ensuring accessibility has been maintained. The process of the modern politician becoming captured by bureaucrats has evolved. Politicians these days are less impressive; they have narrower pre-parliamentary careers than they once did, the political advisers they surround themselves with are more callow and partisan, and governmental departments are larger and more controlling — more partisan, too, which curtails quality public policy debate.

In the media age in which we live, politicians must spend more time acting as performing seals: fronting the cameras, practising their lines and immersing themselves in the theatre of politics, a superficial art. Then there is the time MPs must spend attending party political events and fundraisers.

There are only so many hours in the day and all this means there is less time to think about bold policy reforms. The nature of the modern news cycle makes bold reform that much harder to achieve. There is instant unpicking of ideas on often tedious grounds, with claims and counterclaims that the numbers don't stack up.

But for the numbers to stack up, the ideas first need to have been put through rigorous departmental modelling, which often leaks, killing ideas in their infancy. This also reduces the chances of oppositions developing meaningful policies because they don't have access to such resources.

Bill Shorten's 2019 election defeat with a big-picture agenda — whether one agrees or disagrees with said agenda — makes it that much less likely that we'll see oppositions be so bold in the future. Which means governments are our only hope. One good thing to come out of the global recession the coronavirus caused is the chance for change — the capacity to re-embrace meaningful reforms.

This is the subject of renowned economist Ross Garnaut's new book, Reset: Restoring Australia after the Pandemic Recession. Garnaut's prequel to Reset was his book Superpower, in which he detailed the opportunities associated with pursuing economic reforms around climate change action, also explaining the opportunity costs of not doing so. Reset is his attempt to explain why now is the time to consider radical (but reasoned) ideas that the political system would usually render impossible to achieve.

These include a universal basic income and replacing corporate tax with a tax on cashflows. I'm not going to try to justify such complex and contested propositions in a few hundred words when Garnaut used tens of thousands to do so. Read his book. Or don't, be sceptical and prove the point already made that the superficiality of debate has overtaken a more in-depth way of approaching policy.

Garnaut's book makes a cogent case for why now is the time to reform, thereby observing the old adage about never letting a crisis go to waste. Too often reforming ideas, especially on tax, are met by criticism that such reforms aren't revenue neutral. That is, they will cost the budget in the short term, which makes them politically unpalatable in an era of shallow misinformed debate about the need to get budgets "back in black" for no other reason than because. Does that ring a bell?

But in the wake of the extraordinary spending decisions last year, there will be wall-to-wall deficits in the years ahead and our politicians have become resigned to that. So has the public, which no longer is drawn into political combat tearing down one side or the other for "fiscal recklessness" if it can't chart a short-term course to a balanced budget. This shift, which may not last long, provides politicians and policymakers with the opportunity to institute meaningful reforms that have long-term benefit.

The pandemic and the impact it h its, although they poke a further hole in the budget in the short term. Garnaut articulates the case for a universal basic income on just such grounds. He makes the point that, yes, it is expensive in the short term but across time the impact on the participation rate and innovation and entrepreneurial spirit will pay huge budget dividends, to say nothing of its value as a means of reducing inequality — inequality being something most economists acknowledge has a profound adverse effect on economic growth and prosperity.

As Garnaut writes: "We are kidding ourselves if we think that such extreme divergence of fortune among Australians is consistent with social cohesion and effective democratic government as we deal with intractable domestic and international problems."

Cometh the hour, cometh the man. Prime Minister, over to you.

Taxpayers belted for JobKeeper bungle

13–14 February 2021

Does everybody remember the Building the Education Revolution scheme? The Rudd government announced and quickly implemented it during the global financial crisis. It was stimulus spending designed to ensure people stayed employed, at the same time building much needed infrastructure for schools.

At the margins the scheme was abused, with some (albeit isolated) examples of wasted spending and overspending. Was Labor given understanding for design faults? Of course not. What about understanding because of the need for speed, rolling out the scheme quickly so the stimulus could have the desired effect? Nope.

The Liberals in opposition used a "waste watch" bus to highlight the problems. There was a near daily barrage in the media unpicking the problems. The Rudd and Gillard governments eventually published full details of the spending, which in good time also was reviewed independently.

We know the debt accrued during the GFC has been dwarfed by what has been spent courtesy of the coronavirus recession — understandably, given the scale of the problems caused by the pandemic. But the misuse of JobKeeper dollars within that spending envelope was entirely avoidable and it is high time the government is held to account for the waste — at least as much as Labor was for its relatively insignificant waste during the GFC.

Don't forget, JobKeeper cost tens of billions of dollars in borrowed money that taxpayers will need to pay back eventually.

Labor MP and former economics professor Andrew Leigh valiantly has tried to shine a light on the scale of the potential waste.

"JobKeeper is the single biggest expenditure scheme put in place by an Australian government," he says.

The government designed the scheme on the back of an envelope and used a "one size fits all" approach to pump money out the door. That meant that some companies eligible for the payments ultimately didn't need them. But JobKeeper wasn't designed in a way that allowed the government to claw back the taxpayer money.

In its haste to inject JobKeeper cash into businesses to save jobs, the Coalition put next to zero safeguards in place to ensure the money didn't simply go into bigger dividends for shareholders and large bonuses for executives.

Because the government did not tie a series of key performance indicators to the flow of money, we now are reliant on businesses doing the right thing and voluntarily handing back the money if ultimately they didn't need it.

So far we've seen only a handful of companies do that: Toyota Australia, Super Retail Group, Domino's Pizza and Iluka Resources, for example. This week Nick Scali paid back $3.6m, but that's less than half of what it received from JobKeeper in the first place. The above are the exceptions. As Leigh says: "This is not a legal issue but a moral one."

We know of plenty of companies that are recording record profits and paying out large bonuses but that haven't paid taxpayers back a single cent of JobKeeper supplements.

Premier Investments received $45m in JobKeeper but is paying out $57m in dividends and gave its chief executive a multimillion-dollar bonus. Solomon Lew will receive more than $20m in dividends. Crown Casino received $111m from JobKeeper yet paid a dividend of $203m. Harvey Norman received $9m and is paying out $75m in dividends.

These are just the companies we know about. It is the tip of the

JobKeeper iceberg. Where is the Coalition's waste watch bus when you need it?

The government doesn't want to pressure firms into paying back JobKeeper money because doing so highlights that it stuffed up in the first place. You can't unscramble an egg. I don't blame businesses for taking advantage of the government's largesse. It is the job of public-policy makers to get the settings right in the first place, which they clearly did not.

Yet on Thursday Scott Morrison had the gall to claim that his government cautiously planned out its spending programs during the pandemic.

Courtesy of JobKeeper, businesses that didn't need the funds in the first place or recovered sufficiently that they can pay the money back instead have been able to increase profits and bonuses on the taxpayers' dime — at the same time that the government quibbles about lifting Newstart or protecting the rights of workers.

Keep in mind that the Liberal Party is the major party with the closest links into business. Draw your own conclusions about that.

The Liberal Party also claims to be the party of fiscal conservatism, focusing on paying down debt and being cautious with taxpayers' money. The speed with which conservatives have pivoted from claims of a "debt and deficit disaster" to profligate and irresponsible splashing of cash is remarkable. They need to be held to account for the massive hole they have left in the budget, one that easily could have been avoided with better policy design.

The likes of the Prime Minister and Josh Frydenberg would be squealing if Labor did the equivalent in government. In fact they did just that when it came to any waste attached to stimulus spending during the GFC, even though the scale of the waste was nothing compared with JobKeeper.

Yet the Treasurer won't even disclose the full list of which companies have taken JobKeeper, reported profits and paid out dividends and bonuses. That is the very least that should happen.

Not that we should be surprised by the hypocrisy. It was the same with the home insulation scheme during the GFC. A handful of deaths that a royal commission found weren't even a consequence of the scheme's design were dangled in front of Labor via vicious political attacks, including frequent accusations by Coalition MPs that Labor had "blood on their hands".

Yet when the Coalition's Robodebt scheme was found to be illegal after it had led to countless suicides by vulnerable Australians injured by the capricious design features concocted by Morrison as social services minister, extracting even an apology was hard — despite a class settlement stinging taxpayers to the tune of more than $1bn. Nor was there a royal commission to get to the bottom of what went so very wrong.

At least when it comes to JobKeeper, the scale of the waste may soon be revealed, alongside any other irregularities. That's because the Auditor-General is launching an investigation. No wonder the last budget saw the government cut funding to the Auditor-General's office. Independent scrutiny and accountability isn't an ethos the Morrison government subscribes to.

Where's the leadership for real reform?

5 February 2021

The Labor Party has lost seven of the last nine federal elections and is on track to make that eight out of 10 later this year. Such failure is an under-discussed phenomenon in modern Australian politics. In a two-party system, which is therefore a two-horse race, winning only 20 per cent of elections is simply woeful. When you consider that one of the only two victories Labor has had during the past quarter of a century was to form a minority government (the Gillard government in 2010), the scale of the problem amplifies.

Labor has managed to form majority government only once since its 1993 win under Paul Keating's leadership. That was Kevin Rudd's 2007 victory. It makes you wonder why so many of us were so quick to assume that Bill Shorten was on track to win the 2019 election, given Shorten's personal polling numbers and the historical failures of modern Labor to get over the electoral line.

While the two-party vote was consistently in Labor's favour during the previous electoral cycle, that fact needed to be put in the wider context of the party's track record: snatching defeat from the jaws of victory. It's a well-worn tradition. Time and time again Labor comes close to winning but doesn't quite get over the line.

The 1998 election should have been Kim Beazley's for the taking, given that John Howard campaigned on introducing a GST, the same policy script John Hewson failed to sell to the electorate in 1993. It wasn't to be; Howard was returned despite securing less than 50 per cent of the two-party vote, winning the campaign ground game in the marginal seats that mattered.

Three years later Beazley again looked set for victory — until Howard outflanked Labor on the Tampa asylum-seeker standoff to win the 2001 poll with an expanded majority. Another defeat was snatched from the jaws of victory and Labor's tendency to doubt itself grew. Labor in opposition turned to Mark Latham as leader one year out from the 2004 election, and doing so brought a significant bounce in the opinion polls.

When Howard eventually called the election, his government was still trailing Labor 46 to 54 per cent. It should have been an election winning lead for Labor. Six weeks later, after Latham imploded on the campaign trail, the Coalition increased its majority and picked up seats in every state. By the time of the 2007 election the Howard government was tired and internal leadership tensions dominated the news agenda most weeks.

Rudd learned the art of conservative politicking, outmanoeuvring the Coalition at its own game. But even then Rudd's "historic win" — the only majority Labor government in the past quarter of a century — secured a thin eight-seat majority.

Howard losing his own seat papered over the closeness of the seat-by-seat victory. Remember, that success in 2007 came only off the back of nearly 12 years of continuous Coalition rule. In just three years after Rudd's victory Labor managed to lose the moral high ground on climate change, roll a popular prime minister in what was an unprecedented first-term coup, and at the 2010 election the majority was lost.

Julia Gillard scraped home relying on the support of crossbenchers, including two country independents. By 2013 it was all over. What the true believers had hoped would be a long-term government to match the Hawke and Keating years in power wasn't to be. Just six years after coming to power, Labor was bundled out of office in the biggest electoral rout since Howard vanquished Keating in 1996. The Rudd-Gillard governments had more in common with Gough Whitlam's short-term reign than that of Bob Hawke and Keating, only without the ground-breaking social reforms to be proud of.

Despite the Coalition replicating Rudd and Gillard's internal divisions in the following three years, Malcolm Turnbull did form majority government for the Coalition in 2016 and Scott Morrison marginally increased its share of seats in 2019. Turnbull, one of the most divisive figures in modern conservative politics, still managed to hold together a divided team after ousting Tony Abbott, the spiritual leader of the social conservatives.

Morrison won re-election after the conservatives got their own back against Turnbull, despite his predilection for marketing over policy. The Morrison machine unpicked Labor's ability to appeal to the mainstream and carved out a third term for a thoroughly unimpressive and divided Coalition government, one that now appears to be invincible at the next election despite lacking any sort of vision for the future.

This is the problem with modern Australian politics. The progressive side of the two-party divide is too inept to apply adequate pressure on the conservative side, meaning conservatives stay in government without lifting their game.

Poor opposition makes for poor government. The Westminster system needs a strong opposition to hold a government to account and keep it on its toes. Equally, when progressive governments don't get their professional act together they make it easy for conservatives to fearmonger their way back into office without much of an agenda, without time on the opposition benches to reflect on party philosophy and the purpose behind winning government beyond attaining power for power's sake.

Right now Australia needs a serious set of policy objectives to come out the other side of the pandemic well equipped for the brave new world that lies ahead. Convincing tired voters who just want stability after such a difficult year, and amid ongoing economic uncertainty, that the medicine they really need is more reform isn't easy.

But that is the job of leaders. Instead, this week we had the Prime Minister address the National Press Club and tell those in attendance that he had no plans to do things such as increase taxes because that wasn't tax reform. He says the biggest thing he learned during the pandemic was to listen more, but what he seems to mean by that is following the populist sentiment rather than providing leadership.

Morrison's characterisation of tax increases as not constituting tax reform showed a profound misunderstanding of how tax reform works. Of course it involves increasing taxes. That is what Howard did in 1998 when campaigning for a GST.

The key is to use higher taxes in some areas to reduce less efficient or distorting taxes in other areas. That is how a government maintains its tax take, but with reforms that help stimulate improved productivity and growth. It is also how a political party crafts policy to align with its ideological roots.

If Morrison, as a former treasurer and long-time partisan, doesn't know that, we have a problem. If he knows it but is prepared nonetheless to misrepresent deliberately how tax reform works, we still have a problem. Because either way he is indicating that he can't be bothered to do heavy lifting in what is his first full term as Prime Minister. Inspiring stuff

It is easy to forget that in early 2021 Albo was under considerable internal pressure. There was serious talk that if he didn't improve he might need to be removed.

Pressure mounts for Albanese to lift Labor's game

30–31 January 2021

Parliament resumes next Tuesday and it's likely to be a lopsided affair. Anthony Albanese is under pressure while Scott Morrison and his government continue to enjoy the warm glow attached to Australia successfully managing the pandemic — notwithstanding problems surrounding the vaccine.

Yes, the states have done the lion's share of the heavy lifting, but that doesn't change the reality that Morrison as Prime Minister gets much of the credit for pandemic management, meaning that his re-election come the end of this year is all but guaranteed.

So what can Labor do? Indeed what should Labor do?

There are serious players in the senior ranks of the opposition who believe it should just ride out the down times and live in hope; lose honourably (the polls are OK) or take advantage of an unexpected change in circumstances. They take an "anything can happen" attitude to electoral politics, pointing to the miracle win Morrison pulled off last time. Swings and roundabouts, they say. However, there isn't a great deal of confidence in their voices when they tell you that.

Others say a change from Albanese to a more competitive leader needs to be made this year, but the timing will be important. Put forward Jim

Chalmers too soon and a future talent gets eaten alive by an operator such as Morrison. Tanya Plibersek is someone the party could turn to just before an election to give the opposition momentum. Jacinda Ardern managed to achieve success along those lines despite the strong economic management of the conservative government in New Zealand. But just how analogous such a move would be here, beyond gender comparisons, is difficult to assess.

Chalmers likely waits, he's in no rush. And Labor probably can't find a way to time any shift to Plibersek sufficiently well to overcome doubts about her. Morrison determines the timing of the next election, not Labor.

Then there is Chris Bowen. The senior NSW Right figure is still serving time in the naughty corner for his role in Labor's defeat at the 2019 election, thrust down the ranks of the shadow ministry. As opposition Treasury spokesman in 2019, Bowen bore the brunt of criticism for the economic reforms believed to have cost Labor victory. Alongside Bill Shorten, of course, who still has leadership ambitions by the way. Albanese isn't a mile behind in the opinion polls, but the worry among his colleagues is that if Labor enters an election campaign behind rather than in front, the Coalition is likely to extend its lead and win handsomely.

The fact it was Plibersek who used her position as Labor's deputy leader at the time to insist on high-spending policies, that led Bowen to insist on high-taxing policies to go with them to keep the books in order is a detail lost on sometimes superficial leadership calculations.

Bowen is an articulate politician who, given the chance to prove his wares as treasurer, would have done well, perhaps using the position as a stepping stone to the Lodge.

In the minds of Shorten and Bowen, their leadership team was supposed to resemble that of Bob Hawke and Paul Keating. The agenda they ran on was similarly bold to the one Hawke and Keating enacted. But in the end Shorten didn't have Hawke's charisma and made the task of achieving victory harder by spelling out his agenda before the election, not after it like Hawke. Virtuous and upfront, to be sure, but at a high price as it turned out.

In all the considerations of what Labor needs to do to be competitive at the next election, and who should lead it, there is also the incumbent to consider. Albanese isn't a mile behind in the opinion polls, but the worry among his colleagues is that if Labor enters an election campaign behind rather than in front, the Coalition is likely to extend its lead and win handsomely.

Were that to happen, sitting MPs would lose their seats. That can sometimes be enough to stir them into action when it comes to pushing for a change of leader, notwithstanding Labor's leadership rules that make it hard to remove the incumbent.

Team Morrison, from the moment it was elected, began targeting Labor seats it could win at the next election, remembering the government's majority is thin.

The rough sketch sees the conservatives looking to hold the line in states such as Queensland and Western Australia, where they are dominant, as well as in Tasmania. Morrison then would go on the hunt to pick up seats in NSW, his home state, and Victoria. The former is more likely to see gains than the latter, according to Liberal strategists. What happens in South Australia is up in the air.

This mud map has a bearing on how Labor approaches the next election, too, because whoever leads the party can have an impact on the opposition's strengths and weaknesses in certain parts of the country. A Queenslander such as Chalmers leading Labor may be able to do up north what Kevin Rudd did in 2007. John Howard lost that election in Queensland alone, partly off the back of parochialism.

Labor hasn't been competitive federally in WA since Kim Beazley's leadership. There were signs at the 2019 election of a swing back to Labor, but that was a mirage. At the state level Mark McGowan is dominant for Labor, but there are few signs of that translating federally. The federal Labor team from WA isn't strong.

Morrison's awareness of the need not to lose WA voters is one reason he capitulated on a constitutional challenge to borders and rarely attacks the popular McGowan directly. Morrison doesn't want McGowan going all in for Labor federally. Morrison won't even confirm if he'll head west to help state Liberals campaign ahead of the WA election in March. While evidence is scant that premiers can help turn states their party's way federally, Morrison wouldn't want to see McGowan try. Not with the WA Premier's 90 per cent approval rating dwarfing that of the Prime Minister, or any other leader in the country for that matter.

Besides, there are advantages for premiers in having a prime minister of a different partisan colour. Voters don't consciously choose to balance out representation between the parties at state and federal levels, but the electoral data tells us it often happens that way. This is why Howard was quietly happy to see a gaggle of Labor premiers succeed during his long tenure as prime minister.

The odds remain in Albanese's favour to survive, but it could be a bumpy ride, and survival is anything but certain. He has been dealt a bad hand. After taking over the reins of a shattered party Albanese looked in the box seat a year ago. Morrison's self-pity in the wake of being called out for his jetsetting holiday to Hawaii as his home state burned helped to sink his approval ratings. The contrast to a hands-on Albanese helping out in bushfire-affected areas couldn't have been greater.

But 12 months on it is Morrison who is dominant. Notwithstanding myriad problems on his plate, Morrison has the opposition's measure going into the first week of parliament this year.

Another howler below. If it is the unknown unknowns you have to worry about, that was the botched vaccine rollout for me when writing this column! It forced Scott Morrison to delay the election and the rest is history.

Morrison manages to side-step failures in waltz to election

16–17 January 2021

This year is likely to be the year Scott Morrison wins re-election. Going to the polls early, late in the year rather than in 2022, to take advantage of the positive glow he and his government is enjoying courtesy of the pandemic. The vaccine rollout should be in full swing by then, and as long as the Coalition doesn't stuff that up, Australians will be sufficiently grateful.

It doesn't take too much imagination to realise how much more devastating the virus could have been. Looking around the world makes for grim observation.

Morrison will want to get to the polls before the risk of an economic backlash presents itself. While the Coalition can always fall back on the tired and factually questionable claims that they are the better economic managers compared with Labor, the possibility of a slow recovery with higher than anticipated unemployment presents political uncertainty Team Morrison would rather minimise.

In short it's a more manageable reality at the end of this year than, for example, after a 2022 budget (or end of 2021 financial update) is handed down.

But it's what is likely to get lost in the next election campaign that Australians should be focused on. Yes, pandemic management has been important. But federal Labor wouldn't have made the bad situation any worse. If anything their collective caution may have seen Australia do better, achieving elimination (or slow enough to thereto) like New Zealand. Besides, state governments of both political colours are more responsible for the good outcomes from this pandemic.

The failures, across aged care, disability care, hotel quarantine and border protection are federal responsibilities one and all. Yes the Commonwealth ceded some of those responsibilities to the states, which frankly only rebuts the federal government's bleating about states exceeding their collective remit.

What follows represents a build-up of rats and mice failures beyond the pandemic during this government's last 12 months in office. Big failures to be sure, just not when a once in a generation pandemic is sweeping the globe.

The Robodebt settlement was extraordinary. $1.2bn to silence the expose of failures that led to people committing suicide. To say that Morrison — as the Minister responsible for conceiving of the policy in the first place — should be ashamed is an understatement. The land deal near Sydney's second airport which saw a Liberal Party donor receive ten times the value of the land sold to the Commonwealth ($30m instead of $3m) added to the rorting of sporting grants exposed shortly after the election. Morrison's lack of curiosity about getting to the bottom of these dodgy dealings was in sharp contrast to his sharp and unprofessional response to Christine Holgate's decision as chief executive of Australia Post to award bonuses to some of her executives.

The PM saw an opportunity to slap down a senior businesswoman, and used cowards castle to do it, attacking her in Question Time. Saying he'll make damn sure she steps aside. Never mind that she was entirely within her rights to award the bonuses, they were nominal and endorsed by the chair of her board.

This was all uncovered as part of an investigation after the fact, but the report no doubt clearing Holgate of wrongdoing was suppressed. Cabinet considered it and decided not to release it. Using cabinet confidence to cover-up is one step above using cowards castle to vilify.

One of the little spoken about background to the hostility Holgate faced is that she stood up to the government on a number of occasions when it came to public policy settings affecting Australia Post. While that is her duty as chief executive it was viewed dimly.

Cover-up and payback are contagious within this government. The Office of the Auditor General incurred a similar wrath. As one of the few independent bodies capable of holding government accountable it had its operating budget slashed in the 2020 budget. Less money means fewer investigations, which given all manner of wrongdoing the Auditor General has exposed in recent years the Coalition will clock up as another win. Democracy shouldn't. At a time when parliament is being stymied, the opposition is largely ineffectual and executive government runs rampant, an office like the Auditor General's becomes even more valuable.

None of the above should be considered rats and mice failures, but that's the way a distracted public sees them, if they notice such poor governance at all. The media too shows little interest.

In a sign Morrison isn't weighed down by the collection of poor governance under his stewardship, his first media conference of 2021 was a triumph. The Prime Minister looked relaxed and comfortable, and he hadn't even started his January holiday yet. Morrison announced a change to the national anthem as a substitute for a meaningful response to the Uluru statement and he even seemed at ease with the ongoing border battles. Morrison simply reminded people that such powers are in the hands of the premiers and they will be held accountable for the consequences, good or bad.

Previous frustration with this constitutional reality replaced by acceptance. Confidence borne out of the knowledge that the Coalition has the next election in the bag as long as Morrison doesn't lose his head.

Meanwhile, it is Anthony Albanese who will return from the summer break battered and bruised. Not only did he suffer a near-death experience when his car was hit hard on the driver's side (political leaders always face risks on their right flank but not usually like that), but Albo also faces the risk of being challenged in the first half of this year. Yes Labor's leadership rules help protect him, but they are far from a complete vaccination from the virus of leadership instability.

The state of Australian politics now is a far cry from where it was at this time last year. Back then a miserable Morrison was feeling sorry for himself under siege for his mismanagement of the bushfires. Unable to rise to the challenge after jetting back from a secret holiday in Hawaii while Australia burned.

Credit where credit is due, Morrison took his opportunity to bounce back from the quagmire all of his own making. Battle hardened from the bushfires he used the experience to reclaim both credibility and dominance during the pandemic, coming out the other side the overwhelming favourite to win the next election. How good are pandemics? How good is Scott Morrison? Someone really should write a book about everything that happened.

Apologists discover their inner conviction

9–10 January 2021

Donald Trump hasn't exactly had the best week of his political career. First he tries to strongarm a Republican secretary of state in Georgia into rigging election results and overturning a democratic decision. Then, because of his two-month-long dummy spit at having lost the US presidential election on November 3, he watches his party lose not one but two run-off elections, costing the Republicans control of the Senate.

Then, after publicly attempting to shame Vice-President Mike Pence into acting unconstitutionally, Trump incites a mob to storm the Capitol building in a capricious act of sedition aimed at overturning the presidential election result.

Just as rats always desert a sinking ship, in recent days a conga line of Republicans and conservative commentators has walked away from years of support for Trump. While their collective last-minute finding of a conscience when it comes to this despicable president is welcomed, there is no papering over the fact they have held remarkably strong up until this point.

According to the internet, a lemming is a small rodent that "behaves aggressively towards human observers". And like lemmings approaching a democratic cliff on January 20, so it has been with the collective of Trump apologists who have cheered on this megalomaniac for years, in the full knowledge of what he is really like.

Put plainly, I have watched these dangerous fools bang out column inches year after year and spruik their collective stupidity on television time after time, displaying callous indifference to the risks attached to what and who Trump is: a modern-day demagogue, a leader who seeks to appeal to the prejudices of ordinary citizens rather than to their rational selves.

This week we saw where this could lead: a Capitol building lockdown as staff and politicians sought refuge behind locked doors or pieces of furniture. Authorities with guns drawn attempted to defend the premises. Rioters pillaged historic memorabilia and lounged in the offices of democratically elected leaders. Deaths followed, although not nearly as many as there would have been had these wreckers of democracy been black, not white.

Year after year I've watched conservatives lecture their societies about moral standards, yet where was their morality leading up to this week's events? Instead, they stoked the flames of ill-founded discontent among Trump supporters, for some in a bid to lay claim to becoming the next Trump.

Two Republican senators stood out from the crowd for very different reasons: Ted Cruz and Mitt Romney. The former, who represents Texas, went all in arguing against the democratic wishes of American voters, defending the actions of a president in disrepute despite Trump previously having attacked Cruz's father and Cruz's wife in the most despicable ways. Yet Cruz has become an unflinching Trump advocate and defender. What a pathetic human being.

Romney, in contrast, was the only Republican senator prepared to support the President's impeachment last February. And this week his words condemning Trump have served only to elevate the one-time presidential candidate.

The callow collective of reactionary Australian commentators who regularly attempt to out-do one another in their support for Trump should be thoroughly ashamed of themselves, enablers of dangerous political intolerance one and all. To be sure, they won't show a shred of contrition, courtesy of a mixture of stubbornness and ignorance.

Some have finally begun to condemn the President, albeit with caveats. Most, however, have spent the past two months whinging about the result, some even echoing Trump's claim the election was rigged.

Many current and former politicians also should be included, mouthing off about Trump's virtues while ignoring his vices.

For anyone who tries to argue now that they simply couldn't have seen coming what has transpired this week, that merely shows their lack of research.

Here are a bunch of quotes from leading Republicans about Trump before he took power, figures who have walked alongside him during his presidency despite knowing exactly what he was.

Republican senator Lindsey Graham: "I think he's a kook, I think he's crazy, I think he's unfit for office. He's a race-baiting xenophobic religious bigot." Cruz: "He doesn't know the difference between truth and lies. He lies (with) practically every word that comes out of his mouth. He combines it with being a narcissist at a level I don't think this country has ever seen." Senator Rand Paul: "My concern is that he would grab up that power and really treat the country as sort of his little bully fiefdom." Rick Perry, who served in Trump's cabinet up until 2019 described Trump as "a toxic mix of demagoguery and mean spiritedness and nonsense". Nikki Haley, touted as a future Republican presidential candidate: "Donald Trump is everything I taught my children not to do in kindergarten." Former Republican presidential contender Marco Rubio: "Donald Trump is a con artist. He's been exploiting working Americans for 40 years."

All of the above have been some of Trump's strongest supporters, despite their reservations about their man.

And this week we saw every living former defence secretary sign an open letter expressing concerns that Trump just might try to use the military to seize power, a truly extraordinary collective that included former vice-president Dick Cheney.

Democracy is fragile, which is one of the reasons conservatives historically have defended traditional institutions so strongly. Doing so is at the heart of what it means to be conservative.

Yet during the past four years supposed conservatives have rallied around the populist Trump despite his predilection for tearing down institutions and cultural markers of conservatism. Trump has attacked the courts, the legislature, the media and indeed anyone and everyone who gets in his way. This week it culminated in a cry to "patriots" to storm the Capitol, and an ongoing unwillingness to accept his electoral defeat. Rather, Trump continues to make false claims that voter fraud cost him the election.

Reactionaries like to claim some sort of superiority when it comes to reading the mood of the mainstream, just one reason they were so quick to claim victory on the night Trump went on to lose the election.

Last year, the mainstream delivered reactionaries and Trump a crushing defeat according to the popular vote and the electoral college.

For all the chaos fuelled by a sore loser this week, the good news is most Americans turned their back on Trump. And after what has transpired in recent days, you can bet more will join that worthy protest.

When going got tough, the states stepped up

2–3 January 2021

With 2020 out of the way (thank gawd) we can reflect on the political leaders we have to thank for how well Australia managed the pandemic. As awful as the year was, compared with other parts of the world Australia has excelled, notwithstanding stumbles along the way.

The premiers as a collective have done better than anyone federally. That's important to note. They were the ones who initially dragged the federal government, kicking and screaming behind the scenes, over the line to lock down and ensure COVID-19 didn't spread through the community the way it did in other parts of the world.

However much Scott Morrison is lauded now for his performance during the pandemic, and he does deserve some applause, when the premiers were issuing cautions he was spruiking his desire to attend the footy one last time before restrictions came in.

When state chief health officers were advising their premiers last March that social distancing restrictions might be necessary, the federal chief medical officer rocked up at the ABC Insiders studio shaking hands. Doing so might have been safe because community transmission was low at the time, but it didn't set the right example.

Make no mistake, state governments stepped up when Australians needed them to.

As part of researching for our forthcoming book, How Good is Scott Morrison?, Wayne Errington and I discovered that early on members of federal cabinet were arguing for a Donald Trump style laissez-faire approach to the virus. All will be revealed when we publish in April.

Premiers took a different view, effectively forcing the Prime Minister into what could have been a humiliating backdown from his initially lax approach. To Morrison's credit, he saw the writing on the wall and got on board, projecting unity, albeit reluctantly. Who knew the federation was so powerful?

That was another revelation during this pandemic: federalism is alive and well. Long thought to be in retreat in recent decades, the power of state governments has been glaringly on display throughout the pandemic.

At the federal level the two ministers who deserve the most credit for Australia's record, joining the premiers as deserving of our praise, are Josh Frydenberg and Health Minister Greg Hunt.

Neither was particularly close to Morrison at the beginning of the pandemic, but by the end of it they were invaluable to both the Prime Minister and the nation. They gave Morrison much needed policy ballast last year.

Few realise how hard Hunt worked behind the scenes stockpiling equipment for emergency departments to ensure Australia was well placed when it came to ventilators and masks in the event COVID-19 got out of control.

Equally, the Treasurer was a driving force behind the rollout of payments that saved jobs and businesses. People can condemn his over-the-top criticisms of Victorian Premier Daniel Andrews (as I do), or his structuring of JobKeeper and JobSeeker (which did leave some people behind). But Frydenberg was a Liberal Treasurer who rolled out an agenda that was very different from his ideological beliefs.

Coalition colleagues didn't always agree with the strict health measures and profligate spending. Neither did reactionary commentators who often have more opinions than brains. But without Hunt and Frydenberg the health crisis could have been much worse and the long-term economic recovery could have been far slower and more painful.

Frydenberg sought John Howard's advice throughout the crisis, which helped him stand his ground in cabinet when his suggestions were challenged — including by the Prime Minister.

If the end-of-year financial update proves accurate, the unemployment rate won't rise beyond 7.5 per cent. That is extraordinary given the damage the pandemic caused. Initial estimates were for more than 10 per cent unemployment.

Victoria's second wave was devastating for many, but even with that failure added into the mix, Australia is a world leader on health outcomes.

Hunt and Frydenberg, who squared off for the deputy leadership of the Liberal Party when Malcolm Turnbull and Julie Bishop departed, are close friends. A pair of Victorians — Bill Lawry would be proud.

Morrison doesn't get close to his parliamentary colleagues. Apart from Stuart Robert — who shares Morrison's Pentecostal faith — the Prime Minister has no other real friends in the parliamentary ranks. He's close to Alex Hawke and Ben Morton, but these relationships are transactional as factional and strategic allies.

This time 12 months ago the government looked like the dog that caught the car, unsure what to do with the third term it had secured a little more than seven months earlier. Morrison had recently returned from the US, where he'd joined Donald Trump on stage at a campaign rally. The Prime Minister was taking his lead from a President who proved incapable of winning re-election.

There was little by way of an agenda domestically, and Morrison looked like damaged goods as bushfires raged. He was exposed as a blame shifter, having returned from an overseas holiday he had secretly embarked on while his home state, NSW, burned. He looked sorry for himself, deeply un-prime ministerial.

The level of animosity between Morrison and NSW Premier Gladys Berejiklian was off the charts. The optics of their collegial relationship now paper over those tensions. Perhaps one day the full details of what transpired between the pair during the bushfires and in the early days of the pandemic when Berejiklian sided with Labor premiers will be revealed.

But the Covid crisis saved Morrison's bacon, and he is now invincible in what may turn out to be an election year. He can't lose the next election. He has Labor's measure. The good work managing the pandemic, however, is shared by others: premiers, Frydenberg and Hunt. Even if Morrison gets most of the credit as Prime Minister.

While the lead indicators are that this will be a better year, the effects of COVID-19 are far from over. Australia continues to face threats of community outbreaks, with current clusters in Victoria and NSW. Travel internationally remains largely off limits, and interstate borders remain largely shut. So much depends on the success of the vaccines.

When JobKeeper ends in March, the unemployment rate will rise, even if the Mid-Year Economic and Fiscal Outlook forecasts are accurate and it doesn't lift beyond 7.5 per cent. And then we have the risks attached to our trade relationship with China.

If the economy does recover well, inflation could become a risk. Higher inflation would mean higher interest rates. It would be ironic if a strong recovery out the other side of the recession became a bigger economic problem than the downturn itself. We have seen how problematic, politically speaking, rising interest rates have been in the past for governments.

Last year was certainly one to forget, but there are no guarantees that this year will be one to be remembered.

The royal commission Labor is having into Robodebt may well give us a clearer picture of what the former PM did and didn't know about the myriad of problems in the system. This column resulted in no small amount of complaints from the PM's media team.

Robodebt was a Morrison fiasco at every stage

21–22 November 2020

Scott Morrison and his team have been coated in Teflon since the pandemic struck. A grateful nation has given its incumbent leaders the benefit of the doubt as we look around the world and see abject failure in handling the coronavirus elsewhere.

But such positivity shouldn't blind us to poor conduct, and the Robodebt disaster is without doubt the worst example of maladministration and callous indifference to vulnerable Australians since the Coalition took office in 2013.

The Coalition is a certainty to win the next election despite a long list of deficiencies across the policy and political spectrum. Among them: the sports rorts scandal; Angus Taylor's still unexplained use of a forged document to attack Sydney City Council; water buybacks along the Murray-Darling Basin that simply don't pass the pub test; a $30 million taxpayer purchase of land for Sydney's second airport at 10 times the official valuation, bought from a Liberal Party donor no less.

None of these examples of dubious practices is as bad as what we've witnessed when it comes to Robodebt, however. And none of them directly lands at the feet of the Prime Minister the way the Robodebt saga does.

The Coalition instituted automated payments to collect what it hoped would be billions of dollars of overpayments to welfare recipients. It justified the practice by claiming Labor had done similar in the past. That is a lie, unless comparing oranges and apples is legitimate. Labor never used automated payments for welfare recipients the way Robodebt functioned, which assumed guilt, not innocence, and put the onus on the welfare recipient to prove their case for a reversal. We are talking about people whose vulnerability makes doing so even harder than it might be for the rest of us.

The Robodebt scheme removed human checks from the system, completely automating the process on a scale never seen before. Red flags were raised but the government ignored them. Income averaging was used, which by definition means many vulnerable people automatically would be called on to return payments. The courts struck it out.

Anyone with half a brain knows welfare recipients don't have bundles of cash lying around. Hence, when thousands upon thousands of notices went out demanding repayments and threatening to cut off people's welfare if they didn't, the mental anguish felt was off the charts. Some committed suicide, and many of their families were convinced they did so because of the stress caused by the Robodebt scheme.

This is a shameful moment in Australian history.

Rather than admit its mistake as soon as it came to light, the government fought tooth and nail to defend its missteps, settling only at the last minute before the court case was due to start. The financial cost: $1.2 billion, a record class action settlement.

Now for the most important part of this sorry story — why hasn't anyone been held to account? The answer is simple. If one head has to roll for what has transpired it is that of Morrison. That won't happen.

Morrison was the social services minister when Robodebt was conceived. He charged his junior minister, Alan Tudge, to prosecute the case for the capricious practices Morrison wanted put in place. When the quantum of cash that the Finance Department hoped to collect from Robodebt was realised, the eyes of Treasury lit up. It was just what the bean counters ordered as the government sought to return the budget to balance and make political mileage from doing so. By that time Morrison was the nation's treasurer, right when Treasury was putting the squeeze on the Department of Social Services to deliver the promised windfall on offer from Robodebt.

The surplus was central to the Coalition's re-election strategy, featuring in campaign ads and rhetorically throughout. Within that, the money that Robodebt was to earn was important. With the truth about the scheme's failures already on show, the government defended itself, didn't apologise and continued to leave the vulnerable to rot on the vine.

Morrison was Prime Minister by that point, the ultimate beneficiary of the political strategy.

Knowing what we do about the financial cost of Robodebt ($1.2bn) and the toll on people's lives (even contributing to a loss of life), it is hard to stomach the hypocrisy we see and hear from Morrison. Using the parliament to thunder about former Australia Post chief executive Christine Holgate authorising a $19,000 purchase of Cartier watches as executive bonuses. Demanding she step down. Hearing the Prime Minister constantly refer to Labor as having blood on its hands because of the handful of lives lost during the home insulation program rollout, even though the royal commission the Coalition called found that the scheme was not responsible for those deaths.

The scale of devastation from Robodebt dwarfs any and all such failures. Yet not one head will roll because the only one that should is Morrison's: he is the glue that held together every poor decision on Robodebt for years. He won't sack himself. Morrison has barely apologised for what happened.

US president Harry S. Truman had a sign on his desk that read "The buck stops here". You will never find such a sign on Morrison's desk. I can't be sure Morrison knew the extent of the problem he was unleashing when he contrived Robodebt. More likely he had no idea.

Marketing, not public policy, is his shtick. I suspect he saw the chance to hit welfare recipients with bills to help the budget bottom line. A win-win for a Liberal government that doesn't get votes from those on welfare but does score political points for its management of the economy. A chance to look tough. More red meat for the party's base.

But surely on reflection the Prime Minister realises how low he went. How much damage he caused. How many lives he ruined. Maybe not. It's not as if this devout Christian ever took the time to reflect on his asylum-seeker policies in that way.

For operators such as Morrison who've lived their entire adult lives inside the partisan world of politics, they know politics is a blood sport, which means sometimes blood gets spilt.

Opposition kerfuffle steals spotlight from the Coalition

14–15 November 2020

A week in which the government should have been under pressure instead saw Labor dealing with what is an as yet unresolved rolling crisis. The pandemic hasn't made it easy for oppositions to gain political traction but this week Labor stole the focus for all the wrong reasons.

Opposition agriculture and resources spokesman Joel Fitzgibbon quit the frontbench on Tuesday in disgust over what he said was the party's failure to get the balance right on climate change. Fitzgibbon thinks it is a second-order issue in the context of the recession and job losses, but others don't agree. Reports emerged of a shouting match in the shadow cabinet meeting between Fitzgibbon and opposition legal affairs spokesman Mark Dreyfus.

Fitzgibbon told Dreyfus to "shut up, you idiot". Dreyfus took to morning radio the next day and publicly attacked Fitzgibbon for being out of touch with his party and with most Australians when it came to climate change. It is an irony that this dispute is occurring in the context of Joe Biden winning the US presidency on a platform to do more on climate change, a shift that should put the pressure on the Coalition. If the public scolding Dreyfus delivered was supposed to quieten Fitzgibbon down, it had the opposite effect.

He in turn used the media to call for opposition climate change and energy spokesman Mark Butler to be sacked. The South Australian left-wing factional heavyweight is a close ally of Anthony Albanese, who is also from the left. Fitzgibbon's argument is that Butler has been in the climate spokesman role across two failed elections where climate change policy deficiencies were at the heart of the losses.

We all remember the way Bill Shorten was caught out on the costings of emissions reductions policies during the election campaign last year. Labor deputy leader Richard Marles defended Butler, but not before admitting that "it's going to be bumpy" as the opposition navigates these debates.

The divisions are personal and policy driven. Equally, personal ambition isn't far below the surface. Marles would like to be seen as the next Labor leader in waiting. The NSW right thinks it should be one of its own (Chris Bowen or Tony Burke). Jim Chalmers thinks Labor's best chances of returning to government is to have a Queenslander leading the party, an affiliation he just happens to have. Tanya Plibersek wonders why it can't be a woman when Labor has boosted its gender representation.

I know if Penny Wong were in the house, not the Senate, it would be a woman right now and Labor would likely already be in government. Meanwhile, Shorten wonders whether the phrase "third time lucky" can become a real thing.

Senior Labor figures attempted to hose down the divisions late in the week, claiming Fitzgibbon was isolated and on the way out. Apparently there was always a deal that he'd quit shadow cabinet by the end of this year to make way for fellow NSW right traveller Ed Husic, who frankly should have been on Labor's frontbench half a lifetime ago given his talents.

While it is true Fitzgibbon is on the way out, it's also true that past leadership challenges have been ignited by none other than Fitzgibbon. This is his shtick. And Fitzgibbon isn't a Lone Ranger within Labor when it comes to concerns the party is out of touch with so-called mainstream voters.

On Thursday evening at the end of what was a bruising week, Fitzgibbon dined at Otis restaurant in the Canberra suburb of Kingston with the national convener of the right faction, Don Farrell. It was the same restaurant where the pair established the Otis Club, a collection of Labor MPs who want Albanese to do more for blue-collar workers and their communities. Fitzgibbon's departure means Labor no longer has a regional MP in shadow cabinet. The agriculture portfolio therefore has been given to the newbie, Husic, a city dweller.

The Nationals have had a great time pointing out there aren't too many farms in the western Sydney electorate of Chifley. Labor's disconnection with the regions has rarely been more apparent than it is right now, which is a problem far greater than its tensions on what to do on climate policy. Queensland is always a crucial battleground in federal elections, and it has a vast regional population federal Labor just isn't appealing to.

Albanese will likely reshuffle his line-up this year when Scott Morrison does the same, but he can't create regional representatives out of thin air. The confusion in Labor ranks wasn't limited to all of the above this week, however. On Thursday afternoon Albanese called an emergency shadow cabinet meeting to clarify what the opposition's policy was when it came to personal relationships between MPs and staff.

Even though this was the issue that put the government under pressure at the beginning of the week, Labor has had its fair share of controversies in that space through the years. Albanese misspoke on Wednesday evening when trying to talk ABC host Leigh Sales through Labor's policy on what's known informally as the "bonking ban". He thought they already had one; most Labor MPs did not. It turns out Albo should have phoned a friend and checked with the masses in his party because they were right, as the Prime Minister had pointed out in his media conference on Tuesday.

When Malcolm Turnbull announced a "bonking ban" for ministers and their staff in 2018, Shorten said he'd keep the policy were Labor elected into government. It wasn't, which left Labor without a policy on this issue in the current parliament. Labor's senior women weren't impressed, understandably so, and demanded that Albanese do something about it.

But after he overreached on television, shadow cabinet had to come together the next day and mop up the mess. So we got to the end of the mid-November sitting period and Labor is back in the headlines but for all the wrong reasons. If the government had hoped to move the media cycle on from its difficult start to the week, it needn't have worried about how to manufacture such a political outcome. Labor did it for the Coalition and the challenges the week threw up for Labor aren't going away any time soon.

How Scomo swapped his Hawaiian shirt for a hero's cape

31 October 2020

Scott Morrison's political dominance is such that it's hard to conjure up circumstances that would see him lose the next election. Morrison may have been the underdog at the last election, but he's the firm favourite at the next. Every advantage is his.

Prime ministers choose the timing of federal elections, which only adds to his chances of winning, by picking the exact moment in the electoral cycle to force Labor to the polls. The summer of 2019–20 feels like a lifetime ago now. Morrison was under pressure, having returned from Hawaii, caught out for trying to secretly holiday while Australia burned.

On his return he struck all the wrong chords when confronted about his failure. The Morrison of today doesn't make those mistakes. The ups and downs of managing the pandemic have hardened him politically but softened him in the eyes of many Australians. The PM's critics sometimes find that hard to accept, because all they see is the rat cunning, which to be sure is still there.

There is a hint of the left's response to Howard in the way Morrison's critics spitefully hiss at him. It can leave swinging voters who aren't enamoured with Morrison defending him against the worst of insults they feel are over-the-top, just as swinging voters did with Howard. Australians are appreciative for where the country is at versus how other nations are struggling through Covid, and they largely give Morrison the credit for that.

Anthony Albanese and the Labor Party aren't that many seats short of the elusive majority, but the issues aren't running their way. Not even close. In the post pandemic world, incumbency advantage is high, as long as those in power haven't mishandled the virus. Donald Trump is the example of what happens to a leader when they do mismanage something so important.

The Coalition government certainly hasn't failed when it comes to COVID-19, and even the few pockets of failure along the way have been glazed over in the name of applauding the wider successes Australia has enjoyed. Because it has been a global pandemic, comparisons with other nations are easy. Whether it's minimising the health impacts or evading the worst of the economic downturn, compared with neighbours near and far, Australia looks pretty good. Morrison — the master of shifting blame or absolving himself of responsibility — has been able to do exactly that each time question marks have arisen about mismanagement.

We almost waited too long before shutting the border to the US. The disembarkation of the Ruby Princess was found to be a failure of the NSW Health Department. The problems in the aged-care sector in Victoria only grew because of the second wave, which became the state Labor government's responsibility, courtesy of its mishandling of hotel quarantining and poor contact tracing procedures.

There is little doubt aged-care problems are the closest Morrison has been to coming unstuck in this pandemic. Even then, if the problem had grown out of control, he could have cut the minister, Richard Colbeck, loose — just as he did with Bridget McKenzie when the sports rorts scandal was gaining traction.

Federal Labor is talking of "the Morrison-Frydenberg recession", but nobody is seriously buying into that. Not when the recession is global in scale. To the extent that the surplus target was both unnecessary and perhaps even unachievable in the wake of the bushfires, COVID-19 almost instantly insulated the Coalition from criticism, including for its "back in black" gloating before it had even been delivered.

Labor would have been pilloried for the size and breadth of spending on schemes such as JobKeeper and JobSeeker had it delivered them. The conservative side of politics being so bold, in contrast, was applauded. Even the decision to wind back the payments, while difficult for some, can be seen through the prism of encouraging people back into work and attempting a return to normality.

The bushfires saw an alarmingly quick decline in Morrison's personal support, however, those days are over. Just like state leaders right around the country, including Victorian Premier Daniel Andrews, the PM's personal numbers are significantly higher than the Opposition Leader he squares off against, and his satisfaction rating is sky-high.

Criticisms of potential lost opportunities when it comes to reform in the aftermath of a crisis, while valid, will not resonate among mainstream voters. This is Morrison's heartland, and he is savvy enough to know how to feed it red meat when he needs to.

A hint of nationalism when rebuffing British PM Boris Johnson for having the temerity to suggest Australia needs to adopt zero emissions targets. A sprinkle of hope that a further lowering of taxes to help with the cost of living is just over the horizon. The PM also knows how to instil fear into these voters. Don't risk a return to Labor, he says, lest it makes a bad situation worse. This is followed up by a positive message: trust the Coalition to steer the country the rest of the way out of this pandemic.

Let us finish what we started. Labor knows it is facing an uphill task to be competitive at the next election, much less win it. Already we are seeing signs of turf wars over unity and individual survivalism over collective hope of victory. Albanese will battle this all the way up until polling day. Team Morrison is also well served by its campaign unit.

At last year's election, new Liberal Party federal director Andrew Hirst may have been the difference between victory and defeat, with his deployment of ground-game tactics and a cut-through advertising campaign targeting Bill Shorten. He is already planning his line of attack for Albanese, not to mention alternative leaders in Labor's caucus should change happen on the eve of the election.

The one-time novice director will go into the next campaign more seasoned but still hungry for further success. Unlike in years past, the Coalition is now every bit as good as Labor at online campaigning and fundraising. Context is everything when it comes to the next election, and the Coalition will fight that campaign having successfully steered Australia through the Covid recession and out the other side of the pandemic.

Labor could have benefited from a similar halo effect at the 2010 election, having survived the global financial crisis, had it not been for the fact that it removed the leader who did that just months before polling day. There is no chance of Morrison suffering the same fate.

It is easy to forget just how many excuses the Coalition had for failing to enact a federal integrity commission. This was one of the early excuses: the pandemic means we can't walk and chew gum at the same time!

Pandemic a poor excuse for delaying Integrity Commission

24–25 October 2020

The return of parliament for the first full week of sittings post the budget saw the Prime Minister batting away questions as to why he still hadn't established a federal integrity commission. Despite having committed to doing so nearly two years ago, shortly after becoming PM.

Scott Morrison claims that he and his government haven't had the time they need to make it happen, using the floor of parliament to cite the pandemic as the reason. Given that he spent the full previous week in Queensland campaigning for the state LNP ahead of the election due at the end of this month, the hollowness of the excuse was there for all to see.

It has been a frequently used excuse in 2020. The pandemic has meant parliament couldn't sit, we were told, the virtual world seemingly escaping the PM's attention. Ironically on Wednesday morning this week he gave a speech about the importance of business embracing the digital world in the wake of COVID-19.

Nearly 12 months ago, federal Attorney-General Christian Porter received an exposure draft on legislation for an integrity commission, but this week he cited the need for extensive consultation before draft legislation could be presented to parliament. Again the pandemic was the excuse. Ain't the virtual world grand. It really does seem that this male-dominated government can't do two things at once.

What happens with the integrity commission going forward will be a fascinating case study in just how dominant the Coalition is in the wake of the pandemic. And how strategic it can be at outflanking opponents.

Trust in government has never been higher, benefiting incumbents at state and federal levels. The Labor Party federally is banking on that changing if the Coalition doesn't move quickly on the integrity commission. Coalition strategists disagree, believing Anthony Albanese is clutching at straws and appears out of touch with the priorities of Australians: jobs and the economy, their material needs.

The scholar Ronald Inglehart identified the concept of "post-material" voting tendencies in his 1977 book The Silent Revolution. Its thesis was that as Western societies saw material needs increasingly satisfied, post-material values such as the environment would rise up as important factors in how voters cast their ballots. Since that time, of course, elections have ebbed and flowed based on issues that could reasonably fall into one of these two categories. Depending on everything from conflict to recession to the individual circumstances of particular voting cohorts.

But in the wake of a pandemic that has thrust the world into recession and seen countless jobs lost and debt ballooning, it is hard to see voters putting too much stock in post-material tendencies. Which would mean Labor may be barking up the wrong tree when it comes to the integrity commission, unless it can link that debate to material voting preferences.

A Liberal Party donor receiving a sale price 10 times the value of land he sold to the Commonwealth as part of a purchase surrounding Sydney's second airport could provide that link. It stinks and it sees political insiders getting rich at a time when mainstream voters are struggling to keep their families financially secure. But the link is still a long bow for Labor to draw, and people need to be paying attention, which they probably aren't. That said, the issue will likely be in the government's rear-view mirror as a strategic dilemma before the end of 2020.

Crossbench MP Helen Haines is tabling a private member's bill on Monday outlining her own version of a national integrity commission, and she has used the past 12 months to consult widely with parliamentary colleagues on both sides of the major party divide to gauge their support for what she's proposing.

It is a fair and reasonable compromise between the government's apparently undercooked options, which would largely see politicians and staffers immune from investigation by such a body, and the more radical models which could see careers ruined on ultimately spurious grounds, as some state anti-corruption bodies have done over the years. This is an important point. At the very least her bill should force the government to harden up its model such that any integrity commission isn't just a toothless tiger.

The Haines bill will be tabled next week, but it won't actually be debated before the final sitting week of the year in December.

There are government MPs planning to cross the floor to vote for the Haines bill to be debated if the government seeks to shut that debate down. And in doing so, there is a good chance that if her bill is opposed by the government they will again cross the floor to see it passed in the House of Representatives.

Remember the Coalition holds only the barest of majorities in the lower house, even if it's politically standing because of the Covid crisis is much stronger now. The Haines bill would certainly pass the Senate if the House passed it, because the Senate has already passed a Greens bill for an integrity commission, signalling where the numbers in the upper house rest. It isn't so clear whether the Senate would pass an unamended government bill for a toothless -integrity commission.

But all of the above is theoretical at this stage. The fact Haines is receiving backing from some Coalition backbenchers will hasten Porter and the PM into action with their own bill. To have it ready for tabling in December, before the Haines bill is due for debate. That should be enough to prevent colleagues crossing the floor. And you can bet between now and then the PM's henchmen in the parliament will be hitting the phones to try to establish who are these rogue MPs willing to cross the floor.

For all the talk in Liberal circles that it's the party which tolerates conscience votes in violation of party solidarity (when Labor officially bans such practices), if you do cross the floor in the Liberal Party you can usually kiss goodbye to frontbench promotion anytime soon.

The fact some MPs are willing to risk that tells you there are people of integrity in the government's ranks. Perhaps their voices will grow louder as politics returns to normal and the pandemic fades into the background.

Major parties to duel on long road to recovery

10–11 October 2020

The fact this week's budget forecast puts the deficit at a whopping $67bn in four years tells us everything we need to know about how much the fiscal political debate in this country has changed. Gone are the days when the conservatives threatened to block lifting the debt ceiling, condemned the use of deficits to help with growth, and attacked the accumulation of more and more debt burdening future generations.

Four years from now we'll have a $67bn deficit, if a vaccine is widely distributed by the end of next year, if next year's growth exceeds 4 per cent and if unemployment doesn't peak beyond 8.5 per cent. That is a delicate and unlikely threesome.

On Tuesday Josh Frydenberg handed down a record-breaking deficit of more than $210bn. National debt will balloon past $1 trillion in the years ahead, keeping in mind this government had already doubled the debt it inherited from Labor before COVID-19 even struck.

Whoever could have imagined a Coalition government would need to eat so much humble pie? However, it is gorging on it, without a hint of contrition for the criticisms it once levelled at Labor during the global financial crisis. Without embarrassment for premature printing of "back in black" mugs.

Yes, this Covid economic crisis is worse than the GFC. Much worse. But the spending principles adopted by Labor then are the same as those being adopted by the Coalition now. Even if the debt numbers being racked up leave what was spent during the GFC looking like chump change.

When the Treasurer was confronted with the obvious charge of hypocrisy on budget night, time and time again he pushed back at the comparison by pointing to failures with some of the spending programs Labor introduced during the GFC. Such as the fiasco of the pink batts home insulation scheme, which cost lives. It remains to be seen how well or badly all the dollars have been spent during this crisis.

But, given the failures and loss of life within aged-care homes during Covid — in part because of federal government system failures, according to the aged-care royal commission — the chutzpah required to raise pink batts is off the charts. But what interests me most about this budget isn't the hypocrisy on the part of the Coalition. It is the brewing standoff between our two major parties over how Australia should chart its way out of this pandemic, and the economic crisis it has caused.

Labor wants JobKeeper lifted back to the levels it was originally set at, expanded to include more casual workers, and pushed out beyond the end of March when it is due to wind up. The budget revealed the government's intent to wind up the program, as had already been flagged. There is no money set aside in the budget to extend it. Equally, the government has already begun reducing JobSeeker payments, viewing them as an inhibitor to people currently unemployed getting back into work. Labor disagrees, wanting the Newstart rate lifted, possibly in line with JobSeeker's current settings. This variation between the parties underpins their differing philosophical approaches to how the economy should be best supported to overcome the worst of the crisis, and how best to reduce unemployment levels back to pre-pandemic levels.

In short, Frydenberg's budget revealed plans that rely on a business-led recovery. Labor, in contrast, wants government to do the heavy lifting. This will present an interesting contrast once the halo comes off the Coalition.

The Liberals may have lost their philosophical lenses when it comes to debt and deficits, but in a sense that was always a political charade anyway. The budget did include substantial amounts of tax credit and tax concession stimulus to encourage businesses to invest more and therefore (hopefully) hire more workers off the unemployment queues.

The youth wage subsidy has received most attention, but the asset write-off opportunities the budget has opened up are more substantial in monetary terms. And I can tell you tax and business professionals are astounded at how far the Treasurer went on Tuesday evening. In an entirely positive way. He clearly understands business.

Labor is left in an interesting position. Will it back all of these concessions for business, or switch to the politics of envy and attack the Coalition for giving too much to business and not enough to lower and middle-income families? So far Anthony Albanese has avoided the temptation to dive in too deep, instead exploiting failures in the budget to look after certain cohorts of the community: women over 35, families dependent on childcare, and older working-class men who will find it hard to compete for jobs in the post-Covid world. Without attacking business.

Finally, a minor funding cut in the budget that deserves being highlighted; the finer details within the budget documents reveal the Australian National Audit Office has had its financing cut by a few million dollars. When billions are being thrown around with little thought it is hardly a big "saving" to help the budget bottom line. Fiscal belt tightening hasn't exactly been a theme of Budget 2020. More likely, the decision to cut its funding is a spiteful one.

The Auditor's office has been responsible for exposing all manner of inappropriate public policy decision-making processes by this Coalition government, including the sports rorts saga, which cost the Nationals deputy leader her frontbench role. If Scott Morrison or one of his praetorian guard didn't have a direct role in that decision I'll eat my hat.

When parliament is diminished, the opposition consigned to irrelevance and processes such as Freedom of Information searches are thwarted, cutting an oversight body such as the National Audit Office is disgraceful. It will have a direct impact on the number of investigations the organisation can do each year, and it sends a warning message: if your findings hurt us, we will hurt you back.

Forgotten, or casualties of the culture war?

26 September 2020

Too many Australians have joined the ranks of the forgotten people during this pandemic, isolated from government support.

Despite record handouts across some sections of Australian society, the young and women disproportionately have missed out. Within these broader groupings more specifically it is casual workers and people employed by (or studying in) universities as well as the arts and entertainment industry who have been especially disadvantaged by government decision-making.

Australians stranded abroad also have been largely forgotten, notwithstanding valiant efforts by the opposition to draw attention to their plight.

On May 22, 1942, Robert Menzies delivered his famous "Forgotten People" speech, which he used as the bedrock for creating the Liberal Party two years later. Menzies claimed too many middle-class Australians had been forgotten by their government. His intention was to recalibrate the right of politics away from speaking up on behalf of big business, as the United Australia Party (which he formerly led) had long done.

Scott Morrison's government has its own forgotten people to worry about, but it is hard to work out if the disadvantage these citizens face bothers him, personally or politically. There is a sense some of the forgetfulness is intentional, as Liberals move to settle ideological and cultural scores with sections of Australian society they have long regarded as hostile, such as universities (hotbeds of left-wing thinking apparently) and the arts sector (too quick to mock the right as social dinosaurs). The pandemic has given this government the capacity to use the power of the state to wage such a culture war with laser-like precision.

The Morrison government made the decision to exclude most casual workers from JobKeeper, putting them in a vulnerable position during the biggest crisis since the Great Depression. In doing so, the young and women suffered disproportionately and continue to. There is nothing polemical in saying that, it's what the data tells us.

Despite this early assault on the welfare of these forgotten Australians, subsequent support packages continued to be tailored towards professions that employed more men than women: the gas announcement; the HomeBuilder scheme; broader infrastructure spending, too. The few exceptions — the childcare package — prove the rule.

The economic effects of the pandemic have been the inverse of the health effects: the elderly are especially vulnerable to the coronavirus itself, whereas young people are the losers when it comes to limited work or study opportunities.

This is one of the reasons leaving universities to wither on the vine courtesy of their collective ineligibility for JobKeeper support has been so brazenly forgetful. The rearguard action we've seen this week to try to save research jobs is too little, too late.

Thousands of higher education jobs have already gone. Throw in the "reforms" that will push the cost of study even higher and it's easy to see how poorly the young have been treated during the pandemic.

Australians are left to wonder just how deliberate the government's forgetfulness is. Is it possible that the Prime Minister isn't as pragmatic as most of us assume, instead prepared to risk the political wrath of these forgotten communities within Australian society in the name of a cultural revolution?

Certainly his treatment of the university and arts and entertainment sectors has been particularly brazen, in the case of the latter even making an announcement in June that money was coming yet months later not one cent has flowed through. The treatment has been so bad that the owner of a Gold Coast studio where Morrison made an arts support package announcement ended up writing to the Prime Minister complaining that he'd been used and hadn't received the promised support.

Come mid-September it was left to the Victorian government to announce $13m in support for local entertainment venues to help them recover from the effects of the second wave. That's a fiscal drop in the ocean compared with the sums of taxpayers' money flying around federally.

Perhaps the most concerning aspect of the Coalition's forgetfulness is the lack of clear policy settings to help those Australians permanently disrupted by the pandemic. A lack of forward planning to be sure. Our lives have been changed forever, and with that social and economic norms too. Even when a vaccine rolls out things won't go back to the way they were, meaning whole sections of society will be worse off.

While Australians have slowly begun returning to their offices, most are working more flexibly than they did before: more time working from home, less commuting, fewer people crammed into elevators. Open-plan offices will likely become the exception in a Covid-safe world. This process of de-urbanisation may work for the few able to rejig our work practices, but what about the millions of Australians who can't do that; indeed, who rely on the commuting workforce? When the average CBD worker spends only three out of five days in the office they spend only 60 per cent of what they once did on everything from transport to coffees, lunches or shopping in the city. The workers in these CBD retail sectors will quickly find themselves out of work. The businesses employing them may become unviable. Tinkering with insolvency provisions, as the Treasurer outlined this week in a speech in Canberra, won't do much to help with that reality.

Then there are the forgotten workers in manual jobs who will lose out because of the uptick in automation embraced during the pandemic. More electronic check-outs replacing retail and wholesale workers, more robots in factories picking products off shelves. These developments in automation have been around for a while now, but they have improved and proliferated during the pandemic and there is no turning back. What about those displaced workers? Again, retraining and upskilling needs to be part of any solution, but our institutes of higher learning — where that can happen — have been marginalised and forgotten.

The question now: Is it deliberate forgetfulness by the Prime Minister down in the Coalition government? Or just poor policymaking leaving so many Australians behind?

Pragmatism is good but only goes so far

19–20 September 2020

The unemployment rate fell dramatically this week, catching analysts off guard. Of course when JobKeeper gets withdrawn next year that is likely to see the rate head north once again, as Treasury has forecast. JobSeeker payments also are coming down, moving back towards the paltry rate Newstart was set at before the coronavirus crisis caused this recession.

Next month Josh Frydenberg will hand down a budget that was supposed to be in surplus. We were told we were already "back in black", remember? Instead the budget will be in deficit, the largest in the history of this nation. That will see national debt, which has already doubled since the Coalition came to office in 2013, continue to balloon.

We know unemployment usually rises far more quickly than it comes down, history has taught us that. The Treasurer made that exact point when moving to legislate the JobKeeper payments to keep people in work.

But there is only so much a government can do.

This week the Australian Council of Social Service released research it commissioned from Deloitte, with modelling showing that reducing JobSeeker payments could put a further 130,000 Australians out of work. At first glance it seems an odd finding, given that people on JobSeeker are already out of work. But the reason is an obvious one.

People on low incomes, which anyone on unemployment benefits certainty is, live hand-to-mouth. That is, they spend what little money they get each fortnight. They don't save, thereby withdrawing money from the economy. Therefore, when their income is reduced, billions of dollars less is being pumped back into the economy each fortnight.

Less money is spent on retail, in particular, which means the jobs that money flow is maintaining are put at risk. That is where the 130,000 figure comes from. In addition to the value the extra payments provide for recipients of government assistance, that money also helps pump-prime the economy, in turn saving jobs.

The price of doing so is more debt, but the hope is a pay-off comes in the longer term: jobs maintained, improved living standards for welfare recipients and hopefully enhanced economic growth (what Paul Keating would call "growing the pie").

Economic conservatives dispute the value of this chain of events, indeed whether it actually happens. They claim higher unemployment benefits can be a disincentive to work, so they need to come down for that reason alone.

They also say that ballooning debt is a first-order problem, and argue we can't burden future generations with it. That said, fewer Coalition MPs are mounting this argument any more in the context of the current crisis.

All of the above is a necessarily nuanced debate, which frankly is beyond the comprehension of many of our elected MPs, untrained in economics and commerce, some lacking in logic and common sense at the best of times. Politics doesn't always lend itself to nuance anyway, modern politics in particular. Simplistic slogans have replaced the weighty economic debates of the past. However, in the wake of this crisis as a nation we need the tone of the debate to lift.

How nations respond to the coronavirus-induced global recession will play a vital role in how prosperous they are when we all come out the other side. Make good decisions and Australia will be on the right side of history, extending our decades long run as the "Lucky Country", as Donald Horne once described us. Make bad decisions and we risk emulating Argentina, which slipped down the global prosperity ratings during the 20th century.

It is therefore an incredibly important time for policymakers. Unfortunately, our political settings aren't match fit for the challenge. Our democratic institutions aren't working adequately. Parliamentary debate is being stifled by the lack of sittings and the exclusions caused by social distancing. The federation is broken as states and the commonwealth squabble over their respective power-sharing arrangements.

Partisan debates on the economy aren't what they used to be: since losing the 1996 election and deserting the proud economic legacy of the Keating era, Labor can't compete in the court of public opinion when it comes to the economy.

With the state of the economy front and centre, and polls confirming Labor is a mile behind the Liberals as preferred economic managers, Scott Morrison has the next election in the bag. If the recovery is swifter than expected, he gets credit. If it's slower, even made worse by poor policy choices, Morrison simply asks voters if they are willing to risk handing the reins of power over to Labor at such an important time. He knows the ballot box answer will be no.

That means a guaranteed four to five more years of Coalition government deciding how Australia reshapes its economy in the wake of the pandemic. So we turn our attention to how well equipped it is to do that.

Genuine economic liberals within the Liberal partyroom are few and far between these days. Economic literacy is even scarcer. Reactionary conservatives instead run rampant within Coalition ranks. The Prime Minister's preferences have long included economic intervention, not economic liberalism. For example, when he clashed with then treasurer Joe Hockey in cabinet in the Coalition's first term over whether the government should subsidise SPC Ardmona, Morrison was all for it. Or this week when he announced plans to build a government-owned gas-fired power plant to compete with the private sector.

At one level Morrison's pragmatism has its upsides. It means he won't put ideological dogma first. But his pragmatism is political, not economic, meaning the pathways he chooses are likely to be all about winning elections, not good policy.

Occasionally the coincidence of duality may arise if we're lucky.

More likely tough but necessary decisions involving economic reform will be shelved rather than enacted, as happened during the Fraser years when the Campbell review (recommending micro-economic reforms) gathered dust on then treasurer John Howard's bookshelf. The do-nothing years of the Fraser government (1975–83) didn't hold Australia back because they gave way to the reforming years of Bob Hawke and Keating.

Who seriously sees such impressive figures on the opposition benches now? And at a time of far greater crisis and need.

Officials' lack of consistency borders on heartless

12–13 September 2020

The state of Australian borders has become high farce. Restrictions are inconsistent, often elitist and deeply unsympathetic to the plight of ordinary Australians. The disagreements between the commonwealth and some states also have exposed serious fractures in the federation, as well as constitutional uncertainty. We are all at sea.

The irony of the poor treatment mainstream Australians are receiving when it comes to borders is that mainstream Australians seem to support the restrictions. That's because most of us aren't adversely affected by them; not directly anyway. But god help you if you're suffering an illness and need understanding to cross a hard border for surgery or check-ups.

Or if you are looking for compassion from a premier to be allowed to bypass a quarantine period to see a parent on death's door or to attend their funeral. The latter is what happened to 26-year-old Canberra resident Sarah Caisip. Even though there have been no COVID-19 cases in the ACT for 60 days in a row, she was denied one last face-to-face visit with her father or the opportunity to comfort her 11-year-old sister at his funeral in Queensland.

What kind of a society have we become? Queensland Premier Annastacia Palaszczuk said it was a decision for the state's Chief Health Officer, Jeannette Young. Hands washed, buck passed, accountability withdrawn. Let's be clear about one thing: politicians make the decisions; not bureaucrats, not health professionals, not academic experts or mobs with pitchforks.

While we expect politicians to take on board all manner of advice, we pay them to show leadership and make decisions for themselves.

Palaszczuk could have overruled her CHO in a heartbeat if she had wanted to. Instead, she hid behind her. I can't respect that. Especially when there are legitimate question marks over exactly why Palaszczuk is being so strident on borders. Is it because with a state election due on October 31 she thinks the lockdown will help her at the polls?

Or is it because the Premier and her CHO have been spooked by the young women who broke rules travelling between Melbourne and Brisbane while infected with Covid? Neither reason is adequate to justify some of the denials of common decency we are witnessing. Caisip's plight is far from an isolated incident. The children of a 39-year-old man with brain cancer have been denied passage across a hard border.

Yet Australian diplomats fly overseas and return to home quarantine as long as their "itinerary is supervised". Hollywood actors get exemptions to fly into some states. Billionaires get exemptions to fly in and out of states, indeed to skip hotel quarantine altogether. Politicians frequently are granted exemptions for interstate travel.

Football codes have been granted all manner of special rights. Yet mainstream Australians are being treated like second-class citizens in their own country. We can't find a way to get kids into hospitals to see their dying parents if they are unlucky enough to reside across artificial borders decided more than a century ago?

Freight drivers can move about anywhere in the country with one Covid swab every seven days. In the words of American journalist Edward R. Murrow: "We will not be driven by fear into an age of unreason". I'm not one of the nutters claiming we should let this virus rip through the community. When the pandemic started I was aghast at Brendan Murphy, the chief medical officer at the time and now secretary of the federal Department of Health, turning up at ABC Insiders for an interview and shaking hands with panellists before the show got started, then going on to pose for photographs with the panel without socially distancing.

I kept my distance, but the photo didn't catch me shaking my head. I thought it set a terrible example, frankly, as did Scott Morrison's comments days before that he wanted to get to the footy one last time. And they wonder why it took Australians time to start adhering to the rules in the days that followed when they all but yelled into their microphones demanding that people did as they said, not as they themselves had been doing so recently.

But fast forward six months, and surely an advanced society such as ours can work out a way to insert compassionate exemptions into a system of border restrictions and lockdowns. If not, can someone please explain the rationale behind the money and power-based exemptions that do exist? I'm told the inconsistency on borders and the volume of exemption requests have generated a regulatory nightmare wherein public health officials are spending more time on who can come in and out of states than they are developing necessary strategies to control Covid. That sounds like a collection of officials who couldn't organise a piss-up at a brewery.

The Prime Minister wants to take issue with premiers on border shutdowns doing economic damage. Indeed, he appears to have a problem with Daniel Andrews's lockdown in Victoria. But he's deeply inconsistent, too. He threw his Attorney-General, Christian Porter, and Senate leader Mathias Cormann under the bus when he walked away from Clive Palmer's High Court challenge to the West Australian border shutdown.

I'm not passing judgment either way on WA Premier Mark McGowan's decision or the constitutionality of it. The courts and the court of public opinion will do that in the fullness of time. But Morrison wants to chastise some premiers (always Labor) and ignore others (always Liberal) on an issue that requires consistency. He's inconsistent because he's too political and too partisan, worried about Liberal seats in the west where a closed border is popular, happy to press Queensland's premier on borders with a state election she might lose just over the horizon.

The Australian Health Protection Principal Committee has descended into irrelevance, largely because of the unilateral actions of chief health officers acting at the behest of premiers who are out of their depth or without direction from premiers who are unable or unwilling to show leadership. And we have a prime minister long on intimidating phone calls (according to at least one premier) and short on consistency. The nation has become rudderless.

Ideological assault on superannuation will leave us worse off

5 September 2020

The Coalition's opportunistic assault on superannuation is nothing short of outrageous. Frankly, it staggers me that anyone would think it's a good idea to dismantle a system that is the envy of the world. In addition to helping people fund their own retirement, Australia's $3 trillion superannuation sector provides important stability to our markets as well as valuable funds that get invested in nation-building infrastructure.

Let's hope the rumblings within the government are nothing more than maverick backbenchers freelancing. The concern, however, is that the assault is much more calculated than that. When asked about plans to junk legislated increases in super contributions, both Scott Morrison and Josh Frydenberg have implied the upcoming budget may include just such a shift.

The compulsory rate of superannuation contributions is due to lift from 9.5 per cent to 10 per cent from July 1 next year, eventually increasing to 12 per cent in 2025. But the fact businesses are doing it tough right now is being used as a fig leaf to conceal an ideological assault on super. And it is sucking in some financial experts who seemingly don't realise that eroding super has long been a partisan goal for conservatives. Because Labor introduced compulsory super, Liberal MPs, who seem to have lost their zeal for necessary reforms in other areas, are hellbent on tearing down the system.

To be sure, super has its problems. Vested interests distort the value of super. Returns are diminished by unnecessarily excessive fees and charges. Yes, compulsory super goes against principles of freedom of choice, and there are some downsides to denying people early access to super in the here and now.

We know the tax arrangements are problematic and too many people burn through their super, only to become a burden on the state-funded pension system, directly contradicting super's primary purpose.

But so what? All of these issues can be fixed without trashing the system.

For many Liberals, dismantling super has become the modern equivalent of dismantling Medicare. That was a raison d'être for economic dries during the 1980s and early '90s until John Howard backed down and supported Medicare from 1995 onwards. It is now a proud bedrock of Australia's social liberalism and held up as one of the best healthcare systems anywhere.

The question is, can Labor use the popularity of super in the community to outmanoeuvre the Coalition if it seeks to erode it, just as Labor did previously on Medicare? It is one of the few issues on which Labor has the potential to win the day. Perhaps that's why the Coalition promised not to adjust the planned increases at last year's federal election.

We know a contribution rate of 9.5 per cent is insufficient to plan for a comfortable retirement, which is why public servants get 15 per cent. It is also why the parliament has legislated to lift the rate incrementally to 12 per cent.

So what has changed? Is it hubris now that the Prime Minister is popular and Labor continues to lick its wounds from last year's unexpected election defeat?

The pandemic hasn't adjusted Liberal thinking. The same voices calling for changes now were doing so before the pandemic. They just have an excuse for breaking the election promise: the pandemic.

Longer life expectancy serves to increase the importance of super. Because people are living longer, we have to save more for retirement.

While libertarians may like to believe people can do that independently for themselves, most do not.

Forced savings via a superannuation scheme is therefore a good idea, and Australia's system (notwithstanding the problems noted) ranks as one of the best in the world. According to the Mercer Global Pension Index, Australia ranks third, trailing only Denmark and The Netherlands.

As Paul Keating so eloquently pointed out this week, the baby-faced Liberal MPs who are trying to prevent super increases taking effect are themselves enjoying public service super rates. Hypocrisy is thy name.

And when you talk to MPs privately on either side of politics, they lament the 2004 ending of the generous parliamentary super scheme in which MPs and senators were paid a percentage of their salary for the rest of their lives.

Keating, of course, introduced super in the first place. His observation — that it's a fallacy that super can't go up as it has been legislated to do because it will depress wages growth — is right. Wages have been depressed for years. They didn't go up after 2013 when the newly elected Coalition government delayed the planned increase in super. For many Australians the subsequent increase in super contributions from 9 per cent to 9.5 per cent has been the only wage rise they have had.

Then we have the vandalism of the decision to let Australians access up to $20,000 from their super during the current economic downturn. More than 40 per cent of people who took advantage of the early access did so despite not having suffered a reduction in their income, and one in 10 gambled the money away.

In what can be described only as an awful public policy decision, the early access to super the Treasurer announced at the height of the pandemic has punched a $30bn hole in the retirement savings of Australians. The multiplier effect of what that will cost Australians retiring decades from now is off the charts.

The decision also has set a very dangerous precedent, which might mean future governments also find excuses to provide early access exceptions, further eroding super savings.

Allowing people to access their super early, with very limited oversight, is diminishing people's capacity to live comfortably in retirement. The Coalition likes to talk about the burden national debt puts on future generations as a reason to try to reduce debt levels. The same logic should see them resist diminishing super savings as they have been. Doing so will put a bigger burden on future generations to fund state pension schemes for the many Australians who have eroded their super.

No chance of policy progress when the cabinet is bare

29 August 2020

The few remaining Liberal MPs with strong ideological views and values are increasingly demanding that the Covid crisis not be wasted. That is, they want economic reforms to be vigorously pursued, even if doing so costs the government support at the ballot box. Their argument is that power for power's sake is meaningless.

This ideological world view butts up against the traditional conservative position that staying in office to keep Labor out of office is an end in and of itself.

While the Liberal Party of the 1980s and '90s was dominated by ideologues, before and since that time traditional conservatism has reigned supreme within the partyroom. Especially when the values and views of the Nationals are incorporated into Coalition decision-making.

It was Winston Churchill, while looking to establish the UN in the wake of World War II, who said "never let a good crisis go to waste". The theory is that in times of crisis, or more accurately the aftermath, people are more willing to accept change. Churchill may have led the Conservative party in Britain, but he was a member of the British Liberal Party before that.

With the nation's economy in recession (like most of the world), and unemployment and debt on the rise, Australia can no longer be complacent about our status as the "lucky country".

To be sure, we have been lucky, better placed than most going into this Covid-induced downturn and geographically well placed to pivot quickly enough to avoid the worst of the health implications of the virus.

But as the world reaches its way out of the downturn, we will see marked differences between nation-states as to what levers they pull on the policy front.

What Australia doesn't want to do is emulate Argentina. From the late 1800s to the late 1900s it went from being the world's sixth wealthiest nation to one of the poorest, driven by bad decision-making in the aftermath of the 1930s Great Depression.

The real heavy lifting our politicians will need to engage in isn't what has been required so far to manage our way through the pandemic itself. It will come in the years ahead. How do we reform our systems to insulate against future shocks and to best stimulate growth and prosperity?

These decisions matter. While much of the theatre of parliamentary democracy creates only marginal differences in the modern era, as the choice between major parties often becomes a case of Tweedledee versus Tweedledum, that may no longer be the case.

Labor is showing signs of wanting to humanise workplace relations laws, welfare processes and bolster rather than cut superannuation contributions. And that is just for starters.

Anthony Albanese has flagged the need for debate over the impact a growing casualisation of the workforce is having on the social contract, on the way families live and the way people balance their personal and working lives.

His vision and what it might mean becomes relevant only if Labor is competitive in the polls. That seems unlikely unless the government pursues economic reforms of its own that perhaps are less popular.

Notwithstanding the failures being picked at in aged care, for example, Scott Morrison has a halo over him these days, and we know from last year's election he also is a savvy political operator when seeking to unpick his opponent.

It's a halo that is likely to see him stare down internal ideological opponents, after which he can run on ideological empty and still beat Labor and its bolder agenda.

This parliamentary sitting week one ideologically driven Liberal backbencher said to me: "If we can't start talking about seriously reforming super and industrial relations now, when we are in a recession, when can we?" The answer is never. If a crisis won't induce a substantive debate about policy settings, nothing will.

So what does that mean for the policy contest between now and the next election?

Here is the depressing reality, readers: very little. You could hide the amount of ideological interest in the cabinet under an overgrown pinky fingernail.

They are a collection of ambitious political operatives who have been elevated to high office. And that's the status of the good ones. The rest are even worse. Barely any of them have goals for their political careers beyond length of service and status in office.

They have become used to benchmarking the most banal key performance indicators, to one day look back on their careers with pride. Balance the budget, pay down debt, stop the boats. These slogans are about as substantive as the modern frontbencher gets. So how can we expect them to be capable of pivoting, thus making cogent arguments for weighty reform ideas? To challenge populism rather than echo it because that's what the economy might need right now?

The answer is we can't.

Deputy Liberal leader Josh Frydenberg recently cited Margaret Thatcher as an ideological inspiration to him. Good on him for at least seeking to up the ideological ante. But I wonder if the Treasurer even read her two-part biography, or merely heard that she was an inspiration to John Howard, which was good enough for him. Thatcher's reforms in Britain, while controversial then and now, were justified to her wavering cabinet at the time with the line "yes, the medicine is harsh, but the patient requires it".

When Frydenberg's Thatcherism pitch was given airtime in the media, he was quickly shot down by the former head of Tourism Australia. The Prime Minister didn't want Australians to worry that his government might be prepared to give voters the medicine they need if it had a sour aftertaste. He'd rather feed them sugar.

So what will happen to the backbenchers agitating for meaningful reforms in the wake of Covid? They will be ignored. Or they will be bought off, as so often happens in modern politics, with frontbench promotions. Picked off one by one. Promotion brings silence, thanks to the rules of cabinet solidarity. Hopeful readers may think: perhaps then they will use their new-found power to argue the case internally. More likely they will not. Even if they do, they will be outnumbered and ultimately outmanoeuvred by the Prime Minister and his entourage, who are primarily focused on winning elections.

A scorecard they look set to achieve, just as Malcolm Fraser did. Hands up who thinks Fraser's legacy is a grand one? The prime minister who sat on his reforming hands through a recession, only to be replaced by Bob Hawke's Labor government. But don't worry, Fraser was prime minister for more than seven years.

Labor must take a good hard look at itself

22 August 2020

I first developed an interest in politics during the late 1980s, when Bob Hawke was prime minister, and Andrew Peacock and John Howard were battling it out to lead the Liberal Party. I was in my early teens and, although my parents weren't political, we did discuss and debate politics at home.

At the time Labor seemed like a powerful organisation. The likes of Graham Richardson and Robert Ray controlled the Labor government's factional and strategic decision-making. Paul Keating gave the government serious policy ballast and no small amount of mongrel in parliament. And Hawke kept the show together with his consensus style of leadership, including in his relationship with the ACTU's Bill Kelty.

Paul Kelly's seminal book *The End of Certainty*, which took in the 1993 election, became my bible for understanding the weighty issue of that era. The fact Keating found a way to come back and defeat John Hewson at that election only solidified the strength of the Labor machine in my mind.

In those days there were heady and divisive debates at the centre of the political showdowns. The Business Council of Australia targeted Labor ferociously even though micro-economic reform was at the centre of the government's agenda. Unions were divided about moves Labor was making but came together under the party's campaign banner. And the media (as always) gave Labor a hard time, more so than the Coalition. The political machine that was the Labor Party appeared strong, strategic, and focused on significant reform for mainstream Australia. There was no sense of disintegration as had occurred when the party split in the 1950s, nor of the variety Joel Fitzgibbon talked about this week as modern Labor battles to find its soul.

At the time the Coalition was a mess. The Nationals broke free from the Coalition at one point, and during most of the 1980s and early '90s it caused no small amount of problems for the Liberal Party. The Joh for PM campaign thwarted Howard's 1987 election ambitions. The disunity in the wake of Howard's political removal put Peacock on the back foot at the 1990 election.

The campaign unit within the Coalition wasn't as dynamic as that of Labor, and the opposition was caught between popularism and political ideology.

By 1993 it found too much of the latter and Labor used populist fearmongering to bring down Hewson. But those years were the exception to the rule in Australian politics, the rule being that federal Labor doesn't dominate and rarely wins. It struggles to maintain unity and is not the natural party of government at the federal level.

Since Robert Menzies was elected as the first Liberal prime minister in 1949, the conservative side of politics has been in power for nearly 70 per cent of the time (49 of 71 years), and of course it is in power today, with few signs of that changing any time soon. In what is one of the world's most rigid two-party systems, that is domination.

The Hawke and Keating years account for most of Labor's relatively limited time in power since World War II. So those of us who grew up learning about politics during that time have a distorted view about the political professionalism of Labor and the extent of division within the conservative side of politics.

Since Keating lost the 1996 election to Howard, the national dominance of the conservatives has been restored. Howard led the nation for nearly 12 years and the incumbent Coalition government (albeit with three successive prime ministers) will govern for at least nine years before

Labor gets the chance to return to government. Not that Labor looks remotely likely to win the next election; it's Scott Morrison's to lose.

All of this needs to be food for thought for federal Labor, which has proven incapable of securing the successes the party has been capable of at the state level. It simply may be that state governments are elected on their capacity to provide service delivery, meaning that Labor finds itself in an even fight as voters swing between the party of the supposed fiscal conservatives and Labor, which is better known for its passion in policy areas such as health and education. In contrast, federally the dominant areas of responsibility are managing the economy, foreign affairs and defence — natural Coalition strengths, according to the opinion polls.

If Anthony Albanese thinks he can win the next election simply by working with an "it's time" factor, he is likely to get a rude shock. That was the campaign theme for Gough Whitlam after 23 years of conservative governance, not a mere nine. Kevin Rudd won against Howard by representing generational change after one leader in his late 60s had been prime minister for nearly 12 years.

Albanese is five years older than Morrison, who will have been Prime Minister for less than four years come the next election. Morrison also will be the first PM other than Howard to have served a full term in office in more than a quarter of a century. These are hardly preconditions for a successful "it's time" campaign. Equally, the Liberals largely have put their political and policy divisions behind them. The departures of Tony Abbott and Malcolm Turnbull ended a decades-old feud between the pair, restoring stability. No one within the federal parliamentary party will challenge Morrison's authority.

The conservative side no longer defines itself by the ideological divides of the 1980s and early '90s. It has returned to the simple principle on which it was founded: to give a voice to the mainstream and keep Labor away from the Treasury benches.

The irony that it doubled the debt Labor accumulated during the global financial crisis, only to be on course to double it again fighting the coronavirus isn't lost on me. But it does appear to be lost on an electorate that believes the Liberals are better economic managers.

And Morrison is fast developing the political skills of Howard. One senior Labor operative told me they thought Morrison might be even better than Howard in terms of political skills, marvelling at his ability to pivot away from questions he doesn't want to answer and deflect blame for responsibilities that clearly fall into his lap. US president Harry S. Truman had a sign on his desk: "The buck stops here". Morrison has a trophy with an asylum-seeker vessel on it with the words "I stopped these".

When you throw in the Prime Minister's marketing background, in particular his time spent as a NSW state director running campaigns, Morrison's capacity for political manoeuvring becomes even clearer. Especially as long as Andrew Hirst remains federal party director. His skills in conjunction with Morrison's relentless campaigning against Bill Shorten snatched their party an unlikely win last year.

For any of us who grew up watching the Labor political machine dominate the conservatives, it's important to remember that was an aberration. The true order sees federal Labor regularly outwitted and outmanoeuvred by the Coalition. There's no sign of that changing.

We've made mistakes, but it might have been worse

8–9 August 2020

Naturally the thoughts of all Australians go out to our fellow countrymen and women enduring stage-four lockdown in Victoria. The spread of the virus there is alarming. The toll of the lockdown on people's mental health must be significant.

The economic impact is disastrous. While many who are simply trying to cope with the situation are supportive of the efforts of the state government, others are highly critical of Premier Daniel Andrews. Failures of hotel quarantine seemingly caused this second wave, and structural problems in Victorian health have meant that the contact tracing system has been second rate. At first glance these are state government let-downs. But the situation isn't that simple.

I have written before about the culpability of the commonwealth in these failures, even if the state government has mismanaged its affairs. Quarantining is explicitly defined as a commonwealth power according to section 51 (ix) of the Constitution. The fact it has become a shared responsibility between tiers of government doesn't change that.

The bottom line is the commonwealth has the power to run quarantining but allowed states to do it in the name of pragmatism. Attempts to thereafter lambaste Victoria for using security guards ignores three things: the commonwealth had the power to insist on a different approach and didn't; the notice period the Victorian government was given to facilitate large-scale hotel quarantining was minimal; and security guards did the same work in Western Australia, where no such failures eventuated.

So yes, the Victorian government wears the blame for the hotel quarantine mistakes, but context matters. And while Victoria's health structures have contributed to inadequate contact tracing, so have the deficiencies with the COVIDSafe app. That was a commonwealth initiative, one we initially were told was "vital" to containing any potential second wave.

Yet long before hotel quarantine failures pushed Melbourne to the brink, the COVIDSafe app was revealed to be an underwhelming tool — and an expensive one at that, riddled with glitches that still haven't been fixed. So it is clear that both the Victorian and commonwealth governments have let their citizens down when it comes to containing this pandemic. Blaming one and not the other is selective. We can conclude that at the same time as recognising that things could be much worse, and the credit for the situation not being worse must go to our politicians.

For example, we could have failed to contain the first wave of the virus, like most European nations, putting pressure on our health system before it was adequately ready to respond. The time Australia bought for itself, courtesy of bettering most of the rest of the world in responding to the first wave, saved lives — there is no doubt about that.

Or we could be in the situation the US is in, never having seriously embraced the need to lock down the country to suppress or eliminate the virus. Under President Donald Trump too many Americans have died from COVID-19 and many more inevitably will. Equally, the impact of the way the health side of the crisis has been mismanaged there has decimated the US economy.

A more than 30 per cent collapse in gross domestic product is truly staggering. But Australians also need to accept that our leaders haven't managed the crisis as well as, for example, somewhere like New Zealand has. Jacinda Ardern's approach aimed for elimination, and it worked. Scott Morrison's suppression strategy had a different goal.

Claims the NZ economy was dealt an unnecessary body blow to achieve such a feat now seem silly. Trying to repair an economy constantly gyrating between lockdowns and lifting restrictions is proving even more damaging. Of course the risk is always there for NZ that the virus returns, and our Kiwi neighbours didn't face the same degree of difficulty that we did: theirs is a smaller, more isolated population, with fewer international arrivals.

Also NZ's unitary political system empowered Ardern in a way Morrison can only dream. Our Prime Minister may have a penchant for cancelling parliament in favour of executive government, but he can't get around the states' service delivery powers. Yet Australia's federation may have saved parts of the country from enduring what Victorians are now going through, because of state governments defying what in hindsight were foolhardy demands by the commonwealth they lift border restrictions.

If Australia's political system matched New Zealand's unitary structure, the federal government could have done what it liked on this score. Where would we be then? Most likely the second wave currently contained to Victoria would be a national disaster, with the assistance other states are providing Victoria drying up as each jurisdiction looked after itself.

This would have stretched resources in a way that would have increased death rates and reduced the capacity of contact tracing, just for starters. Then we have to consider how much worse the economic fallout would be. Sliding doors. Western Australia and Tasmania maintained hard border closures when the federal government demanded they open up. WA Premier Mark McGowan was prepared to stare down a High Court challenge supported by the commonwealth. Morrison has since backflipped and withdrawn his government's support for Clive Palmer's challenge.

Queensland delayed opening its borders (which now are closed again) despite pressure from Morrison and his ministers. After eventually giving in to the political pressure and opening up, Queensland has been rewarded with a renewed risk of community transmissions precisely because of the brief period of free movement the feds insisted on.

South Australia is in a similar boat. NSW never closed its borders the way other states did, because Premier Gladys Berejiklian is close to Morrison and preferred not to defy him. The reward for people living in NSW? Australia's largest state is now the one most at risk from the outbreak in Victoria. Forced to consider lockdowns and endure other states shutting themselves off from NSW because it was too slow to act.

The federal parliament needs to get back to work, too

1–2 August 2020

The next fortnight was supposed to bring a return of parliamentary sittings, but Scott Morrison announced that on the advice of the acting Chief Medical Officer he'd cancelled parliament. Apparently it's too dangerous for Victorian MPs to make their way to Canberra amid the second wave hitting their home state.

The announcement was made at the same time Josh Frydenberg (a Victorian) made his way to Canberra to deliver his budget update. Victorian federal ministers regularly are given travel exemptions without the need to self-isolate. But that inconsistency is the least of the problems with yet another cancellation of parliamentary sittings.

Parliament matters. It is a cornerstone of our democratic polity. That the executive and Prime Minister consider it irrelevant enough to junk sittings isn't something to be applauded or allowed to continue without comment. Australia's parliament sat during the 1919 pandemic and during World War II, far riskier (and deadlier) times than we are witnessing today. Let's be clear about one thing: relying on the advice of the acting CMO as the excuse for the cancellation is a fig leaf.

Paul Kelly isn't saying Victorian MPs can't travel. He's simply saying there are risks if they do en masse, without appropriate quarantining. I'm certain he'd also say there are risks in granting ministers exemptions from quarantine to traverse the continent. But that still goes on because they are deemed acceptable risks.

Victorian MPs, for example, could have made their way to Canberra two weeks earlier and gone into self-isolation. Unlike the rest of us who would need to pay for doing so now, they would be paid for sitting in their hotel rooms ordering room service.

But apparently even that is too much to expect. Why is it good enough for the rest of Australia to self-isolate when travelling for work demands but the political class won't? They expect health workers to quarantine from their families when treating the sick. They want frontline workers to continue doing their jobs despite the risks they face at the coalface. Kids are still attending school. Footballers are forced to spend copious amounts of time away from their families and friends in isolation hubs to ensure playing environments are safe.

But the politicians think they don't have to do their important work in parliament? I thought we were all in this together. To be fair, many politicians do think parliament should sit. Individual MPs don't get to make that decision. The government controlling the numbers in the House of Representatives does. In practical terms that means the Prime Minister.

And, in a show of political capitulation for which federal Labor is becoming known, the opposition gave Morrison bipartisan support for this latest democratic shutdown. A minister remarked to me the other day that the best thing about parliament not sitting was that his own backbenchers couldn't congregate, "causing trouble" for ministers busy dealing with the pandemic.

How respectful of one's colleagues, and of democratic institutions and lines of accountability, centuries in the making. Even if physically returning to parliament were too problematic right now, why couldn't the parliament meet virtually? Other professionals are doing just that to keep their businesses afloat during these pandemic times. My 11 and 13-year-olds were capable of attending Zoom sessions at their school when classes went online. Why is doing so possible for children but beyond the capability of our nation's politicians?

The cabinet meets virtually. So do the national security committee, the expenditure review committee and the national cabinet. Why can't parliament do the same? Unlike these other meetings the public gets to see what happens in parliament. The only answer is that while there is a way, there is no will. Not within the executive and the inner sanctum of the Prime Minister.

There aren't institutional limitations either. Our democratic system is based on the British Westminster system, and British parliamentary democracy has carried on virtually when unable to meet physically since the early stages of this pandemic. The same has happened in other countries. I know many Australians don't think the sitting of parliament is that important.

They are wrong. It's a complacency the executive preys on as it continues to diminish the role of parliament, especially now that the pandemic has shut it down completely. Yes, antics in the chamber often make it on to the nightly news, giving people the impression that when the political class descends on Canberra it is nothing more than kids at a school camp.

But there is a lot more to what goes on during sitting weeks, such as the checks and balances sittings provide — especially in the Senate, which is not controlled by the government of the day. The opportunity for the opposition to ask the government questions in the house. Legislative scrutiny, which often leads to amendments to poorly crafted laws.

Partyroom meetings during sitting weeks ensure government and opposition frontbenches don't become distant from the broader partisan teams. Even the role of the fourth estate is diminished when parliament doesn't sit. Right now our nation is facing up to some of the biggest challenges in a generation. From rising unemployment to a recession that risks becoming a depression, to the scale of government spending — the economic impacts of executive decision-making are enormous. And then of course we have the health crisis, policy options for managing it, and the impact the pandemic is having on the federation.

All of which makes parliamentary sittings more important, not less. The cultural erosion of accountability structures that comes from cancelling parliament as lightly as we have, in unprecedented ways without efforts to find alternative ways of meeting, should not be underestimated. British philosopher Edmund Burke — considered to be the founder of modern conservatism and praised by liberals and conservatives alike — wrote about the importance of parliament to the democratic process.

One of the founders of British parliamentary democracy in the 17th century, John Pym, said: "A Parliament is that to the Commonwealth which the soul is to the body." Shortly after becoming Liberal leader Morrison himself said it was important "to ensure that we not only bring our party back together… but that we bring the parliament back together".

Fast forward to today and the Prime Minister seems content to let his MPs remain isolated, scattered across the country, while parliament sits idle. All the while executive government marches on.

A fluid, vanilla super product is just what we all need

4–5 July 2020

If ever there were an area of public policy in desperate need of reform, it is the superannuation sector. The only problem is that most politicians are running scared from the behemoth that is the super sector writ large, or are in thrall to it.

Some politicians are even ideologically callow enough to deny the value of superannuation altogether, relegating themselves to the dustbin of the debate. None of which diminishes the need for reform. Superannuation is compulsory, meaning every working Australian has a stake in how it is constituted as a policy. It truly is one of those policy scripts to which everyone should pay attention.

The battle between retail and industry funds masks the true issue at hand. So does the "freedom of choice" advocacy by those in favour of self-managed funds. All of the above have a right to co-exist in the super space, but there needs to be a generic, colourless super product that acts as the default fund all Australians are automatically enrolled in.

One run by the Future Fund (which has a track record of strong returns), for example, which has at-cost fees in the order of 0.1 per cent — substantially lower than anything offered by retail or industry funds. One without the downright illegal actions we've seen from some retail funds that rip off their customers. And one without the vested interests of unions and others in industry funds that claim to have the best interests of their members front and centre but are attendant to other needs, too. A generic vanilla product run by the Future Fund would not need to be complicated.

The wholesale nature of the Future Fund easily could be converted to include a retail shopfront for super, keeping fees low by managing accountants as one with payout carve-outs. After all, the Future Fund already covers the costs of public service defined benefits schemes. Any Australian who particularly wanted to join industry or retail funds could opt out of the generic fund and do so. If anyone decided the overheads of a self-managed super fund were a cost worth bearing to independently manage their financial affairs, they could do that, too. Just as they do now.

The My Super policy was supposed to offer a generic product along the lines I have proposed but, without the low fees and universal opt-out policy settings I'm calling for, such a scheme can't be anything more than second-rate. For most of us, the vanilla product I'm suggesting would be more than good enough and it would maximise returns by minimising fees.

The simplicity also would mean swaths of younger Australians would avoid the costly consequences of having multiple funds, as they traverse an increasingly fluid working environment across sectors and industries, without fees eroding the small holdings in each account. The generic fund would follow workers everywhere they go.

With any new employment, their super payments automatically would be deposited into the one fund, with its high returns and low fees. If this reform to super is so obviously beneficial to the public, and so easily implemented, why hasn't it already happened, I hear you ask. Enter the murky world of self-interest and political nepotism.

For a start, many politicians don't want to rock the super boat because the unions have long held affiliations that benefit from the status quo. Because they hope to benefit in the years ahead from board or executive appointments in these funds during their post-parliamentary careers. This is a scourge on both sides of the major party divide.

Equally, because the super sector has become gigantic almost beyond belief — controlling hundreds of billions of dollars — taking it on by reforming it and removing the automatic benefits the whole sector gets (because of the current policy configuration) is risky business. Conservatives worry that the sector will throw its substantial money and weight around, as the mining sector did when Labor sought to introduce a minerals resource rent tax.

Keep in mind that the mining lobby is comparatively tiny compared with the super sector. Direct union links specifically into the industry super sector make the reasons Labor won't join the reforming party even easier to understand. All that we are left with are fringe ideologues within the right of politics calling for super to be scrapped altogether.

That is a stupid proposition when you consider most Australians benefit from the forced savings, especially if their money for retirement can be maximised via targeted reforms. With the rate of super legislated to increase steadily in the years ahead, in line with people's retirement needs (presently the rate of compulsory super isn't sufficient to live off in old age), the time for getting the policy settings right should be now.

Instead of seeing the value of a well-crafted super policy that can ensure, over time, that Australians for the most part pay their own way in retirement, Liberals continue to erode the value of super. The decision to grant people access to their super during these Covid times not only guarantees they will have less money in retirement, it has given people the opportunity to draw down on their savings when the stockmarket has been hit by the pandemic. That has allowed people to access $10,000 last financial year and will again this financial year, when that value is well down on what it might have been six or 12 months ago.

And evidence has emerged, of course, that the money hasn't been used for essentials in this time of need. Rather, much of the draw-down savings have been frittered away on things such as online gambling. Equally, we have seen significant fraud, with limited oversight when it comes to ensuring only the eligible draw down their super. Paul

Keating introduced compulsory super in the 1990s and, in doing so, gave Australia an opportunity to lead the world in retirement planning and policymaking.

However, he could not have foreseen the glitches that would need to be addressed, the vested interests and the weak political players of today who aren't up to the challenge of further refining what he started. Super is good, but it should be so much better than it is. Fixing it is simple, and made hard only because of a lack of political courage.

Morrison proving quick learner of Howard's playbook

27–28 June 2020

There is no denying the dominance of the Prime Minister at the moment, and it is hard to see that changing before the next election. Scott Morrison wins if he successfully manages Australia out of the economic crisis caused by COVID-19. If the economic fallout gets away from the government and mismanagement rears its ugly head, Morrison still wins off the back of a scare campaign warning voters not to risk turning to Labor in a time of crisis, using the Coalition's dominance on economic management as revealed consistently by the polls.

That catch-22 may be a factor preventing Anthony Albanese taking up residence in the Lodge. But there is no denying the successful way Morrison and the Coalition have responded to the Covid crisis; indeed, there is no denying Morrison's political successes since he assumed the prime ministership. Not all political leaders can take advantage of circumstances, even those in their favour.

So far, Morrison's skills suggest he can. Yes, there have been problems along the way. Before COVID-19 hitting, Morrison appeared to be on a downward trajectory courtesy of his botched response to the bushfires and the lingering taint of the sports rorts affair. In that context, the gigantic blunder on robodebt could have been enough to bring his government to its knees.

But not now. Morrison has grown into the role of Prime Minister; even his harshest critics must concede that. John Howard, once comfortable in the job, still presided over a litany of scandals. However, Howard's political acumen allowed him to pivot past them and maintain his dominance.

Morrison looks set to do the same, and much earlier into his tenure than Howard. Morrison's successes to date are all the more remarkable in the context of the previous 12-plus years in Australian politics.

No prime minister since Howard has managed to serve out a full term in office, much less do so and win the subsequent election. If Morrison breaks that drought, he'll have done so carrying his colleagues over the line for a fourth Coalition term in office after close to nine years in power, even though he has been Prime Minister only since August 2018.

From Kevin Rudd to Julia Gillard, back to Rudd, to Tony Abbott and on to Malcolm Turnbull, none learned from their mistakes. Each learned nothing and forgot nothing, contributing to their collective failures in staying in office. Prime ministers need both to win elections and achieve policy outcomes.

Morrison has yet to substantially prove himself on the latter scorecard. But he is on his way — and has been in the job for less than two years. It is easy to forget, for example, the sizeable income tax cuts passed through the parliament immediately after the "miracle" election win last year. As many as 94 per cent of taxpayers soon will have a top marginal tax rate of 30 per cent.

While I may have reservations about such a flat income tax structure, moving towards that outcome is in the DNA of Liberals. Morrison is therefore servicing their ideological needs. But not at the expense of managing the Covid crisis. JobSeeker and JobKeeper aren't the sort of policy scripts Liberals gravitate towards.

Yet Morrison introduced both relatively swiftly, breaking from the conservative economic tradition of letting the market rip even in a time of crisis, which would have seen unemployment skyrocket well into double digits, as it has in other parts of the world, rather than the current 7.1 per cent. Morrison was prepared to throw fiscal caution to the wind to save people's livelihoods.

Doubling the Newstart rate for JobSeeker has cushioned the impact of unemployment for hundreds of thousands of Australians who are experiencing it for the first time. And extending the increase to those who were already unemployed has allowed them to improve their impoverished state in meaningful ways during this crisis while providing vital economic stimulus via their new-found spending capacity. Yes, we know there are plans to wind back JobSeeker and JobKeeper come September. And workers have missed out on JobKeeper for threadbare reasons.

But there are clear indications selective industries will see a version of JobKeeper extended, and the old Newstart rate will be lifted, for the first time since 1994, even if it's well short of the current JobSeeker payments. But for a Liberal prime minister, that is as it should be. Morrison is finding the balance between his ideological right flank, which quite frankly is heartless, and his left-wing critics, who would spend more than Liberals are comfortable with, as Labor did after the global financial crisis, well after the crisis had passed.

It is a pragmatic balancing act and one Morrison is managing successfully so far. Former political commentator Laurie Oakes once said of Howard that he had made every mistake in politics, but only once. Morrison is showing all the indications of similar political learning. He even is putting his predilection for combative media performances behind him, which in time will unite more mainstream Australians behind him and against interviewers asking loaded questions.

Howard made a similar transformation from his first stint as opposition leader to his successful era as prime minister. And "Howard's battlers" rallied around him. We will be able to properly judge Morrison's prime ministership only once it is over, or close enough to, neither of which is on the horizon for now courtesy of his performance.

That was also the case with Howard. Imagine judging Howard's prime ministership less than two years into it: way down in the polls, and substantially so. Howard was deeply unpopular personally and, despite winning a thumping majority in 1996, he was staring down the barrel of losing his first attempt at re-election, his first-term government having been beset by scandals and losing a handful of ministers.

Comparatively speaking Morrison is flying, and doing so during the deepest recession this country looks set to face since the Depression. He may be the first prime minister to preside over a recession in 29 years, but we can hardly blame Morrison for that. The entire world is in recession. In Morrison's short tenure as Prime Minister, he has won an election few thought he would (me included), and he has presided over Australia managing the COVID-19 health crisis as well as any nation.

Now comes the economic recovery, and the task of reforming the economy to cope in the post-Covid world. These will be mammoth tasks that ultimately will affect Morrison's legacy, how history judges him. For now he gets an A+, with a fourth Coalition term all but assured.

Tehan offers a masterclass in bad public policy

20–21 June 2020

Even if we assume the best of intentions by the government when it comes to the higher education reforms announced on Friday, there are significant problems with what has been proposed.

The aim appears simple enough: to increase the fees of courses believed to deliver worse job prospects than those in which fees are set to be decreased. In line with where the government believes the job market is heading in the years ahead.

As far as vocational education goes, that's a reasonable enough goal. Putting to one side that universities are supposed to be more than just job-creating factories. Of course, once fewer people are studying philosophy and the like, there will be fewer people to think about such issues. No doubt an intended consequence of this policy script.

But has the government struck the right balance to achieve what it has primarily set out to do? That is, drive students towards certain subjects and away from others? With the goal of boosting demand in certain areas of employment. In a word, no. It has misunderstood the distinction between areas of employment, which need more people building a career within them (for example, teaching), and areas of study that are already overloaded with graduates (for example, teaching). How can that be?

Because not everyone who gains a teaching degree uses it to teach. That's because of issues with the pay and conditions for teachers, especially within the public school system. So graduates use their degrees to pursue careers in other fields. The same goes for many other areas of study. By dropping the fees for students undertaking such studies, the government isn't addressing the causes behind limited supply in the teaching profession, or many other areas of employment.

There is also an issue with governments picking winners, as is often the case in public policy decision-making. Governments are notoriously bad at picking winners. That is, governments trying to solve problems that might exist now, but won't by the time their solutions take effect. Consider engineering. This reform is because we apparently need more engineering graduates into the future, so fees in that discipline will fall.

However, a few short years ago well-qualified engineers were out of work because of the mining downturn. New graduates had no chance of breaking in. That sector is only now just getting back off the ground, and the construction sector (also a pathway for engineers) is starting to struggle in the wake of COVID-19.

The point is, assuming certain professions will always have greater needs than others is dangerous, and the law of unintended consequences can take over. Like it did with China's one child policy, for example.

What seemed like a good way of curbing population growth became a demographic time bomb. There are other relatively minor issues with what the government plans to do in higher education: it appears to be driven by an ideological aim of curbing the arts and humanities, which it perceives (not entirely unreasonably) as anti-conservative.

The extent of consultation was limited, meaning the reforms have barely been pressure-tested. Details are still thin on the ground following Education Minister Dan Tehan's National Press Club speech. And there is the pragmatic barrier that any changes need to pass through the Senate anyway, which is far from a certainty. We may simply be witnessing the early stages of another failed attempt to reform the sector.

But by far the biggest failure with this ham-fisted policy announcement is the dire fiscal impact it will have on universities already struggling, not to mention the counter-productive flow-on effect it will have on the goals of the government. The Coalition is thrusting this reform on the university sector right at a time when it is already reeling from the impact of COVID-19.

A massive downturn in international student numbers, which supported their budget bottom lines. No access to JobKeeper. The challenge of increasingly moving to online learning and developing strategies to cope with social distancing into the medium to longer term. In the midst of all that, the government plans to make students studying in areas like arts, law and commerce pay more to do so.

These are some of the few disciplines in which government subsidies per student are less than the cost of teaching them. Unlike in the very disciplines it wants to see student numbers swell. In other words, it is putting in place a price barrier, which if its goal is achieved will deter students from studying in the humanities.

But these are the disciplines in which universities can actually make money. Why? Because the overheads are far lower than in the sciences. No labs, no expensive equipment. All that arts, law and commerce students require are the internet, PowerPoint, a basic lecture theatre and the occasional book. These students are already subsidising the students doing STEM degrees.

The more of these students universities have, the more spare cash per student they can use to subsidise those in the more expensive disciplines such as medicine and nursing. However, this policy deters students from studying in the humanities, encouraging them instead to take up STEM subjects. Costing universities more at the very same time as imposing price-point disincentives for students wishing to study in the areas that generally help subsidise such disciplines. It is a massive fiscal fail by the government — a sure sign this policy has been crafted on the back of an envelope, and without adequate sector-wide consultation.

Or thought through for the unintended consequences it might

provoke. Basic ingredients of good public policy-making. So how will the already cash-strapped universities respond to this additional fiscal burden being imposed on them? The Group of Eight unis will have no choice but to wear it: they cannot close down expensive areas of study. They must remain multifaceted in their offerings to maintain their Go8 status. This policy will worsen their fiscal positions in a time of crisis.

But the remaining non-Go8 universities may decide to cut their losses and completely shut down faculties that cost more to run than the government tips in funding. Which are those faculties? The very same ones these reforms are designed to drive more students into. Slow clap, Dan Tehan. This policy is nothing short of a joke from start to finish. If I were crafting a new course from scratch on how not to enact public policy appropriately, this would be the very first case study in the outline.

As we rush towards the exit, cautious steps get the boot

30–31 May 2020

We are moving too quickly through the three steps the national cabinet set for lifting lockdown restrictions, thereby risking the success Australia has had to date in combating COVID-19. For many, this is a difficult argument to hear; not because the medical experts disagree but because of the damage the lockdown has done and the desperation we all have to get past it.

However, we must not rush to failure. Make no mistake: rushing towards a brighter economic future risks our capacity to sustain any advancements made. Reopening the economy too quickly in a bid to revive it, only to cause a second wave of infections that would force further restrictions, would do even greater economic harm than has been done already.

Importantly, it would risk a health crisis similar to what we have seen abroad but that we have been lucky enough to avoid here. The politicians, in their growing haste to kick-start the economy and keep a restless public onside, need to be careful. We all want restrictions eased as soon as possible for our individual sanity, to help save jobs and to try to resume normal life.

So many people already have lost their jobs or have been severely affected by lost income. Few Australians are untouched by this crisis. The toll on the mental health of people has been immense. But there was a reason the national cabinet set in place a three-stage process across three-week intervals, presumably on the advice of the medical experts. That's because we need to be careful, tracking the data during each period of eased restrictions to ensure the steps taken are fit for purpose.

The whole concept of conservatism is built around caution: don't support changes too quickly without strong evidence, lest the law of unintended consequences kicks in. Some right-wingers have questioned the reaction to the pandemic from day one, claiming conservatism was ignored in a rush to lockdown. However, that misunderstands the ideology.

Being conservative doesn't mean simply being slow to act in a crisis. It is a proof-based ideology that requires caution. In the context of current public policy challenges the proof of the virus spreading swiftly out of control overseas coupled with what we knew about the threats it posed required the pandemic response we saw. It may be that a non-conservative approach to lifting restrictions has the unintended consequence of bringing back all the dangers that so far have been managed well.

The problem is that the premiers and Scott Morrison are alert to and alarmed by the damage being done to the economy and less focused on the health crisis that has been narrowly avoided. As a result they are breaking their own agreed rules — intentionally or unintentionally — and adjusting restrictions within the stipulated three-week period outlined at the national cabinet meeting more than a fortnight ago.

This was confirmed at the most recent meeting on Friday. The agreed three-step process negotiated at the national cabinet made it abundantly clear that while each state could and should operate independently in terms of how it chose to lift restrictions, changes were to be set in stone for those three-week intervals. From a public policy perspective that was a sound approach. Let federalism work its magic using the different approaches from each state and territory as a series of case studies to assess successes and failures.

As an unintended consequence of state border restrictions, the experimental value of the variables state by state was enhanced —

remember, the Australian Health Protection Principal Committee never recommended closing state borders in the first place. That too was politicians making decisions not commensurate with the medical advice. State by state variations evaluated according to the impact of changes across a three-week period would provide a strong sample set with good scientific methodology — assuming, that is, the guidelines agreed to were followed.

We are still within the first three-week period, and already some states — with the backing of the federal government — are moving more quickly than originally outlined and agreed to. NSW, for example, initially moved to open up pubs and restaurants with a maximum of 10 patrons at any one time.

Under the three-stage process the national cabinet agreed to, that should have been the permitted maximum in NSW for three weeks, without change, as data was accumulated, assessed and as caution sat front of mind. Instead, it didn't take long for Premier Gladys Berejiklian to announce that NSW would be lifting the limit to 50 come this Monday.

Making that announcement during the first stage — rather than after it has ended and once an evaluation of the first tranche of changes has been made — is risky in the extreme. It also caught many businesses off guard, as excited as they are with any easing of restrictions to help them reopen their doors.

One suspects vested interest groups lobbying for a quicker easing of restrictions are carrying too much sway over some politicians. As a nation we have embraced individual public health measures — using hand sanitiser and frequent handwashing, keeping 1.5m apart and so on. Community measures — that is, how we choose to congregate in larger gatherings — are just as important. This is the delicate area of decision-making in the three stages of reopening and we must get it right to avoid a second wave of COVID-19 infection.

NSW hasn't been alone in making mistakes, distorting the sample set for stage one. Other states have done similar. You have to wonder what the medical experts are telling the politicians making these decisions. We are constantly told the medical advice is being followed. Is that the case here? Australia needs to be cautious, because there are numerous examples of nations that lifted restrictions too soon, only to be hit by a second wave of the virus.

The latest is South Korea, once the pin-up country for how to successfully manage this virus. On Thursday it had the biggest spike in new virus cases in nearly two months — a doubling of cases from the previous day. All of its early good work controlling the virus is now at risk. That could be Australia's fate if caution doesn't prevail.

We ain't seen nothing yet as China flexes bullying muscles

23–24 May 2020

The bad news just keeps on coming during this crisis.

Our children are set to enter a very different world when they start their working lives than the one we all anticipated (and hoped for) just months ago. How Australia recovers from this health and economic crisis will define whether we remain the lucky country.

History is littered with nations that have catapulted down the international wealth index courtesy of poor decision-making.

The 20th century example etched in my brain is that of Argentina. In his 2008 book The Ascent of Money: A Financial History of the World, historian Niall Ferguson details how poor choices led to Argentina's transformation "from the world's sixth richest country in the 1880s into the inflation-ridden basket case of the 1980s".

Nations the world over will face important policy choices in the here and now that will determine their future, and those decisions will shape (or perhaps reshape) the world order.

Protectionist tendencies are likely to be fuelled by hyper-nationalism in the aftermath of this crisis. Debt will inevitably balloon, such that it consumes a growing portion of gross domestic product, reducing the government's capacity to spend on everything from health and education to welfare. How we choose to respond to this reality will shape our destiny.

Less travel and tighter social restrictions will change the way we culturally interact with one another. This will feed some people's feelings of isolation, with potentially profound mental health consequences. It will also affect the electorate's attitude towards the political class and the decisions of government.

Do we become more contrarian and, if so, with what cultural ramifications? Or does compliance take hold in our political culture, giving government the imprimatur to erode rights without political consequences?

We already know that in the short to medium term the unemployment queues will be longer, and underemployment will increasingly define the working lives of many of us still gainfully employed. This will hamper the budget bottom line, but it will also rock the national psyche. Do Australians turn to higher education, as they traditionally do when jobs are scarce? Perhaps not this time, because of the reconfiguration of that sector, which has been gutted by the crisis. Lower enrolments in further education in the aftermath of the crisis may reduce the country's capacity to come out the other side of it successfully, as we have in the past.

The budget will come under increasing pressure because of closed borders and what The Economist describes as the new 90 per cent economy, where capacity constraints drive down growth. That, sadly, is an optimistic forecast in the current climate.

I have seen plenty of attempts at glass-half-full analysis of the future: more flexible working conditions, improved hygiene, new inventive ways of doing business, more time with family creating a better appreciation of work-life balance. None of these are out of the question, but they come hand in glove with the downsides, which will likely be far more defining and more difficult to navigate.

A less prosperous world awaits us. But as the Argentinian example highlights, there are better choices to be made. We are already seeing the consequences of a rising China in the context of a declining US. The latter has long been the butt of jokes and attacked for its self-interested soft diplomacy. But the world ain't seen nothing yet. A rising China will see democratic institutions tested like never before. China as a stand-alone superpower — assuming the US falls completely off its perch, as some are predicting — is a scary thought. It does not respect the rule of law, the rights of individuals, international norms or democratic institutions. It outwardly projects its power with a bullying streak.

The Soviet Union always faced a powerful Cold War enemy in the US. China is a far bigger threat than the Soviet Union ever was. We are now in an era of trade interdependence, with a greater global reach than ever. Unlike the Soviet Union, China is an insider within this system, able to benefit from it economically, as well as throw its weight around. This context matters not only in a security sense as we look forward, but economically as well.

All of the above will require the best of the best making the political and public policy decisions in Canberra and in state parliaments. This is where things get particularly scary.

Who reading this honestly believes that our nation is served by a stellar line-up of qualified political leaders, across state parliaments as well as federally? Because if this crisis has taught us anything, it is that the federation is more robust than previously thought. State governments are not subservient to Canberra beyond vertical fiscal imbalance. Their autonomy of decision-making and importance on the service delivery side of government has been made abundantly clear as premiers have regularly defied the Prime Minister during this crisis.

Even if you do have a healthy regard for the quality of our politicians, that is likely because your partisan rose-coloured glasses lead you to believe that one side of politics is excellent while the other side is a joke. In other words, your partisan bias distorts your views. To truly believe that we have first-rate political leaders, you have to believe they are represented on both sides of the major party divide, not just one.

Most Australians haven't felt that way for years. Certainly not since the glory days of Bob Hawke, Paul Keating, John Howard and Peter Costello, who led partisan teams capable of making tough decisions.

To be sure, tough decisions are reforming decisions, which are not necessarily always popular. These do not include spending our way out of the global financial crisis, or indeed this crisis. While doing so may (or may not) be the right course of action, deciding to spend money isn't a difficult decision. It is a big decision, but not a difficult one. Difficult decisions are the ones that challenge your base, are hard to sell, and require a passion and belief to do so.

That is what Hawke's micro-economic reforms were, and Howard's gun reforms.

In contrast, the COVIDSafe app — which apparently is "vital" and "necessary" and "paramount" to defeating this virus — is optional. As the number of Australians who have downloaded it stagnates at a quarter of that which experts tell us must use it for it to be effective, we hear no noises that the government will up the ante to ensure its deliverance.

That is surely weak politicking. Unless they overstated its importance in the first place.

Difficult decision-making also needs to include being able to sell one's ideas effectively, otherwise it's just foolhardy politicking. If you can't take the people with you eventually, you may as well not bother because in a democratic polity winning elections is a necessary ingredient in achieve difficult reforms.

Julia Gillard failed this test with her climate change policies, as did Tony Abbott with his early attempts to fix the budget.

The aftermath of this crisis is going to be all important, and we need politicians who can do more than hand out money and preside. Otherwise our days as the lucky country will soon come to an end.

Voters ignore the dark arts to keep calm and muddle on

16–17 May 2020

Buying time — that is what the JobKeeper package has done, as evidenced by the various employment numbers released on Thursday. Hopefully it won't merely have provided a stay of execution for millions of workers. The figures paint a frighteningly bad picture, highlighting the risks to the economy in the coming years.

Very few Australians have job security any more in an economic climate such as this. Our children are likely to grow up in a very different world. Parents have sought to take comfort in the generally positive news that kids aren't as badly affected by the coronavirus as adults. But unless the economy snaps back, they will be the ones entering a drastically changed workplace environment in the years to come.

Nearly 600,000 Australians joined the unemployment queues last month. In just one month the rate went up from 5.2 per cent to 6.2 per cent, according to the Australian Bureau of Statistics. On Tuesday, Josh Frydenberg told us Treasury was forecasting the unemployment rate to hit 10 per cent. If we are lucky. The participation rate went down by 2.5 per cent.

That is a sharper fall than at any time since the rate was first recorded back in 1978. There are 500,000 fewer people even bothering to look for work, hidden from the headline unemployment rate of 6.2 per cent because they have given up looking, knowing there just aren't jobs out there at the moment, or because their partners are still employed and they don't qualify for unemployment benefits.

Were these casualties of the economic fallout from the coronavirus added to the unemployment rate it would already be nudging 10 per cent. But the bad news doesn't end there. The JobKeeper scheme is keeping potentially millions of Australians in jobs they otherwise would have been fired from. The businesses they worked for closed down. Such a dire outcome would make reassembling the economy even more problematic on the other side of this pandemic.

Changes to industrial relations laws allowing employers to temporarily reduce people's working hours to part time also has kept the unemployment rate artificially lower. Highlighting this reality, the underemployment rate rose last month from 4.9 per cent to a whopping 13.8 per cent. JobKeeper is buying the government much-needed time as it tries to work out what to do about the new unemployment problem.

Australia is better placed to do this than most other nations. Why? Because we started this crisis with relatively low debt and a AAA credit rating. But don't thank either side of politics for that. Thank the politicians from previous generations: Bob Hawke, Paul Keating, John Howard and Peter Costello. They legislated micro-economic reforms, improved the tax and IR systems and paid down net government debt to zero.

The most recent generation of Labor used debt to fight off the global financial crisis, and perhaps for that reason didn't extend Australia's tradition of major economic reform. The current government doubled the debt for no good reason: no GFC, no nation-building infrastructure program. We entered this crisis well placed to muddle through it despite this generation's politicians, not because of them.

We now depend on them to get us through it and out the other side. Labor says the structure of the JobKeeper package is faulty, which it certainly is. A teenager earning beer money while studying, earning $200 a week while living with their parents, is eligible for the $1500 fortnightly JobKeeper payment, yet a single mother working full-time hours in a casual job for the past 11 months isn't eligible.

Labor makes the point that while JobKeeper is saving jobs, a wider net would have saved even more jobs; noting, as the Treasurer has, that when the unemployment rate goes up it takes years to come back down. Nevertheless, without JobKeeper, and IR changes allowing employers to push down working hours of employees, the headline unemployment rate could be nearly 20 per cent.

That, ladies and gentlemen, is Great Depression territory. A sobering reality worth considering when criticising the job Frydenberg is doing. But we are a long way from being out of the woods just yet. The virus continues to linger. International borders remain closed indefinitely. Global trade is being disrupted. China is acting menacingly. And the billions of taxpayer dollars going out the door can't go on forever. If we lose our AAA credit rating, borrowing costs go up. If the economy doesn't fire back up soon, we will be at risk of the unemployment rate hitting double figures as it continues to head further north.

It seems like a lifetime ago Scott Morrison arrogantly bragged about returning the budget to surplus, going so far as to claim it was already there — authorising the production of "back in black" mugs (yes, I have one for posterity) produced by Liberal Party HQ. We probably wouldn't have achieved the surplus anyway because of the damage done by the bushfires and the sluggish growth and productivity in the first quarter of the year.

But the coronavirus fallout and the stimulus and job saving responses have replaced that hoped-for surplus with the biggest deficit in the history of the country. The budget won't be handed down until October. The political questions from here include how do Australians respond to the hardship being thrust upon them?

Do they reward the government for its response? Do they criticise it on the edges, like Labor is doing now? Even if voters are hurt and unhappy, do they trust Labor as the alternative government to do any better?

Indeed, do they grant what has been a dysfunctional government a fourth term when the next election comes around, despite all the changes of leader and scandals such as sports rorts? Most likely people don't care about any of that right now. Their focus is on their families and their livelihoods.

That means voters are switched off to the political contest, and that's likely to remain the case until much closer to the next election.

Good old days of consensus were not what they seem

2–3 May 2020

The government slowly has started shifting the discussion around COVID-19 to what happens in the aftermath of the pandemic; that is, what reforms may be necessary to supercharge the national economy. Australia is likely to go into recession. Coming out of it will require more than basic managerialism by our politicians.

But are they up to the task, do they know what they are getting themselves into, and do they even have ideas worthy of implementation? Scott Morrison has flagged broad areas of reform worth looking at, but when specific changes are mooted they tend to get ruled out all too quickly; for example, adjusting the GST.

The problem with the rule-in, rule-out game is that it immediately distorts the reform debate, diminishing it to a simple political calculation. Although Josh Frydenberg and the Prime Minister were keen to claim ideology had no place in the stimulus rollout — because that suited them, given the quantum of the spend goes completely against their party's ideological instincts — what happens after the crisis will necessarily be deeply ideological.

That's because choices surrounding which reforms are worth including or discarding go to the core of party political ideologies. And when that happens, differences emerge, just as they did in the 1980s when Bob Hawke's government undertook wide-ranging micro-economic reforms. Those reforms laid the foundations for the sustained economic growth and prosperity Australia has enjoyed ever since.

As government MPs, including Morrison, discuss embarking on an array of reforms that is similarly grand in scale, it's important they realise what they are getting themselves into. The rose-coloured glasses being used to look back on the '80s as a period of consensus don't show the level of contestation at the time, the extent of disagreements on what the reform mix needed to look like.

Morrison wants any reforms he pursues in the aftermath of this pandemic to be part of a consensus-driven policymaking process, citing the national cabinet as a mechanism to help achieve that. But major reforms rarely play out that way, something a national leader should know. More likely what the Prime Minister really wants is to minimise dissent to help make the reforming challenge easier. I don't know if it is a deliberate rewriting of history or just a lack of depth of understanding about what transpired in the '80s, but Morrison and others overstate the extent of bipartisanship when Hawke and Paul Keating embarked on their reforms.

They should read Paul Kelly's The End of Certainty. They might learn something. Yes, John Howard in opposition supported some of the micro-economic reforms Labor legislated: floating the dollar, financial market deregulation and tariff reductions, for example. But he certainly did not support all the reforms and definitely not the new taxes designed to offset the tax cuts as part of rejigging the tax system.

Even then Howard had to battle opponents within the Liberal Party and among MPs within the junior Coalition partner, the Nationals. The Coalition opposed the assets test on the Age Pension, fringe benefits taxes, capital gains taxes and non-deductibility of business entertainment expenses. These changes were used to pay for reductions in the personal income tax rates, including bringing the top tax rate down from 60 per cent (that is not a typo; yes, it was that high) to 49 per cent, as well as reducing the company tax rate from 46 per cent to 39 per cent (also not a typo). Labor saw the benefits of increasing Australia's international competitiveness by bringing down such stiflingly high tax rates.

But ideologically it never would have supported doing so without commensurate changes elsewhere to ensure the size of government was such that social spending could continue. Another tax change saw the introduction of the petroleum resource rent tax.

We saw how the modern-day Coalition reacted when Wayne Swan as treasurer proposed the similarly designed minerals resource rent tax during Kevin Rudd's prime ministership. In the '80s, Liberals in opposition were able to support Hawke's tax cuts without the tax increases Labor also introduced because its policy was to do away with Medicare, for example.

And Liberals wanted to go further on the industrial relations reforming front than Labor's Accords with the unions did. The point is that to characterise the reforms of the 80s as a bipartisan love-in is deeply misguided, and false. That some within the government think that's what happened says more about how poorly read they are than it does about the nature of what went on at the time. Perhaps it's wilful ignorance. If government MPs and ministers think they can propose post COVID-19 major economic reforms singing Kumbaya and receive limited to no dissent, they are going to get a rude shock.

They should not expect a consensus-driven approach to major reforms. It just doesn't work that way, as history has taught us. And they cannot expect the opposition to roll over and support whatever is put forward either. That didn't happen in the '80s and it won't happen today, precisely because ideological divides dictate that differences will emerge on everything from the size of government to the role of government.

The Prime Minister won't be able to use his well-worn strategy of claiming the high moral ground either, dismissing criticisms as inappropriate because of the crisis at hand. Debate and dissent over major changes is what is supposed to happen in a vibrant democracy with wide and varied ideological opinions.

Hawke and Keating couldn't even rely on each other's full support as they embarked on their micro-economic mission. Keating's advocacy for a broad-based consumption tax was opposed by the trade union movement and Hawke ultimately acceded to its demands.

Equally, the unions didn't support the entry of foreign banks and complained loudly, making life hard for the parliamentary party. And let's not forget how loudly the Business Council of Australia criticised the Hawke government. This Coalition government can expect similarly vocal criticisms from special interest groups that don't naturally align with it when reforms cut across the interest of their members.

Reform is hard and it is contested. It always has been.

Denying unis a lifeline is ideological wilful ignorance

25–26 April 2020

The potential damaging impacts of the coronavirus are all around us. And while the health challenge seems to be under control — with semi-normal life close to resuming and the curve officially flattening — the economic effects may last a generation.

Profound changes are likely across the economy, and that includes higher education. Australia's second largest export sector will be hit hard by the consequences of limited international travel in the years ahead, and so far at least the government appears unwilling or unable to face up to the problems created by a dearth of international students.

We don't know yet whether this wave of infections will be the first and last, or merely the beginning of a rolling crisis for years to come. Australia is better placed than most nations to quarantine: a benefit of our status as a geographically isolated island. We can therefore function as a somewhat self-contained domestic entity with a certain amount of comfort: when it comes to everything from food production to quality of living, Australia truly is the lucky country.

But there will be many changes. A closer look at domestic manufacturing is in the spotlight, for example. The tourism industry will be hit hard. Some exports, such as iron ore, will continue to do well. However, higher education won't. Its value as an export sector has been in attracting overseas students to study here. That, at least for now, has ground to a halt. The best we can offer is continuing study online, which is not the reason foreign students choose to study at Australian universities.

Yes, the online learning capabilities of most higher education providers in this country are first-rate. So the product being offered can compete on a global stage.

But the comparative advantage Australian universities have enjoyed has been built on location, location, location. That is, the lifestyle benefits of studying here and experiencing Australia, alongside the potential to migrate Down Under once you are finished.

The backdoor visa system for foreign students at the completion of their studies has been the dirty little secret of the success of Australia's second largest export sector. It is why so many students in our region have chosen Australian universities over universities in other parts of the world. Migrate to a great place to live, not too far from home.

Yes, our institutions punch above their weight — with several Australian universities ranked in the world's top 100; proportionately high by global standards for a nation such as ours.

But the growth in the Chinese student market has mostly been about the immigration potential of studying here. Governments have welcomed it because it is skilled labour, meaning early social and economic dislocation issues migrants can face are minimised, and the extra numbers help prop up national accounts growth and tax receipts.

If online learning is the only option at Australian universities, Chinese students, for one, will study on campus elsewhere in the world or stay at home and chose a cheaper local institution. The expansion of Chinese universities in recent years has been huge and many have powered up the rankings.

Here in Australia, foreign students also have helped paper over the government cuts in funding for higher education; that is, cuts relative to the extra investment in universities we have seen by governments overseas and also relative to the growth in domestic student numbers.

Politicians like to crow about the fact more Australians are funnelling through our universities than ever. That growth has not been financed by adequate government investment but, rather, by full-fee-paying international students. With that market drying up because of the coronavirus crisis, Houston, we have a problem.

The government needs to face up to some stark choices: fund universities better to cover the emerging shortfall from fewer full-fee-paying overseas students; or accept a significant decline in domestic student numbers, alongside smaller, more boutique higher education institutions.

Usually in economic downturns more people enrol in further education, rather than simply going on to welfare, for example. But the rise and rise of HECS costs — as governments transfer more of the cost of studying on to students in a nod to the user-pays principle — has diminished that likelihood during this economic crisis. Besides, domestic fees aren't enough to cover the costs of research, hence the dependence on foreign student fees.

While most people think of universities as teaching institutions that is only half their role. Research output is the bedrock of higher learning.

Governments could choose to let our institutions wither on the vine in terms of research capacity. But in an era in which university research is leading the charge to find a vaccine for COVID-19, and given it is largely research that maintains higher rankings for institutions internationally, that would be perhaps the dumbest play of all.

To make matters worse for universities, in recent years inadequate research funding by governments has seen the sector turn towards collaboration to find funds. While some ideological warriors (yes, the culture wars strike again) like to attack our institutions for accepting funding from abroad (yes, not always in ways I approve of), the simple fact is shortfalls in domestic funding precipitated this approach.

And, with companies the world over turning inward and cutting costs, linked grants with universities are going to become only harder to come by.

So far the package the government has put forward to help universities has been limited, to say the least. Only the entertainment and arts sector has more to complain about. Australia's second largest export sector certainly hasn't received the kind of support we have seen handed out to other parts of the economy. It is hard not to see that failure through any prism other than cultural cringe, tall-poppy syndrome and certainly anti-intellectualism.

The war on expertise continues. There is a conspiracy theory within the Coalition that universities are hotbeds of left-wing ideological fervour. As though the broadbased behemoths most universities have become are defined by pockets of arts faculty-driven anti-Coalition sentiment that cling to life in some institutions. They might at times be loud, but they do not define the sector as a whole, nor do they limit its importance to the nation.

Decisions, decisions — why it's essential we get them right

18–19 April 2020

Never have the mechanics of public policymaking been more interesting than they are right now. And the matrix of decision making our political leaders must work through will get only more interesting in the weeks and months ahead as they tentatively begin restarting the economy.

The stakes are high. The health crisis threatens the lives and wellbeing of millions of Australians. The economic challenges associated with it are enormous. Getting the balance right will require all manner of out-of-the-box thinking, coupled with a more mundane capacity to test and rebuild the various parts of our society. What should come first?

Why pick one sector over another? When is too soon to make major moves? Can we, or should we, see variations in how the return to normal is upscaled from state to state? If so, why? Because of differences between states managing the crisis? Or because a federation affords us the opportunity to test different methodologies between states with similar demographics to upscale or wind back the approaches taken, learning by trial and error as we go along?

These are the big public policy decisions Canberra and the state and territory leaders will need to consider. When they do so, they must avoid groupthink. But groups still need to work together effectively. The media needs to hold these decision-makers accountable when they fail. The fourth estate isn't a mouthpiece for government. But it must balance that duty with not scaremongering. So, leaving aside the questions of when, where should the reopening begin?

Some say schools, even though the health advice is split (Victoria's

Chief Health Officer disagrees with the federal Chief Medical Officer). Which is to say nothing of the varied responses to schools opening or closing right around the world, and on what terms. Vital industries such as the mining sector perhaps need to start to reopen first, given the quantum of revenue they generate. But areas such as retail and trade employ many more Australians, so is there a way we can move towards reopening, say, pubs and restaurants safely?

Not only for the sake of the businesses and employees but also for the social and cultural benefits of citizens who have been locked down. Or is the $130bn rescue package enough to keep the hibernation going for a long while yet, because the health advice must come first on this one? There is a sense that it may be a while before pubs and clubs reopen, but with the greater awareness of the need for social distancing now compared with when they were shut, perhaps that can help reduce the wait — as long as cases of the coronavirus remain low and testing rates keep rising, of course.

Are geographical shutdowns the next step in battling this virus? Sub-regions within states, even within local government areas. Perhaps that becomes the next way in which we can control the health risks without wider economic stagnation. But to do that successfully under the biosecurity laws governments are entrusted to use, they say tracking people with their phone data is important.

How comfortable are we granting such powers to our politicians, especially when federal parliament isn't regularly sitting and the opposition has been excluded from the national cabinet? Silencing dissent is easier when institutions are not in operation. Do we worry that our rights won't fully return when we come out the other side of this crisis?

There is a debate about when is the right time to open up sporting codes, with or without crowds (even with social distancing). But contact sports can't socially distance when playing, and these human Petri dishes fly or drive from region to region, a concerning prospect to say the least. Games without crowds could help media companies crying out for content, but with few businesses advertising at the moment anyway, how important is that? Some media operators seem happy in the current fiscal climate not paying their broadcast rights while codes are suspended.

But policymakers also need to consider the social value for people in lockdown getting to watch sports. It's the same reason Roman emperors put on gladiatorial contests — to keep the masses from revolting. That may sound trite, but it's not. If civil order erodes and civil disobedience rises, the health challenge can suddenly become much more acute, and we only have to look abroad to remind ourselves why that is something to be avoided.

Every policy choice needs to be considered and worked through in detail, so that unintended consequences are foreseen. All of the above are micro policy decision-making considerations that don't even go to the macro decisions needed for the longer term: how long is international travel off-limits? Perhaps years. To what extent should government start investing more in national industries; in protectionist policies even?

And what do we even mean by investing? Nationalising sectors, for example, or simply offering targeted support? These are all such interesting decisions. They will be every bit as important as decisions taken by governments in centuries past. Not that long ago, Argentina was once one of the richest countries, before poor choices saw it fall away. For centuries China was the world's richest country.

However, by the 18th century most of Europe had caught up or overtaken it. Decisions taken by policymakers in the US throughout the 19th and 20th centuries set up the prosperity it has since enjoyed, as well as the cultural markers it laid out. How Japan and Germany were managed after World War II set up years of economic success for both nations.

For all the downsides of what this crisis has unleashed, we do live in interesting times. The decisions taken by governments will matter more than they would in the ordinary course of events, when the ship of state can be set on autopilot and the bureaucrats left to run the country, Yes Minister style.

Are our leaders up to the task? We have spent years lamenting the quality of those who seek public office. Is the media up to the task of speaking truth to power? Even if it does, who is listening in the social media era? In an age in which experts are ignored or pilloried (think climate change), can society backflip and see the wisdom in what they recommend? Speaking of wisdom, is there enough of it to go around in our modern world?

The final irony of this health and economic crisis is that COVID-19 targets the elderly right at a time when there are few people left who experienced major upheavals of the past to help the younger generations get through this one.

Some columns you feel more strongly about than others, and the below is one of those. Having studied, researched and taught politics now for decades, I am strongly of the view that the role of the politician is to listen to an array of advice then make a decision. It was becoming increasingly clear our so-called leaders were hiding behind advice rather than taking it all in and making important judgement calls. Anyone who believes in democracy can't be comfortable with elected leaders handing their responsibility over the civil servants, however well qualified some might be.

Not good enough for our leaders to just be followers

28–29 March 2020

"We are following the expert advice." That is what our leaders keep telling us during this crisis. They are following. It is partly designed to reassure us, it is partly designed to insulate them from blame. But it isn't leadership.

Knowing our leaders are followers shouldn't be reassuring and it certainly shouldn't insulate them from criticism. Not when parliament has been suspended indefinitely and some media outlets are already dialling back their coverage. Not when the opposition has been shut out of the national cabinet. Oversight of executive government is never more important than during times of crisis.

For context, parliament continued to operate during both world wars, the Spanish flu pandemic of 1919 and the Depression. To be sure, our decision-makers have an incredibly difficult task, sifting through options to combat the health and economic crises the coronavirus presents. But hiding behind experts in their chosen fields when making decisions with wide-ranging ramifications isn't good enough, whether it is just a communications strategy or a reality as to how backroom planning is being done.

History is littered with examples of politicians making the right and the wrong decisions in times of crisis. Rarely, if ever, is the advice from any one expert discipline the only advice that matters. Even more rarely is there a consensus within any one discipline over a chosen course of action.

Yet we have commentators in this country blindly peddling the lines the politicians do. That advice is clear cut and uncontested. Remember: topic matter experts aren't necessarily also experts at policy implementation. They often aren't. And in the ultimate of ironies, many of the commentators I refer to (and political decision-makers, for that matter) are the same ones who question the near scientific consensus on climate change. Challenging the experts on their expertise.

While I have always accepted the near climate change consensus among scientists, I also have noted the divergent views among public policy experts on how best to act on that information. Zealots on both sides can lose sight of the nuance. Turning our attention to the debate over whether public schools should remain open is a classic example of the misuse of expert advice and leaders acting as followers during this crisis.

Let me start by making absolutely clear I do not have a firm view one way or the other about closing public schools. I recognise the multi-layered elements that must be considered before reaching such a decision. But not once has Scott Morrison recognised the obvious complexity when making public utterances.

Right from the earliest decision to keep public schools open, the Prime Minister fell back on the "expert medical advice" as the reason. Let's logically test that claim. Does anyone think, in a perfect test-tube case, medical advice would say it is safer to keep schools open than close them and lock down households?

I can't imagine too many medical experts would say keeping them open is the better option in that artificial binary choice. Why? Because it exposes teachers to "super spreader" children, as the Chief Medical Officer once described kids. Because social distancing among children is hard. Because slowly but surely other mass gatherings have been shut down.

Also, well more than 100 countries have closed schools already. The list goes on, but it doesn't necessarily mean the decision to keep public schools open in this country was wrong, just that doing so can't logically have been based only on medical advice. There may be many valid reasons schools should stay open, in some capacity anyway, namely poorly resourced public schools: to help emergency workers with childcare if a lockdown isn't yet in place (a whole other decision-making matrix, which deserves to be tested for the slowness to move), because online learning is inadequate and for other social reasons.

The point is, decision-makers might hide behind the advice they get from one compartmentalised expert discipline, but they shouldn't. And they certainly shouldn't be guided by only one element that goes into a complex decision-making matrix. As it turned out there wasn't (and isn't) a consensus on what is best for schools, not among medical or policy experts. Private schools did their own thing, with their better resources, and so far have been vindicated, despite incurring political criticism.

And now states are closing schools off their own bats, despite the Prime Minister advocating "kids should go to school". We also have seen evidence emerge that the medical community — and, yes, even among the medical experts the government hears from directly — is divided on what to do about lockdowns and, by extension, what to do about schools.

One school of thought says go hard, go early. The other says space out your move towards full lockdown. Leadership is difficult; commentary, by way of comparison, is easy — I freely acknowledge that. But that doesn't mean we should give our leaders a leave pass for acting like followers, and timid ones at that: willing to hide behind narrow bands of expert advice, misrepresenting the extent of the consensus among those same experts.

Equally, however, we all have to understand that this crisis — even if handled well — inevitably will see mistakes made and backflips enacted. Some are less significant, such as allowing hairdressers to spend more than 30 minutes with their clients. Some are more serious, such as the delay in beginning social distancing.

It was only two weekends ago the Prime Minister wanted to go to the football and his Chief Medical Office was shaking hands, extolling how relaxed he was about doing so. Then last weekend they scolded Australians for not practising socially distancing and heading to the beach in vast numbers, defying directives not to. Australia should be able to manage this crisis better than most other countries, partly because we are so geographically isolated and because it hit elsewhere first, giving us a chance to learn from the right and wrong responses in other nations.

For that to happen, everyone has to do their part, which includes political leaders leading by example and doing so early, knowing that it takes time for messages to sink in. That is why the Prime Minister was wrong to sound as relaxed as he did about mass gatherings two weeks ago. It is why this paper's editorials were right to criticise him for that.

Morrison's shaky integrity might fail the confidence test

7–8 March 2020

Should the federal Coalition be lampooned for its "back in black" gloating when handing down last year's budget, now that the promised surplus this year appears dead, buried and cremated? In a word, absolutely. Not because the coronavirus outbreak could be predicted; of course it couldn't. Not because during the past 12 months the federal government has mismanaged the books; it hasn't. Not in any meaningful way, anyway.

The Coalition deserves to be lampooned for its back-in-black gloating because it got ahead of itself, displaying hubris while counting chickens. And the Coalition showed Labor no quarter when it over-promised and underdelivered in government on its surplus pledge in the wake of the global financial crisis.

What goes around comes around. That said, the more likely scenario is that the Coalition gets away with the hypocrisy and the KPI failure. Partly because Australians want spending and action to curb or perhaps help control the fallout of coronavirus. Partly because the research tells us voters have more faith in the Coalition when it comes to economic management than they do in Labor.

Hence changing economic circumstances can be successfully explained away using well-worded political rhetoric. I can only imagine how much the double standard must irritate Labor MPs and strategists. Readers might not remember, but the Coalition made its back-in-black pledge when delivering a budget it brought forward to April last year as an election strategy so that it could draw a distinction between its own economic management record and that of the previous Labor government. The words were used by Josh Frydenberg when handing down the budget on the night, and again at regular intervals during the campaign.

However, it now appears the two sides of politics are two peas in a pod: promising surpluses that don't materialise; pledging to bring down debt when it continues to build; using stimulus packages to ward off recession. The national debt has more than doubled since the Coalition came into office, and that was before COVID-19 and the bushfires hit.

The Coalition's build-up of debt has come despite its MPs regularly attacking the build-up of debt on Labor's watch. While Wayne Swan certainly got ahead of himself promising surpluses that never eventuated, he didn't preside over the production of coffee mugs gloating about something yet to happen as the Liberal Party did. I picked one up for a bargain $35 months ago, just in case the Treasurer didn't get there come the May budget.

Apparently the mugs have now sold out. More likely they have been removed from stock. They can no longer be ordered online. Scott Morrison gloated at one of the election debates against Bill Shorten that his government "brought the budget back into surplus, next year". The (mis)use of tenses saw the debate audience laugh at his use of language.

Satirical ABC program The Weekly did an entire skit on it. The GDP growth figures for the December quarter released on Wednesday spoke to the changing expectations within the Australian economy. The 0.5 per cent growth rate was stronger than anticipated, putting the annual figure at 2.2 per cent. That also exceeded expectations, but is well below long-term growth assumptions, and below where growth was when the Coalition came into office.

A low-growth environment is the new black, a consequence of both sides of politics failing to embrace the sort of economic reforms previous governments of both partisan stripes had the courage to do. We therefore have sluggish wages growth, high underemployment and weak productivity growth as a way of life. Australia enters this coronavirus-induced phase less resilient than we entered the early stages of the GFC. Back then debt was non-existent.

Growth was higher to begin with. The Reserve Bank had plenty of room to move when it came to lowering interest rates to help stimulate the economy. None of the above are positive features today. And make no mistake, the seriousness of this health crisis should not be underestimated. Even if the mortality rate is lower than current projections of 1–3 per cent, depending on how contagious the virus is — and experts say it is extremely contagious — if it takes hold here millions of Australians could get it.

Many could die. But it's not just the tragedy of that occurrence that will shake the economy to its core (not to mention people's lives). Those who get sick will understandably panic. The health system will be stretched. People will stop going to work. Children will stop going to school. Social and sporting events will be cancelled. The fabric of our community will change, at least for a while.

These tangible impacts will gut confidence and translate into the economy potentially grinding to a halt. The most important thing at such times is confidence, namely confidence in government: what it communicates to us and how it responds. But will Australians have confidence in Morrison's government?

The polls confirm the Coalition as preferred economic manager, but that isn't necessarily the same thing as trust in a government to manage a crisis. We are already seeing evidence of the bushfires recovery being mismanaged. The Hawaiian adventure sapped confidence in the Prime Minister's immediate personal response to a crisis. At least the nature of COVID-19 means he won't want to travel overseas again. Then we have those colour-coded spreadsheets from the sports rorts saga.

I assume the government won't allocate necessary health assistance and expenditure in a similar way: targeting marginal seats and favouring its own electorates. If the government finds that suggestion offensive, too bad. It has form. Finally, community confidence comes down to believing what politicians tell us.

The Prime Minister's office hid his trip to Hawaii, and this week Morrison confirmed his misleading dismissals of questions about whether he invited controversial pastor Brian Houston to a White House dinner were wrong. He did invite Houston, even though he brushed off questions on the issue as mere "gossip". These are micro-issues, to be sure, but they go to character and honesty, both of which build or erode trust. It was Albert Einstein who once wrote: "Whoever is careless with truth in small matters cannot be trusted in important affairs."

These were the days, writing only in passing about Covid unaware what it would become, before moving onto other issues which stank to high heaven!

Government pork-barrelling saga stinks to high heaven

22–23 February 2020

The government's focus this week was on how to manage the fallout (health-wise and economically) from the novel coronavirus epidemic, alongside releasing details on the royal commission into this summer's bushfires. Important issues, to be sure. In contrast, it hoped that attention on the sports rorts saga simply would fade further from view. That should not happen, nor will it, at least as far as I'm concerned.

The reason is simple: nothing of substance has happened to ensure such flagrant misuse of taxpayer dollars won't happen again. On the contrary, evidence appears to be mounting that the pork-barrelling just before the federal election last year that led the Auditor-General to condemn the $100m sports grants system also has occurred in other programs — for example, when it comes to regional grants.

More Australian National Audit Office reports are pending, apparently. Then we have the fact the government won't even admit it has a problem when it comes to the partisan allocation of sports funding, with Scott Morrison going so far as to commission his own compromised report by his former political chief of staff (now head of the Department of Prime Minister and Cabinet), Phil Gaetjens. Anyone who knows the first thing about good governance knows the head of the Prime Minister's own department doing a review into a scheme that had tentacles reaching into the Prime Minister's office (as evidence from the Senate inquiry already has highlighted) is poor public policy practice.

But wait, it doesn't stop there. The Prime Minister, not wanting to release the Gaetjens report (what does he have to hide?), had it marked up as an official cabinet document. Not because it has been seen by cabinet, which it has not. Or because there are plans for cabinet to see the report anytime soon; there are no such plans. Only the governance committee of cabinet has been entrusted with seeing the report.

That is, the Prime Minister, the Deputy Prime Minister, the Treasurer and the Attorney-General: four members of a cabinet of 23. As crossbencher Rex Patrick said, the Prime Minister sprinkled cabinet dust over the Gaetjens report, wheeling it through the cabinet room in a trolley, simply to ensure that Freedom of Information searches can't access it. And so the Senate inquiry can't either. The whole thing stinks to high heaven.

Morrison seeks to justify what appears a cover-up by claiming it is common practice for such materials not to be revealed publicly. This week he said: "It is not the policy of our government or any government to have cabinet-in-confidence materials, of the governance committee in particular, released."

That is true, except that it is false. In 2014 Tony Abbott, then prime minister, approved the release of cabinet documents for the royal commission he called into Kevin Rudd's botched home insulation scheme. Transparency seems to matter when Labor is being held to account but not when it's the Coalition's turn. The weasel words don't end there. Before the evidence given at the Senate committee hearings by the Auditor-General and his office, Team Morrison had a clear and consistent line when it came to deflecting criticism of the allocation of sports grants: all grants went to eligible projects.

It turns out about 43 per cent of grants approved by the minister did not. The Prime Minister even told parliament that all successful grants were eligible. (Reminder: it is illegal to deliberately mislead the parliament.) Now that we know that wasn't the case, rather than admit the error Team Morrison is doubling down.

As George Costanza told Jerry in Seinfeld: "Just remember, it's not a lie if you believe it." The change of rhetoric now involves claiming "no project was deemed ineligible by Sport Australia". Putting to one side the principle that merit, not eligibility, should be the way grants are selected, how does the government logically find a way to craft the above excuse? It goes like this: ineligible projects were never assessed by Sport Australia, so ipso facto they weren't "deemed ineligible by Sport Australia". It's the sort of rhetorical gymnastics someone who has worked their entire life inside the political bubble actually thinks is clever.

Which it is, if (and only if) we let them get away with it. Speaking of merit versus eligibility, it is ironic that the leader of a political party that has claimed merit must always win out as its excuse for not embracing gender quotas now clings to the loose and weak argument that all is OK when it comes to the allocation of sports rorts grants because successful applicants were eligible. Oops, that's right, 43 per cent weren't eligible.

Let me rephrase: successful applicants weren't ineligible. Oops again! Close to half were ineligible. Give me one more chance to rephrase: successful applicants weren't deemed ineligible by Sport Australia (because Sport Australia never even saw many of the applicants to assess their eligibility or otherwise). I have increasing sympathy for the ministers who are required to spin their way out of this.

It isn't easy! I suppose it is easier if you don't truly believe in the philosophy of accountability and due process underpinning our Westminster system, or the principles of democracy that should be a core value for all elected MPs and senators. The sports rorts saga is far from the worst example in our history of members of the political class putting self-interest ahead of the community's best interests.

And it's certainly not the worst example of maladministration or corruption at the commonwealth level. But it is unique in the unwillingness of the Prime Minister and those around him to admit error and do something (anything) to rectify the situation. The scandal should therefore dog him and everyone complicit in it for the remainder of their collective political careers.

In the meantime, it is incumbent on all of us not to let the matter rest because time since the rort happened continues to pass, which is the government's entire political strategy to wash over this disgrace.

For the PM, sorry seems to be the hardest word to say

8–9 February 2020

The first parliamentary week of the year confirmed one thing: the Coalition won't be admitting mistakes when it comes to the sports rorts saga. Scott Morrison certainly won't be taking a leaf out of the book of former Queensland premier Peter Beattie, who turned apologising for errors into an art form.

Every time Beattie did so, his opponents looked more churlish for not accepting the apology and moving on to the next issue. Instead, the Prime Minister conforms to the never-backdown, never-concede school of thought. Those who know him well say it fits with his personality. But does it align to the personality voters thought he had when they elected him in May last year? Perhaps not.

And if not, there are political risks attached to Morrison's stubbornness on an issue that touches local communities so closely. Nobody likes to find out they fought for government financial assistance for a local community organisation under a process they believed was fair and merit-based when it wasn't, only to discover that the minister had the power to overrule the guidelines those applying for assistance assumed were in place to be adhered to.

But the government and the Prime Minister are unrepentant. Even though Bridget McKenzie — the sports minister who presided over the partisan allocation of funding grants — resigned, albeit on a technicality. Notwithstanding an Auditor-General's report confirming pork-barrelling took place. Not to mention evidence that the sports rorts decision making seeped all the way to the Prime Minister's office.

Despite all of this, McKenzie was praised loudly this week by her Nationals leader, Michael McCormack, for the wonderful job she did. In a television interview with the ABC, McCormack explicitly congratulated her on how she handled the sports rorts funding carve-up. It was brazen stuff.

Then, as quickly as she was removed from the ministry, McKenzie was back as Nationals Senate leader — proving that comebacks don't need to take time to eventuate. On Thursday, Josh Frydenberg refused to answer whether he was "ethically comfortable" as Treasurer with taxpayer dollars being used as part of the sports rorts scandal. Instead, he fell back on that intellectually bereft line, included in the government's officially distributed talking points, that all grant recipients were "eligible" to receive funding. Reminder: that's actually not true because some successful applicants applied after the closing date.

But even if Frydenberg's defence were true, eligibility isn't the point. The scheme was supposed to be merit-based, yet grants reviewed with a rating of 98 out of 100 by Sport Australia were overlooked for grants given just a 50- point rating. It is a disgrace. When quizzed in question time whether the projects that received funding had the most merit, the Prime Minister responded by saying: "I believe funding community sports infrastructure always has merit."

But if Morrison really believes that, how does he justify shafting meritorious projects in favour of those judged to be inferior but gave him a partisan advantage ahead of the election? It is an impossible circle to square. And it emerged during the week that one of Morrison's own staff members urged members of a sporting club in the Prime Minister's electorate to vote Liberal when handing over a taxpayer grant.

The election campaign also included Liberal candidates handing over cheques to organisations rather than local Labor MPs. If these examples don't highlight the partisan purpose of the grants I don't know what does. Yet the government is standing firm, admitting no wrongdoing. How it even hopes to take aim at corrupt unions without facing the charge of hypocrisy is beyond me.

The likes of Morrison and Frydenberg were two of the loudest voices condemning the banks in the wake of the royal commission, or Westpac specifically when the Austrac scandal came to light. The sports rorts scandal has exposed conduct that is no better. Yet the Coalition hopes the issue will just go away, without a mea culpa. A Senate inquiry into the whole shameful saga was formally put in train this week, which means witnesses will be called and evidence will be pored over.

But not everything will be available for scrutiny. For example, the review Morrison ordered by the head of the Department of Prime Minister and Cabinet, Phil Gaetjens, has been marked cabinet in confidence. So it will never see the light of day, at least not until decades from now.

Morrison relied on that review — conducted by a man who used to be his political chief of staff — to rebut the findings of the independent Auditor-General. If that weren't laughable enough, not releasing the Gaetjens report means we cannot know if he is cherry picking from its findings or accurately reflecting what is in it. Given Morrison's track record for openness, I'm not filled with confidence. Nor is former NSW auditor-general Tony Harris, with whom I spoke during the week.

And guess what Team Morrison's argument for not releasing the Gaetjens review was? They don't want to set a precedent of doing so because that will mean the next time such a review is conducted journalists and the public will also expect it to be released. How frightening; people expecting transparency.

It was Morrison last Sunday, when announcing McKenzie would be stepping down, who spruiked the importance of accountability and transparency — before batting away questions about why he wouldn't release the report he selectively quotes from.

Meanwhile, keep an eye out for the government's proposed religious discrimination act. The issue risks dividing the Liberal Party more even than climate change has. The Attorney-General has been asked to find a pathway through the middle, but the government's right and left flanks aren't happy with how the legislation has been crafted. To say MPs and senators are prepared to cross the floor is an understatement. Morrison is passionate about the need to firm up religious protections for organisations in the wake of same-sex marriage laws being enacted, and following the dispute between Rugby Australia and Israel Folau.

But true liberals within Liberal ranks (yes, they do still exist) are equally passionate about avoiding a scenario whereby individuals can be discriminated against by religiously affiliated organisations. Especially organisations receiving taxpayer assistance. Legislation that guarantees that right, even expanding on it, leaves many within the government feeling deeply uncomfortable. Watch this space.

It seems appropriate that this is the final column in the collection. A smart-arse piece of prose which as it turns out replied on the now-PM to make it work. Enjoy and thanks for getting this far! PVO

Morrison learns to listen to advice from his life coach

18–19 January 2020

Everybody needs a life coach and, judging by his recent performances, few more so than Scott Morrison. Life coaches can give sage advice, but it is important to listen to what they have to say to get the maximum benefit.

During this bushfire season Anthony Albanese effectively has become Morrison's life coach, helpfully offering suggestions on what the government and the Prime Minister should be doing.

Unfortunately, for too long Morrison wasn't listening, openly rejecting the advice the Opposition Leader offered. But credit where credit is due: Morrison now has started to follow Albanese's advice. Not that the man himself would ever admit that.

If Morrison had listened to Albanese from the start he might still be preferred prime minister in the latest polls. In fact, if Morrison also had listened to the advice of his other life coach, John Howard, he wouldn't be in his present political pickle.

One of Howard's golden rules as prime minister was not to take overseas holidays. That was perhaps too cautious, which of course was Howard's way. But suggesting a prime minister avoid two overseas holidays in one year, the second during an emergency in his home state, is probably advice no life coach would think needed to be passed on.

Albanese wrote to Morrison back in November last year, before the bushfires became the issue that they are now and before the Prime Minister jetted off to Hawaii. Albanese's advice included looking into ways to reward volunteer firefighters appropriately for the work they were doing. It came from having spent time on the ground talking to these selfless volunteers. Noting the time volunteers were spending away from their employment, Albanese also suggested improved leave arrangements.

In a series of doorstop interviews soon after he returned from his beachside holiday, Morrison dismissed such a policy change, citing everything from firefighters falling under the responsibility of the states to any debate about conditions not being appropriate in the midst of the fires. Besides, as he said, the volunteer firefighters liked being out there.

Yet sure enough, as the political heat turned up, the Prime Minister eventually adopted the ideas his life coach recommended.

In that same November letter to Morrison, Albanese suggested "expanding the capacity of Australia's National Aerial Firefighting Centre", with appropriate funding to boot. This was a natural follow-on from the policy Labor took to the election last year: to develop a national firefighting fleet for times of crisis such as now.

At least on this occasion the Prime Minister didn't instantly dismiss the suggestion. But he was slow to respond. With the fires in full swing come December, the Coalition boosted funding for aerial firefighting.

The recent military deployment of reservists has been touted by Morrison as some sort of grand initiative he, and only he, had thought up. Never before done in this nation's history. Put to one side that Kevin Rudd called in reservists to help with the 2009 Black Saturday bushfires. Last month Albanese publicly called on Morrison to do more when it came to defence involvement in the fires effort. Come the new year, Morrison issued his call-out to reservists.

One of the things Morrison has been loath to concede is that dealing with the fires requires a national response, which must be frustrating for his life coach who, at a doorstop on December 11, called for exactly that. As the crisis worsened, Morrison adopted the Albanese proposal and established an agency to co-ordinate a national response to the disaster.

The recent announcement by Morrison and Health Minister Greg Hunt about mental health provisions for those affected by the fires also was a follow-up rather than an original idea. Albanese and Chris Bowen suggested it the week before, almost precisely as it was announced later by the government. Morrison's speed in following his life coach's suggestion (on that score at least) showed important learning.

Similarly, Albanese's announcement with his environment spokesman, Mark Butler, that an assessment of the impact of the fires on native habitat and wildlife was needed — with funding to follow — was also swiftly picked up by Morrison. Five days later, the government tipped $50m into Albanese's suggestion.

While these indications of the Prime Minister learning on the job are positives, unfortunately he has yet to fully accept other advice his life coach has been dishing out. Albanese wanted the Council of Australian Governments to come together to help with "Australia's natural disaster preparedness". This request also was in his November letter to the Prime Minister. Sadly, especially given the extent of the tragedies this summer since that time, Morrison responded (in writing) saying such a meeting would one day be considered "should the need arise".

Sear those words into your collective brains, readers: "should the need arise".

Now the government — in a cynical bid to shift the discussion — is attempting to pivot towards "adaptation" rather than further action on climate change as a response to the fires, yet Albanese offered advice on that score too. In his November letter to Morrison, Albanese targeted adaptation initiatives. And this week we learned the government cut funding to the National Climate Change Adaptation Research Facility at Griffith University while Morrison was treasurer, no less.

Labor, unlike the government, can talk about the importance of adaptation planning with its credibility on climate change action intact because it wants to walk and chew gum at the same time.

Policies to reduce emissions in this country were at their most successful when Labor was in office. Nearly half of the emissions reduction target of 26–28 per cent required in the Paris Agreement was achieved on Labor's watch. Since that time reductions in emissions have flatlined, even though the government keeps saying we will "meet and beat" our Paris targets.

Yes we will, but only because of the heavy lifting done by Labor and only because "carry-over credits" from Kyoto will get us the rest of the way there. Carry-over credits aren't the same as emissions reductions; not at all. They are a neat accounting trick. So while Morrison is crowing about us meeting and beating our targets, we don't get there by reducing emissions any further.

With more than two years before the next election is due, the Prime Minister has plenty of time to lift his game. He will take comfort from my prediction that he will do exactly that, and win that election. But his tin ear needs to become a thing of the past.

About the Author

Dr Peter van Onselen has been the Contributing Editor at The Australian since 2009 and the Political Editor at Network 10 since 2018. He is also a professor of politics and public policy at the University of Western Australia and was appointed its foundation chair of journalism in 2011. Peter has been awarded a Bachelor of Arts with first class honours, a Master of Commerce, a Master of Policy Studies and a PhD in political science. Peter has written seven books, including four best sellers. His biography on John Howard was ranked by the Wall Street Journal as the best biography of 2007. Peter has won Walkley and Logie awards for his broadcast journalism and a News Award for his feature and opinion writing.